A History of Appalachia

A History of Appalachia

RICHARD B. DRAKE

THE UNIVERSITY PRESS OF KENTUCKY

Publication of this volume was made possible in part by grants from the E.O. Robinson Mountain Fund and the National Endowment for the Humanities.

Scholarly publisher for the Commonwealth,
serving Bellarmine University, Berea College, Centre College of Kentucky, Eastern Kentucky University, The Filson Club Historical Society, Georgetown College, Kentucky Historical Society, Kentucky State University, Morehead State University, Murray State University, Northern Kentucky University, Transylvania University, University of Kentucky, University of Louisville, and Western Kentucky University.

Editorial and Sales Offices: The University Press of Kentucky
663 South Limestone Street, Lexington, Kentucky 40508–4008

05 04 03 02 01 5 4 3 2 1

Library of Congress Cataloging-in-Publication Data

Drake, Richard B., 1925–
    A history of Appalachia / Richard B. Drake.
        p.   cm.
    ISBN 0-8131-2169-8 (cloth : alk. paper)
    1. Appalachian Region—History. I. Title.
F106 .D73 2001
974—dc21   00-032059

This book is printed on acid-free recycled paper meeting the requirements of the American National Standard for Permanence of Paper for Printed Library Materials.

Manufactured in the United States of America

Contents

Illustrations follow page 148

Maps

Introduction

MANY ARE THOSE WHO CONSIDER Appalachia a mysterious region. Even in the seventeenth century, when the French Huguenot developer Charles Rochefort promoted a colony he called "Apalache" in the Georgia uplands, and even before, when the high country behind the Apalache Indians of northern Florida appeared on maps as the "Apalachean Mountains," the definition of these mountains has been inexact. Modern scholars even today often approach the region having in mind different areas within the eastern mountains of the United States. The region's principal geographic study presents a useful review of the many designations of Appalachia used within the past century, but concludes by appropriating within "Appalachia" vast non-mountain areas, including the Southern Piedmont.

On the other hand, there are those who reserve as Appalachian only those areas of the Southern Appalachians that are "the real mountains." In Horace Kephart's view, this area included only the Smokies and the Unakas along the Tennessee–North Carolina border. And the historian Ralph Mann has recently been at considerable pains to exclude from Appalachia the Valley of Virginia, the Tennessee Valley, as well as the Piedmont. James Still, perhaps the region's premier poet, while admitting that Appalachia is a "somewhat mythical region," insists that "the heart of it [is] in the hills of Eastern Kentucky."

The Appalachia discussed in this book will be quite inclusive, extending to those portions of Appalachia including all of the provinces of the Southern Appalachians—the Blue Ridge, the Ridge and Valley section, and the Cumberland–Allegheny Highlands. In fact, this narrative will encompass much of Appalachian Pennsylvania during the period before 1820, when western Pennsylvania's history was closely tied to that of Virginia. After the War of 1812, Pennsylvania's story drifted away from the more southern story due to different experiences with slavery as well as the massive immigration into Pennsylvania from southern and eastern Europe.

James Still has referred to the "myth of Appalachia." In fact, con-

PHYSIOGRAPHIC SUBREGIONS

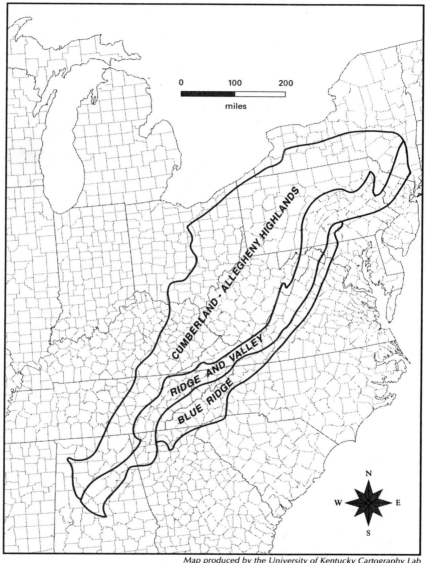

Map produced by the University of Kentucky Cartography Lab

siderable scholarly literature has emerged in recent years claiming that Appalachia, especially as related to the people who live within its perceived boundaries, is really an invention of certain writers during the late nineteenth century. Since the appearance of Henry D. Shapiro's *Appalachia on Our Mind* in 1978, probably most scholars of the region have accepted the view that the notion of "Appalachia" was really an invention of northern writers, who perceived of a "peculiar people" with particular stereotypical characteristics.

Shapiro's study should be viewed as an intellectual historian's study of the growing awareness of Appalachia that developed among certain mainline American intellectuals. Shapiro's notion that a particular picture emerged in the minds of northern, literate Americans seems quite clear. But to conclude that Appalachia existed *only* in this northern, literate mind—thus a myth agreed upon by these writers—seems to me an overly Platonic conclusion. The overwhelming evidence from contemporary observers—teachers who worked with the region's youth, as well as those Appalachians who have left a record of the overwhelmingly rural society that existed before 1930—all this seems to indicate that a unique and distinctive people existed in the region.

This book will be clearly influenced by five basic themes or interpretations. The first is the belief that Appalachia represents a significant and distinct region within the larger American society. Appalachia is not merely a figment of a reformist, mainline imagination in the nineteenth century. It is true that the term "Appalachian" was applied especially to the folk of the Southern Appalachian area by missionaries and writers prior to 1920. But in fact a sense of separateness has been a historic reality for many years, for most of those in the region, whether they called themselves "backwoodsmen" or "Cohees" in the antebellum period, or saw themselves as "mountaineers" or "Appalachians" in more modern times.

A second theme will be the emergence of a regional economy largely dependent upon outside sources of cash, and the concomitant loss of economic control of the region's resources as development took place. This has led many scholars of the region to see Appalachia as a mineral colony of industrial America. Indeed, Appalachian coal and other fossil fuels have fired the engine of American industry from the earliest days of industrial development.

Other scholars have shown how Appalachia became an exploited periphery in the development of world capitalism that has spread since the fifteenth century. Clearly this colonial notion is a view that must be taken seriously in any narrative of the Appalachian experience. But the Appalachian experience has been even more complex than a colonial interpretation can encompass. There are at least three other themes that significantly inform the Appalachian experience. One is the remarkable persistence in the region of what can be termed a "yeomanesque mentality" or attitude—essentially an ideology of agriculture that approaches farming as a largely self-sustaining activity. In this view, land was seen as a resource that provided for the family; it was not a commodity to be bought or sold. Such an approach to farming can provide for family sustenance in a well-watered area such as Appalachia, but it can never lead to much wealth and comfort.

Clearly, yeomanesque self-sufficiency existed for most American farmers before about 1820. But as transportation and technology have developed, an increasing number of farmers have come to produce for local and national markets. In the more remote mountain regions of the Appalachian South, however, yeoman-style agriculture has persisted rather remarkably until World War II and after.

Another unusual Appalachian characteristic that will enlighten this narrative is the strong and continuing presence of wilderness. Early in the Euro–American settlement of Appalachia, this wilderness was seen as a massive, seemingly inexhaustible area full of wild animals and Indians. Some traders and mountain men found this wilderness-dominated region challenging, but most Euro–Americans saw the wilderness as something to be overcome. Even before transportation technology penetrated parts of the region, first the Indian societies, then the yeomanesque, Euro–American settlers, claimed parts of the wilderness for farming.

As time went on, this wilderness receded, so that today there are many who fear that civilization may have already gone too far in replacing this matchless Appalachian wilderness. Air and water pollution are already well advanced in many areas, yet there are still areas of the Appalachian wilderness that can hide an Eric Rudolph, a suspected terrorist in the late 1990s and skilled survivalist, who cannot be found in western North Carolina's dense forests.

Lastly, it must also be said that this vast and varied region is so complex and perplexing that practically any point of view may find some verification. There is grotesque poverty and persisting ignorance, yet the area also has elite suburbs and world-class universities. There are indeed folk who fit the region's most degrading stereotypes, yet multibillion-dollar corporations make their headquarters here.

From an early date, people have seen the region in unusual and sometimes disturbing ways. William Byrd II, for one, as early as 1728 saw the folk of backwoods North Carolina as "Lubbers," who wasted away their lives in laziness. Yet John Filson made such a hero of Daniel Boone, his idealized Kentucky backwoodsman, that the romantically inclined saw Boone as a man without flaw.

Seceding Southern flatlanders saw their mountain neighbors as troublesome unionists, while Northern abolitionists looked upon Southern mountaineers as potential allies in the struggle over slavery. Yet slavery, and later racism, persisted in most of Appalachia, especially in the mountains of Virginia, North Carolina, Alabama, and Georgia. Later captains of industry believed they were bringing great opportunity to mill workers and miners, yet the wage scale imposed and the villages established created feudal dependence. In fact, the schemes of numerous regional developers have merely driven many in the region into a deeper, tragic dependence.

Appalachia has proven to be a particularly enigmatic region. The law of unintended consequences has operated so frequently in this region that even the most sophisticated and well-intentioned efforts have often gone badly awry. During the War on Poverty, for example, the idealistic poverty warriors so successfully convinced their charges that they were eligible for entitlements, that many Appalachian yeomen gave up their gardens and ceased planting corn or growing hogs and chickens.

As others before it, this book will likely prove inadequate to present the full picture of this complex region. There are aspects of the Appalachian experience that have escaped this book's notice or that have not been property emphasized. Already I plead guilty to overlooking parts of this complex experience that has been Appalachian history. But hopefully I have touched on enough of this fascinating experience that future historians will approach the study of this region aware of both the width and variety of the Appalachian Experience.

Part 1

The Contest
for Appalachia

The mountainous area of eastern North America was fought over, first by numerous Indian nations. Then came the Spanish, Dutch, French and English from across the Atlantic Ocean, to establish settlement in the coastal areas, then to spread slowly into the Appalachian Mountains. Finally the European-derived United States, largely with English institutions, extended its control over this mountainous area.

1

The Indian Era

THE APPALACHIAN MOUNTAINS are located entirely within the temperate zone, from about 33 to 48 degrees north latitude. The significant climatic difference between the valley floors, some at less than one thousand feet and the peaks at six thousand feet and more, assures a great variety of natural life. All the area enjoys adequate rainfall, from 40 to 120 inches annually. The diversity of life that has developed in these mountains is spectacular. Varieties of azalea, laurel, and hundreds of other plants may have originated here. Bird life is as varied in Appalachia as anywhere in the world. And in pre–Columbian times, deer, bison, mountain lion, fox, wolf and beaver roamed the mountain forests in great variety and quantity. Humans too came to these mountains, initially in quest of fish and game and the nuts, berries, and seeds that could be gathered.

The first people who came to Appalachia were descendants of people who had migrated from Asia. It is clear that humans did not originate in the Western Hemisphere, as we have no remains of primordial apes in the New World, nor have we found any sites that can be classified as paleolithic.

Much nonsense has been written about the history of the American Indian. But the writing about American Indian history has changed remarkably over the past fifty years. As recently as 1945, Indian history was an amalgam of racial myth, arguments between feuding schools of archaeology, eyewitness accounts, papers attacking the way whites have treated Indians, and romantic musings. To be sure, there were accurate and useful descriptions that subsequent historians and archaeologists could depend upon, such as James Mooney's studies of the Cherokee in the late nineteenth century conducted for the Bureau of American Ethnology. And in the history of American anthropology, the studies of Indian societies played a significant role in that discipline's "Golden Age."

On the whole, however, the literature of American Indian history still remains confusing. For examples, some supposedly authoritative books have assured us that American Indian history could not possibly be older than 10,000 B.C. Others have insisted on an ancient Western Hemisphere past beginning around 30,000 B.C. Some nineteenth-century authors were certain that, since the American Indian was of a "savage race," the remains left by the Mound Builders must have been left by some Old World migrants, such as the Ten Lost Tribes of Israel or the Phoenecians. Other tales insisted that these Indian ruins were left by the Welsh or the Norsemen. Some recent archaeologists have even posited that the ancient Maya of Mexico gained their civilization from some Chinese monk who found his way across the central Pacific.

The story of the American Indian is still an uncertain one. Records are spotty. We have only recently begun to read the ancient languages of Central America; however, all Indian societies in the eastern part of the present-day United States were preliterate. But thanks to the significant researches of a host of scholars—Charles Hudson, Francis Jennings, James Crawford, Charles Faulkner, Raymond Fogelson, Jack F. Kilpatrick, Theda Perdue, Whitcomb Washburn, John R. Swanton, John Finger, Roy S. Dickens Jr.—as well as Native American scholars finding their own voice, Indian history has finally "arrived." No longer can students of American history ignore the Native American past and present.

Archaeologists generally divide Indian time in eastern North America into five cultural periods: 1) the Paleo–Indian Period, 2) the Archaic Period, 3) the Woodland Tradition, 4) the Mississippian Period, and 5) the Historic Era. The Paleo–Indian Period is the most ancient. During this phase of time, the American Indian followed large game across the plains and forests of North America. In eastern North America, it appears that the Ohio Valley was peopled by these ancient Indians, who were constantly on the move.

More information is available about the Archaic Period. Beginning about eight thousand years ago, societies that had become less dependent upon hunting large animals developed a more diversified economy of gathering various vegetables, fishing, and hunting small game. Such a society could settle a specific area and establish a home.

Appalachia was occupied by Indian societies at least as early as the Archaic Period. At the Russell Cave site in Madison County in northern Alabama, particularly rich remains indicate that the site was occupied as far back as 6000 B.C. The Quad site near Birmingham,

Alabama, may in fact date back to the Paleo–Indian Period. In this more settled period, caves were carefully selected for more-or-less permanent homes. Certain areas of Appalachia would be most attractive to such societies, as in the Red River Gorge area of Kentucky, where about one hundred appropriate caves are concentrated, and which evidence suggests was inhabited by a sizeable population during the Archaic Period.

The Woodland Tradition in eastern North America began around 1000 B.C. and dominated the area until about A.D. 700 or 1000. Charles Hudson calls this culture "the most completely indigenous culture ever to exist in eastern North America," for it enjoyed not only the traditional agricultural culture of the American Indian, based on growing corn and squash, but it also developed in unique ways through its pottery, cooking, building, and earthworks. It was within this Woodland Tradition that the several mound builder cultures developed.

The Woodland Tradition developed most notably in the Mississippi and Ohio Valleys, but it spread widely into Appalachia. One of its finest sites, Old Stone Fort, is in central Tennessee near Manchester. There, a fifty-acre area is protected by cliffs on two sides, and rambling earthwork walls enclose it on the other two. One wall is forty-six hundred feet long. In the case of Old Stone Fort, the earthwork mounds were probably defensive, but other mounds built by Woodland folk were for other purposes—burial, religious, civic, etc. Some were built in animal effigy shapes.

The Adena culture in southern Ohio, West Virginia, and Kentucky is one of the most interesting societies of the Woodland Tradition. The Adena were farmers and built their villages along rivers in clusters of round houses made of saplings and bark. These communities were gathered about a conical burial mound sometimes seventy feet high, and often were surrounded by an earthen wall. Furthermore, the Adena were excellent potters, who may have learned their technique of limestone tempering from the small Candy Creek culture in East Tennesee. Adena stonework and ornamentation in copper and mica was outstanding.

One of the most remarkable of all Woodland Indian societies was the Hopewell culture. Like the Adena, the Hopewell built mounds, though they were far more elaborate than those of the Adena. The Hopewell's period, from A.D. 900 to 1300, is usually referred to as the Burial Mound II Period. Southern Ohio was also the center of Hopewell influence. But this culture spread to Illinois, West Virginia, and perhaps into Kentucky and Tennessee.

The Hopewell mounds are their most impressive ruin. Indeed, these people seem to have been so enamored by their burial rites that a high proportion of their surplus was spent on death, particularly for the burial rites of their chieftains. In Hamilton County, Ohio, mounds can be found that span a mile and more. Hopewell burial remains within the conical mounds have yielded copper and iron breastplates and necklaces, antlered head-plates made of copper, rings, beads, necklaces of pearls—one site yielded forty-eight thousand pearls—elaborate obsidian knives, conch shells, and alligator teeth. These artifacts indicate an active trade system stretching to the Rocky Mountains, northern Michigan, and south to Florida.

Socially, the Hopewell lived in an elaborate and stratified society, with considerable local control in the hands of the chieftain. The various villages in the Hopewell system appear to have been held together in a loose confederacy. It may have been that the only thing that held the far-flung Hopewell together was the burial cult and the elaborate system of trade that was necessary to support it.

For some reason, from 1200 or 1300, the Hopewell culture went into decline. It may have been that the riches they had gathered for their dead were too attractive to their more military neighbors. Or perhaps their institutions could not handle their enlarging populations. In any event, raiding and warfare became endemic, and the Hopewell sites moved away from riverbanks to hilltops, which they fortified with elaborate earthworks, as at Fort Ancient just north of Cincinnati. It may have been a remnant Hopewell group in this declining military period that fortified an Appalachian mountaintop in southern Madison County, Kentucky.

With the decline of the Hopewell, though the Woodland culture remained a strong tradition throughout the north, the major cultural event in the southern area of the present United States during the subsequent years prior to the coming of the Europeans, was the emergence of the Temple Mound culture, or the Middle Mississippian Tradition. One of the most dramatic ruins of this culture is at Cahokia, near East St. Louis, Illinois. Eighty-five mounds and a large city extended along the river for six miles. The largest mound at Cahokia was one hundred feet high and covered sixteen acres at its base. The mounds built in the Mississippian Tradition were square or rectangular and built in truncated pyramid fashion, with a ramp leading to the top—perhaps an influence of the Mayas and the Aztecs. It is likely these mounds were used for chief's houses or temples.

The Mississippian Tradition persisted into historic times, as did the Woodland Tradition. Many European accounts describe societies that shared both cultures. The Mississippians were apparently organized into village, even city-states, and the impressive earthen walls seem to imply much warfare. The size of some of these settlements and the earthworks that surrounded them indicate that they were the products of sizeable populations. At Cahokia estimates are that thirty-eight thousand people lived within the five-and-one-half square miles of the city walls. Within the Appalachian region, the principal society influenced by Mississippian culture was the Cherokee.

Mississippian sites that have been excavated in Southern Appalachia include the Tellico and Dallas sites in East Tennessee, the King site in northern Georgia, and the Koger Island site in northern Alabama. This variant of Mississippian culture has been termed "Southern Appalachian Mississippian," which modified the flat-topped pyramidal mound and also retained some Woodland characteristics. Sites of this Southern Appalachian Mississippian culture have been found in Georgia, South Carolina, and in western North Carolina. Its best examples are in northern Georgia—in the Nacoochee Valley near Cleveland and at Etowah near Calhoun. In fact, most of the Southeast Indians in historic times—the Cherokee, Creek, and Choctaw—were essentially Mississippian in culture.

Clear archaeological scholarship traces Cherokee beginnings back at least to the beginning of the Mississippian Period, or to about A.D. 1000. By 1650, the Cherokee economy had developed upon a broad agricultural base and had a sophisticated trade system that dealt with Europeans and a wide variety of Indian nations—some of them quite distant.

When Europeans came into these mountains, the Cherokee dominated the Southern Appalachians by means of a loose confederacy held together by ties of language, kinship, trade, and custom. Alien and hostile groups surrounded the Cherokee—the Creeks, Catawba, and Chickasaws mainly to the south, west, and east. Although most shared a common Temple Mound culture, they were of different language traditions. After the year 1600, until about 1780, the Cherokee were the dominant power in the Southern Appalachians.

For most of the period of their major importance the Cherokee were situated in some seventy towns, with a total population of perhaps twenty thousand, though some estimates exceed ten times that population before European contact. These towns were clustered in four general areas—the Lower Cherokee on the upper Savannah River in Georgia and South Carolina; the Middle Cherokee on the

Tuckasegee and the headwaters of the Little Tennessee in western North Carolina; the Upper Cherokee on the Hiwassee, also in North Carolina; and the Overhill Cherokee on the Lower Little Tennessee. Cherokee used lands that were far more widespread, and at the height of their population, they hunted and gathered regularly in Kentucky, half of West Virginia, as well as parts of northern Georgia and northern Alabama.

The Cherokee called themselves "Aniyunwiya," meaning "the principal people." Probably, they had moved to their southern home from the north, where they had been part of the Iroquois people. The Cherokee speak an Iroquoian language, and linguists believe the Cherokee separated from the main body of Iroquois even thousands of years ago. The Cherokee believe that their original town in the south was Kituwah in Swain County, North Carolina, from which they grew to their later strength.

There is now a general consensus that the Cherokee were in the mountains at the time of the de Soto expedition in 1540. The Cherokee political system and method of warfare were largely male-oriented and involved organization to overcome perceived insult and vengeance. War to the Cherokee was not conceived of as having long-run effects and was organized more as a retaliatory raid. Generally, Cherokee warriors fought one battle and promptly returned home.

During the time when the Cherokee were in firm control of Southern Appalachia, they principally contested with the Catawba, centered in the Carolina Piedmont, and with the powerful Creek, centered in tidewater Georgia and Alabama on their south and west. But the Cherokee were also confronted by a development of Indian nations on their north as well. To the north of the Cherokee nation in the mountainous areas of Pennsylvania, West Virginia, and Virginia was a complex of mostly migrating Algonquian groups, particularly the Shawnee, Delaware, and Conestoga. From about 1630 to 1730, a kind of "Indian haven" emerged in Pennsylvania's Susquehanna Valley that connected Cherokee trade with the powerful Iroquois Confederacy in what is now the state of New York. These various Indian nations all shared the Woodland cultural tradition and fit together a temporary concentration of Indian peoples who, though some had been driven from their original lands along the Atlantic coast, fit themselves into a British–Iroquois alliance system some scholars refer to as the "Covenant Chain." This Covenant Chain was disrupted in Pennsylvania by the grants of land made by the sons of William Penn in the 1730s, and the affected Indian groups were forced to migrate again into areas farther west, particularly the mountains of West Virginia and southern Ohio. The Covenant Chain remained in effect for another generation or so with the Iroquois in western New York State.

During the sixteenth century in New York, meanwhile, the politically powerful Iroquois Confederacy was pieced together so effectively that no Indian power during the seventeenth and eighteenth century in northeastern America was able to stand against them. It had been around 1570 that the prophet Deganawidah, about whom tradition claimed a virgin birth, established the "Great Peace" between the squabbling five tribes of the Mohawk, Oneida, Onondaga, Cayuga, and Seneca nations. He had a dream in which a giant evergreen tree reached into the sky as far as the hand of the Master of Life. The roots of the tree were the Five Nations of the Iroquois. Deganawidah's vision became reality through the labors of a Mohawk statesman, Hiawatha, who is said to have argued so persistently for union that he was banished by his own tribe and was forced to live with another. But years of traveling from one Iroquoian nation to another resulted in an unwritten constitution that established a Great Council for the making of decisions about common war policy. In the late sixteenth century, the Iroquois Confederacy had become a fact. By the time Europeans had arrived in Quebec, Massachusetts, and New York, the Iroquois preeminence was a reality with which the Europeans had to deal.

Some admirers claimed that the power of the Five Nations, the confederacy of five Iroquoian-speaking Indian nations in the north, influenced the political affairs of Indian peoples as far east as New Brunswick, as far west as Nebraska, as far south as Carolina and the Cherokee lands, and north to Hudson Bay. The warriors of the Iroquois' Five Nations, in fact, developed a frightful military reputation that struck terror into the hearts of their enemies. Cadwallader Colden, an English governor of New York and great admirer of the Iroquois, said of them in the 1760s: "I have been told by old men in New England, who remember the Time when the Mohawks made War on their Indians, that as soon as a single Mohawk was discovered in the Country, their Indians raised the cry from Hill to Hill, A Mohawk! A Mohawk! Upon which they all fled like sheep before wolves, without attempting to make the least resistance, whatever Odds were on their side."

The terror loosed by the Iroquois was most effective for centuries. However, Francis Jennings, the principal historian of the Iroquois, claims that their hold on such a vast area was based less on military success than upon diplomatic effectiveness through the Covenant Chain relations with the British colonies of Pennsylvania and New York. The Hurons, Erie, Neutrals, Delaware, and Conestogas, however, were unfortunate enough to be outside the confederacy itself, and to be occupying adjoining lands in Ontario or Pennsylvania; these nations were defeated and in some cases utterly destroyed. The Cherokee were indeed fortunate to have established themselves in the southern mountains by 1600, but even the Cherokee carried on intermittent warfare with their northern cousins throughout most of the eighteenth century.

Most of the Indians of eastern North America spoke languages included in the Algonkin family of languages. On this sea of Algonkin tribes, the Iroquoian-speaking nations of Appalachia sat in troubled domination—the Iroquois Confederation of the Five Nations to the north in Appalachian New York, and the Cherokee to the south, centered in East Tennessee, northern Georgia and western North Carolina. Politically, however, the most significant and most persisting threat to the Cherokee in their southern mountain homeland was the Muskogean-speaking tribes that dominated the southern coastal plain, particularly the Creeks. Culturally the Cherokee and the Creeks were similar—they had both adopted the ways of the Mississippian culture. Their villages had temple mounds and were walled when appropriate. Elaborate assembly halls were prominent. William Bartram, who visited the Cherokee town of Whatoga in the 1770s, wrote the following about that town: "Riding through this large town, the road carried me winding about through their little plantations of corn, Beans, and up to the councilhouse, which was a very large dome or rotunda, situated on the top of an ancient artificial mount, and here my road terminated. All before me and on every side, appeared little plantations of Corn, Beans and divided from each other by narrow strips or borders of grass, which marked the bounds of each one's property, their habitation standing in the midst."

Bartram also visited the Overhill Cherokee town of Cowe, which consisted of "about one hundred dwellings, near the banks of the Tanase." The homes were "one oblong four square building" made of logs "stripped of their bark, notched at their ends" in a manner by then imitative of European log buildings. In the midst of the dwellings was a "town-house," a large rotunda capable of accommodating several hundred people which was built "on the top of an artificial mount of earth . . . the whole an elevation of about sixty feet."

Unlike the Cherokee, the Five Nations of the Iroquois Confederacy, as well as the Shawnee, Delaware, and Conestoga, had adopted few Mississippian customs and retained most of the older Woodland Tradition. Their villages, though often fortified by wooden stockades, were collections of log houses built of saplings and bark. No burial or temple mounds appear in Iroquois or Shawnee villages. Though they were agriculturalists as well as hunters, fur traders, and fisherman, the Five Nations appear not to have had much artistic or architectural genius. Their accomplishments were primarily political and military.

Both traditional Iroquoian and Cherokee societies were matrilineal; in other words, both arranged family and social connections according to female ancestry. Women served as heads of households in charge of houses, the agricultural and economic arrangements, as well as child rearing. The sexual division of labor in Cherokee society meant that farming was the responsibility of the women, while the men hunted and fought the wars of vengeance. Among the tribes of the Iroquois Confederacy, the military and diplomatic functions were so time-consuming that the men were constantly traveling among the groups tributary to the Iroquois. Their diplomatic and military duties so totally dominated their time that Iroquoian society at home came to be dominated by the women, who also carried on local governance. On the other hand, historian Theda Perdue is of the opinion that the power of Iroquois women, which was derived from the matrilineal kinship system and their very major role in agriculture, began to erode when the fur trade increasingly dominated the economy. Thus a complex and changing situation faced Cherokee and Iroquois society as the eighteenth century proceeded.

Indian politics and warfare were fierce enough even before 1680. By that time, the demand of Europeans for furs and deerskins, which the Indians could take from the Appalachian forests, created even more fierce economic rivalries, thus serving to reinforce traditional animosities. In the Southeast, the invasion of various Muskogean peoples, the Creeks particularly, served to disrupt the earlier control of the Shawnee and the Catawbas—the former a wandering Algonkin-speaking nation, the latter a Siouxan-speaking nation far from their fellows on the High Plains. Consequently, kinship differences combined with conflicting political and economic interests to keep warfare an ever-present possibility for Indian nations during the eighteenth century.

By modern standards, the pressure on the land and resources in this period does not seem to be exceptionally great. Realizing that any estimates of Indian populations can only be most tentative, in historic times, the Cherokee population was probably never much more than twenty thousand. The Creek population was similar, as was that of the Choctaws. And the Chickasaws were probably never much more than six thousand; while even the combined Iroquois Confederation could never command more than twenty-four hundred fighting braves. Indian agriculture was fairly efficient, and land seemed plentiful. The wild game in the forest and the fish in the streams remained bountiful enough to provide plenty for all. But when a European fur market intruded, the contest for hunting grounds became an increasingly important factor in Indian politics. It has been suggested that it was not until the white trader came among the Indians that hunting become a source of profit and hunting grounds a subject of major contention.

When Europeans arrived in North America, they were intruders into an existing system of intertribal relations. There was an Indian state system in which Indian leaders, such as Powhatan in Virginia, saw the European newcomers as potential enemies or allies who might be used in relation to their traditional allies and enemies. Initially, Europeans were not necessarily perceived as enemies, and the military weapons superiority that Europeans enjoyed—muzzle-loading rifles, ships, iron implements of many kinds—made them either formidable allies or dangerous enemies.

When the Spanish conquistador Hernando de Soto led his party of several hundred gentlemen adventurers, soldiers, black slaves, and allies from Florida, across Georgia and South Carolina, and then westward toward the Mississippi River, he passed through lands of many Indian nations—the Appalachee, Ocate, and Chalque—and then into the lands of those groups that lived in Appalachia—the Guaquill, Xuala, Guasili, Canasoga, Chiaha, and Coste.

Charles Hudson claims that the Cherokee were firmly entrenched in Southern Appalachia by the time de Soto arrived in 1540. Professor Hudson is very clear that de Soto and his party of 600 soldiers, 100 camp followers, and 220 horses, ruthlessly fought their way through the American Southeast, burning villages and killing Indian hostages and guides. Some Indian groups abandoned their towns as the de Soto party passed through, while others severely harassed the Spaniards. In middle Georgia, the Spanish captured the female chieftainess, "The Lady of Cofitachequi," the leader of the most impressive society that they had met up to this time. After plundering this society, the Spaniards left for the northwest, taking the Lady of

Cofitachequi as hostage. Hudson believes that she led them further and further into the mountains, as far as western North Carolina's Blue Ridge.

During much of the Indian Era, the Appalachian Mountains provided the home for the most prosperous and powerful Indian nations of eastern North America. Part of the reason Indian nations in Appalachia thrived, at least until 1650, may have been due to the fact that the high mountain altitude made diseases less common than what was found in lower-lying regions. The coming of Europeans and Africans, however, brought diseases to the American Indian that he had no way to combat, and the effect was catastrophic. Some estimates of the decline of Indian population in all of North America and the Caribbean are as high as 95 percent over the two hundred years before 1750, due to smallpox, syphilis, gonorrhea, tuberculosis, malaria, and other new diseases.

In pre–Columbian times, the most advanced and powerful of the Indian nations were the Aztecs in Mexico and the Incas in faraway Peru. But within the area of the present-day United States, the most advanced societies were those able to have the closest contact with Mexico, as with the Pueblos in the Southwest and the Mississippian Tradition of the Central South. In eastern North America the controlling groups were Iroquoian speaking, and these were strategically situated in or close to the Appalachian Mountains. These were the mighty Confederacy of the Five Nations, in the Mohawk Valley and Finger Lakes Region of New York, and the Cherokee, based in the heartland of Southern Appalachia. Though the Cherokee were not "in control" in the south as the Iroquois Confederacy dominated the north, they were a significant part of the balance of power that had developed in the south, which also included the Creeks, Catawbas, and Choctaws. The Appalachian Indians, thus, were much respected and even feared by their flatland compatriots.

The Old World Backgrounds

THE EUROPEAN WORLD that came into contact with the North American Indian world during the sixteenth and seventeenth centuries was a vibrant, confident one. This was the Europe that produced the Commercial Revolution, early capitalism, the dramatic discoveries of Christopher Columbus and Vasco da Gama, the Renaissance, and the religious revolution known as the Reformation. By the sixteenth century, European politics was controlled by new, dynamic national monarchies in Spain, France, England, Portugal, and Holland. Suddenly the Atlantic Ocean became Europe's door to the world, and the society in western Europe that had been a backwater in a Mediterranean-oriented Europe now found itself on a new frontier of trade and discovery. Old authorities found themselves confronted by new ideas.

As the new era dawned for the people of western Europe, new men emerged. Gaining their strength from wealth acquired by manufacture and trade, some of these new men—middle-class businessmen—made an alliance with the rising national monarchies in Portugal, Spain, Holland, France, and England. Through their taxes, this business class provided the economic sustenance for these national monarchies to wage their internal wars against a troublesome nobility and to extend their empire abroad. Beginning in the 1460s with Portugal's exploration of the African coast, modern capitalism spread wherever Europe's national monarchies expanded. It continued with the dramatic voyages of Columbus, da Gama, Magellan, and the conquests of Cortez, Pizarro, and Albuquerque. When France, England, and the Dutch began challenging Spain and Portugal in the sixteenth century, the political and economic center of Europe shifted from southwestern Europe to northwestern Europe. Paris, Antwerp, and London became the dominant centers, and the business classes in those cities rose to increasing significance.

Another important class of new persons was the group coming into control of the land. To be sure, some of the old nobility turned their inheritances into vast land-based fortunes, as with the Russells, the Cavendishes, and the Percys in England. But particularly after 1688, most of the lands in England came to be controlled by a group of land speculators, old petty nobility and businessmen, who became England's country gentleman class. This "squirearchy" was essentially an entrepreneurial group who invested in agriculture, and when they operated farms, they sought to make a profit by growing crops for a market. On the continent, the old nobility pretty much retained their ownership of the land, though a new group appeared here, too, as German areas in particular recovered from the ravages of the Thirty Years' War.

As this new age dawned, another group very much larger than the agricultural middle class or the "squirearchy" developed. These were the former peasants who chose not to enter entrepreneurial enterprises and aspired to modest, self-sufficient land ownership. This group probably made up a majority of the population in England and in most of western Europe as well. In France in particular, a rich peasant class emerged to control local agriculture, though many of the old feudal usages remained. Certainly if those who aspired to an independent farmer or "yeoman" status, as it was called in England, are included along with tenants ("meiers" in Germany) and cottagers ("kotters" in Germany), who were never able to acquire title to the lands they tilled, these would be a clear majority. But though their numbers were great, their power was never substantial. Called by various names as medieval agriculture disintegrated—"yeomen" or "yongemen," "franklands" or "vallets," and on the continent, "stricklanders," "kotters," or "meiers"—they had in common the view that one lived one's life best if one owned and controlled one's own land and worked it oneself. To such a person, land was the basis of the good life, as it had been in the medieval period. True, the frugal yeoman or stricklander might rise beyond petty landowning to large holdings, but then he passed into the world of the capitalistic middle class, where wealth was the aim and land was considered only as one of the means toward wealth. But the yeomen, were never able to wrest lands sufficient for their desires from the growing landed capitalist class in England or Germany. In England, the gentleman farmer, and in Germany and on the continent, the seigneurs or Junker class, came to dominate rural life.

When England first established her North American colonies in the seventeenth century, religious differences and political turmoil so dominated English life that the migrant to the colonies was usually one who sought to escape the prevailing political and religious troubles in England. But after the "Glorious Revolution" of 1688 and the "Settlement" that followed, British politics became quite stable and even prosperous for those defined within this "Settlement." But life was very different for those left "outside the Settlement." The pioneers who came to the "backwoods" of the English colonies during the eighteenth century tended to be migrants from England from these aggrieved classes and areas who did not prosper under the "Settlement of 1688," or from the often overrun Rhineland areas of Germany.

David H. Fischer's widely read study of British migration to North America in the seventeenth and eighteenth centuries reinforces this emphasis upon the different kinds of people who left England at different times. Fischer makes much of the various areas in Britain from which migrants came. Those who migrated to the Appalachian "backcountry" after 1717 were, he insists, largely folk from the borderlands of North Britain and were mainly from the six most northern counties of England, Lowland Scotland, and Ulster. This area had been fought over for more than seven hundred years, and the resultant poverty, instability, and violence in that area had created a social system designed to support fairly continual military operations. When frustrations such as difficulty of acquiring land, or religious and political discrimination, combined with want and crop failures, these border folk left England's borderlands, Ulster, and Lowland Scotland for the American colonies.

The principal class who migrated to America after 1715 were mostly folk who aspired to small, independent land ownership, and who shared a "yeomanesque mentality"—a desire for land to support their basically simple lives. These small, often frustrated, farmers were the "sturdy yeoman" long celebrated in English history. The term "yeoman," or "yeaman," had been used in medieval times to designate some sort of service to another, often referring to military service. But by the sixteenth century, the word was largely applied to the class of small farmers who owned their own land. This class developed considerable importance as early as Queen Elizabeth's day. As one writer has put it, these small landowners were faced with both opportunities and dangers as a dynamic market for farm products developed. While some successful yeomen rose to the class of gentleman farmer, others often fell into a status of landlessness.

As the forces of the Commercial Revolution disrupted the medieval economy, the structures of the old society gave way, old ties were destroyed, old institutions were undermined, and new ways of doing things were adopted. One of these new impulses, largely produced by ex-peasant aspirations, was an immense land hunger. This yeomanesque aspiration for land was of critical importance in the settlement of North America.

When the Puritans, and later the Catholic-leaning Stuarts themselves, were driven from power, and stability was restored to English society after 1688, conservative or establishmentarian classes, mostly the gentry, were able to gain control of Parliament and get that legislative body to do its bidding by passing what in that day was considered "progressive" farm legislation. This meant the enclosure of "common lands," i.e. the lands that everyone before had access to. This encouraged the successful administration of the "gathered farm" with scientific practices. By 1700, it was clear that the small yeoman farmer would not be able to compete with the gentleman farmer for control of the English lands and countryside.

Within England a large class of landless and powerless people trailed off below the yeomanry. These were the working husbandmen, the farm laborers, "masterless men," and persons of "the meaner sorte," probably making up nearly half of England's population. These economically powerless people, along with debtors and outright prison refugees, were always a significant portion of the people who migrated to North America in the eighteenth century during an "Augustan Age" that is generally considered a prosperous period for most Englishmen. Many, in fact, were driven from European society by poverty and population pressure, and the abiding dream of most who migrated was a yeomanesque one of the opportunity to acquire land in America. During the eighteenth century, the economic status of those who migrated to America from the British Isles was often desperately poor, and many were a part of those restless, rootless drifters into England's towns and cities. A majority of those who came did so as indentured servants, persons without money even to pay for their trans-Atlantic passage and who worked a specified number of years for the American planter or gentleman who bought his indenture in order to secure his labor.

The Rhineland area of Germany during the eighteenth century

had a social structure similar to that of England, but with two notable exceptions. First, because of the failure of national monarchy in Germany, the nobility was much stronger. Germany at this time was a patchwork of hundreds of dukedoms and principalities that invited constant political meddling by neighboring national monarchies, especially by France. The Thirty Years' War period, 1618–1648, left Germany overrun and devastated. And at a later date, the Rhineland was especially vulnerable to French invasion, particularly during the reign of Louis XIV from 1689 to 1715. Though recovery came after 1715, Germany was still a much-wounded area. The second major difference with the English situation was the persistence of the status of serfdom in Germany, a condition that tied many individual peasants to the soil so that they were not free to move. Unlike England, where actual serfdom had disappeared, Germany experienced a substantial persistence of the institution into the eighteenth century.

In Germany after the Thirty Years' War, the powerful princes and their allies—the Junkers, a class similar to the English country gentlemen yet perhaps even more august—had little interest in farming itself. The Junker's concern was maintenance of his power and position and sufficient income from his lands to support that status, even if he lived in a town. A remnant of the serfs remained, but there was a complex class of petty farmers, tenants, kotters, gartners, stricklanders or meiers that emerged. Such stricklanders were interested in farming but found it difficult to obtain title to the land they worked. Their position was so difficult that they were ready for any new opportunity that might present itself, even if that meant a trans-Atlantic migration. Rents, lease fees, and feudal dues continued to hamper the rural Rhinelander's desire for land in Germany. Furthermore, religious persecution and the movement of vast French, Austrian, and English armies across his unprotected acres coincided with his desire for land, making the Rhinelander more than willing to migrate.

But why to the English colonies in North America? In the eighteenth century there was not yet a unified Germany, and of course no German empire. Furthermore, the English king after 1714 was also the Elector of Hanover, an important German principality on the lower Rhine. The King of England during the eighteenth century was a Hanoverian German, and the Hanoverian kings were more at home in German language than in English until 1760.

Thanks to its peasant past, yeoman culture in eighteenth-century

Germany and England was already many centuries old and was not capitalist in any important way. This culture placed a high value on land, not in a mercantile commercial sense, but in the "human sense," which saw the land as the source of one's life and well-being. Yet it was a culture that had mastered a quite sophisticated technology. By the eighteenth century, it possessed the multiharnessed loom, several varieties of spinning wheels, techniques for dyeing yarn and cloth, and for making soap from animal fat and ashes (lye). It knew how to grow wheat, barley, rye, grapes, apples, and many other crops, and knew about raising animals—cows, hogs, horses, sheep, chickens, and ducks. It knew of the proper care of draft animals and about the proper slaughter of animals for food. It also knew how to process some of these crops into alcoholic form. It knew how to break the soil with a plow and how to till it with a hoe. It knew how to make its own iron implements. By the eighteenth century, this yeoman culture had learned the art of quilt making from the Arabs. When this culture crossed the Atlantic, it brought these skills with it.

By the eighteenth century, too, religion had become a different kind of force in European society than it had been in the earlier centuries. During the Medieval Period, religion gave meaning to life as a preparation for heaven. During the seventeenth century, religion became more "this-worldly" and broadened to become a significant economic and political force. More and more it became a vehicle for defining one's political citizenship. In Germany, religion divided prince from prince but helped unite at least northern Germany against an Italian pope. Likewise in seventeenth century England, the issues most likely to bring about a political clash and the questioning of authority were questions related to religion.

By the eighteenth century, religion became a force that divided the classes. With the "Great Awakening" of the eighteenth century, modern religious revivalism found its mass movement manifestation. Suspicious of the rationalism that dominated the intellectual life of the elite, along with the "latitudinarianism" and rationalism that characterized the elite churches, the mass revivals in England and Germany placed emphasis upon the religious feeling of everyone, even the common people. In Germany this was reflected in the rise of "pietism," which began to take shape in the last decade of the seventeenth century and continued to increase in force during the whole of the eighteenth century. The religious pioneer Philipp Jakob Spener (1635–1705) called for a return to Biblical authority and a simple faith in Christ's saving power. The emergence of the Church of the Brethren (Dunkers), the Moravians, followers of Count Zinzendorf (1700–1760), the Schwenkfelders, and the Evangelical Church in Germany, were all reflections of the force of this religious revival in Germany. The appeal of evangelical religion in Germany was particularly powerful among the rural poor and among those Germans who migrated to America.

In England and her North American colonies, revival also characterized most of the "new" churches of the Great Awakening. England's Great Awakening was led by George Whitefield (1714–1770), John Wesley (1703–1791), and Charles Wesley (1707–1788). Its major institutional manifestations in England were the growth of the Methodist movement and the strengthening of the mass-based dissenter churches, such as the Baptists and the Quakers. In England's North American colonies, this Great Awakening was also an active religious force, and both Whitefield and John Wesley traveled in the colonies and kept a close eye on American religious developments. This eighteenth-century great revival shaped both the immigrants who came and the churches that served those immigrants.

The migration of the eighteenth century, then, brought quite a different kind of person to Britain's North American colonies than the migrations of the seventeenth century. Historian Bernard Bailyn notes that the eighteenth-century English migration, in comparison with the seventeenth-century migration, reflected a geographical difference within Britain as well. During the earlier century, migrants had come largely from the nation's "core in Southeastern England." The areas of migration spread in later times, Bailyn notes, to those "alien periphories" in the former marches in England's backcountry, such as Wales, the Northern Country of England, in Scotland, and Northern Ireland. Thus, the Scotch–Irish, or "Protestant Irish" as they were then called, provided the largest new group of English migrants to the colonies between 1688 and 1776. Such "Englishmen" from "periphoral" areas outside the center of English life in southeast England were clearly a different people. And in the eighteenth century at least, the Rhineland Germans can be considered as another "peripheral" type who related to England's core and made their way to the backwoods of the British colonies of North America.

Some scholars of Appalachian background—Cratis Williams, W.D. Weatherford, Norman Simkins, Forrest MacDonald, Grady McWhiney and others—have presented what they call a "Celtic Thesis" to explain this new kind of emigrant during the eighteenth century, thus focusing on racial differences. Noting the presence of the

Scotch–Irish (thus, Celtic as opposed to Anglo–Saxons) and the persistence of agricultural practices that always included the raising of animals—cattle, hogs, chickens—along with hard drinking and whiskey making and certain language peculiarities, these scholars contend that the eighteenth-century migrant to North America brought an essentially Celtic culture to the backwoods of the British colonies.

The Celtic interpretation has certain merits, but its racial biases are troubling. In fact, racial mixing was well advanced within Great Britain by 1700. To the earlier Celtic Britain of the Scots, Irish, Picts, and Welsh, was added by A.D. 200 a Roman elite. With the Anglo–Saxon invasion of the fourth and fifth centuries, another infusion of peoples occurred. Then came the Danes, in the eighth and ninth centuries, and the Normans and French, in the twelfth and thirteenth centuries. To this add Jews, French Huguenots, and Belgians, who migrated to the British Isles later, and we have a most complex cultural and racial mix, which was Great Britain even before a single Englishman made his way to America. A more meaningful explanation of British life and migration appears to follow Bailyn and Fischer's suggestion, which separates London and southeastern England from the more remote areas of England in the southwest, Wales, the North Country, the borderland areas, Scotland, and Northern Ireland.

A recent interpretation of the Appalachian background submitted by Rodger Cunningham suggests a modification of this "Celtic Thesis" by seeing this a continuing "Periphery Culture," or a persisting "Atlantic Culture," which Cunningham claims emerged as far back as the twelfth century in Lowland Scotland. To the English north, to Wales, Scotland, and later, to Ireland, the "center" in London and England's southeast sent representatives of "Western Civilization" to subdue the "wild lands" then on the fringes of English culture. This "peripheral society," according to Cunningham, developed such successful techniques for dealing with the "wild Scots," and later, the "wild Irish," that when the North American colonies were established, this group was again called upon to subdue the "wild Indian" on England's frontier in North America. Thus, a permanent population of "peripheral people" emerged to fight the center's battles on its imperial frontiers, only to become "Apples on the Flood" in England's centuries-long task of subduing its frontier lands.

Cunningham's interpretation fits rather nicely with Bailyn's insights, as well as recent treatments about the dynamics of the expansion of the World System of capitalism as outlined by Immanual

Wallerstein and Wilma Dunaway. And Cunningham's explanation goes a long way in suggesting how different those in the backwoods or border cultures were always considered by those in the center in southeast England. But in my view, Cunningham makes too much of twelfth-century developments, at the expense of the specific eighteenth-century developments that were more closely related to the actual migration to the British colonies. The evidence that seems most impressive is the testimony of the migrants themselves, and they were obviously impressed with the opportunity available to acquire land and the chance to be free to live and worship as they pleased. The clear "carrot" of land availability seems much more important than any "stick" wielded by any London elites that might drive them to the far American frontiers. Surely the backwoods settler played a military role as an Indian fighter and settler. However, actual settlement came not in the midst of warfare, but usually came immediately following a successful war and Indian removal.

Furthermore, the Rhineland of Germany must be fit into the picture of the expansion of the British Empire during the eighteenth century. After 1714, the Elector of Hanover was then also the King of England. Both George I (1714–1727) and George II (1727–1760) were more German than they were English. A major concern of English policy in these years was the security of Hanover within Germany. With an English King more at home in German than the English language, it should not be surprising to find that agents for William Penn and other colonial proprietors were recruiting thousands of New World immigrants within the Rhineland area. Though German settlement also spread eastward in these years, Germany had no other overseas areas to focus her attention upon, and Britain's empire was generously administered and seemed an excellent place for the German rural poor. Unable to secure land at home, the poor Rhinelander could find fruition for his dreams in America.

But part of the Old World that faced the Atlantic was Africa! Africans did not come to the New World willingly, however, for they came during the seventeenth, eighteenth, and early nineteenth centuries as slaves. The American demand for such labor seemed insatiable. Slavery had been first established in the sugar-growing areas of the West Indies, and by 1680 Negro slavery became the principal answer to the labor problem in the southern British colonies of North America as well. The British had first tried to solve their labor problem by recruiting the poor and powerless from England. The indentured servant had been the major seventeenth-century source of labor in England's North American colonies. The indentured servant, however, saw immigration as an opportunity for himself to become a landowner—a yeoman. An indentured laborer could not be held permanently in a servile laborer's status, but black African slaves *could* be held, because their skin pigmentation could define them permanently as laborers.

Africa supplied these slaves and transplanted some seven million people to the New World in the eighteenth century alone. There were important African kingdoms, particularly Ashanti, Dahomey and Oyo, that made a regular practice of warring on their neighbors for the purpose of capturing them and selling them as slaves to the European merchants who had established themselves at certain fortified trading posts along the African coast. The trade had begun with the Portuguese in about 1450, and by 1700 the system was an essential part of the Atlantic system of trade, with fortified trading posts, slave ships, and regular New World markets.

The region of Africa from which North American slaves came was the west coast from Senegal and Gambia to the Congo. Tragically, the area suffered immense political instability. In the western part of West Africa, the expanding empires of Denkyira and Akwamu were conquered by the Ashanti after 1700. In the Niger River region, Benin and the Ewe state were first conquered by Dahomey, then by the Oyo state of the Yoruba. The wildly competitive state system in the whole Gold Coast and Slave Coast area ensured a steady flow of captured slaves for this terrible trade throughout the sixteenth, seventeenth, and eighteenth centuries. During this time, an Ashanti–Faute confederated empire pieced itself into a troubled dominance of other chiefdoms in the westernmost areas. In fact, the whole area seemed in continual struggle throughout these tragic centuries of insecurity and violence.

Intrastate class divisions intruded into the political struggles of the many West African states as well, for the ruling class of successful African states were apparently clear of any danger of being enslaved. In fact, this ruling group appeared to be engaged in a partnership of exploitation with the Europeans. With a variety of devices, they protected themselves from any particular concern about the trade, including increasingly harsh law codes that defined slaves more and more as "criminals," thus subject to deportation.

At first slaves were gathered as wartime captives, thus the slave trade was initially a by-product of interstate warfare. By the eighteenth century, however, the slave trade so dominated West African life that the procurement of captives for sale became a principal motivation for the endless conflicts. Though some states had been built on the conditions of the development of the slave trade in West Africa—the Ashanti Empire for example—most states completely disintegrated under the destructiveness of the system. The whole era of the slave trade in West Africa became a tragic and insecure time.

Thus, the African and European environments led many people to migrate, either forcibly or voluntarily, across the Atlantic into the backwoods in the great Appalachian arc that was the British frontier in North America from 1730 to 1775.

The Coming of
the Europeans

THE FIRST EUROPEANS to come into the Indian-dominated world in North America were the Spanish. The initial center of Spanish concern was the Caribbean, where the island of Santo Domingo fell under Spanish control soon after Columbus' voyages of the 1490s. Spanish interest then reached to Mexico in the 1520s, where the fabled wealth of the Aztecs was won. Then conquest focused on another rich land full of immediately exploitable wealth—the Inca civilization in Peru conquered by Pizarro in 1536.

The Spanish awareness north of Mexico and the Caribbean was focused on what they called, "La Florida." Florida itself was discovered by Ponce de León in 1513. This province was ultimately to grow to include Spanish efforts in most of the southeastern part of the present United States. Lucas Vasquez de Ayllon attempted the first settlement of the area of the Carolinas in 1526. In 1539 and 1540, two Spanish exploration parties were sent into areas of the present United States. One led by Coronado went from Mexico into the high plains as far north as Kansas. The other was from the Tampa Bay area in Florida and went into the southeastern part of the present-day United States under the command of Hernando de Soto.

De Soto set out in the late winter of 1539 and made his way through the settlements of the Apalache Indians in northern Florida and southern Georgia. Led by at least seventy conquistadores on horseback, this party of several hundred was principally searching for gold. In March of 1540, the de Soto party left the Indian village called Apalache on the west Florida coast headed for a kingdom "governed by a woman" who had "many neighboring lords her tributaries." In May, de Soto found this ruler, the "Cacica," on the upper Savannah River, probably in the neighborhood of modern Hartwell,

Georgia. The Spanish took the Cacica hostage, forcing her to lead them to the "cities" in the mountains. Though rich valleys were encountered, the whole endeavor proved a great disappointment. And to make matters worse, the Cacica slipped away from the Spaniards, and the de Soto party was forced to find its way out of the Georgia–Carolina mountains unaided. Before the Cacica escaped, the de Soto party may have gone as far northward as Brevard, or possibly to Franklin, North Carolina, then came back to the coastal plain by way of the Etowah and Coosa Rivers. The three Spanish accounts of the expedition agree that none of the societies in the mountains were particularly impressive, certainly not as impressive as other major Temple Mound cities that they contacted later along the Mississippi River.

At least two other Spanish parties explored the Appalachian region soon after de Soto's visit. In 1559 and 1560, Tristán de Luna y Arellano, governor of Florida, led a party up the Alabama River to the Coosa River, then westward across northern Alabama. Then in 1566, a military camp under the command of Juan Pardo was established by the Spanish for some months in the Carolina upcountry on the eastern slope of the Blue Ridge. The Pardo party may have left some permanent traces of its time in North Carolina, for there are still mysterious ruined mines in the Mount Mitchell area of the state that may date from the sixteenth century. In 1567, this party also explored the area of East Tennesee. Clearly, Spanish designs were not easily discouraged, but little was found in the eastern part of the present United States that was as attractive to them as Mexico or Peru, aside from a far-flung but temporary mission system anchored at St. Augustine.

From the first contacts with Europeans, the Indians, with their already sophisticated trading system, found that some benefits could be gained from trade with the Europeans for furs. Europe's demand for furs was already well established by 1600. Prior to the discovery of the forests of North America, furs had been supplied earliest by western Europe's forests, then during the fifteenth and sixteenth centuries by the forests of Siberia. In the seventeenth century, American furs and pelts were of a vastly superior quality to even those taken from Siberia, and the new American forests were entered eagerly, especially by the Dutch, English, and French.

The French from Quebec, which they founded as a colony in 1608, opened the earliest significant fur trade system in North America. They did this by exploiting the forests drained by the St. Lawrence

River and the Great Lakes, the great highway to the heart of the continent.

By 1630, the Dutch from Fort Orange (later Albany when the British took it over in the 1660s) had made important contacts with the Iroquois Confederacy. The Dutch were able to develop a sizeable fur trading enterprise by merely placing their operations in the hands of the Iroquois, then the major power in eastern North America.

The first recorded explorations into the Southern Appalachians were by fur traders associated with the Englishman Abraham Wood. These explorations began about 1650 from Wood's headquarters at Fort Henry in Virginia, at the falls of the James River. Over the next twenty-five years, General Wood, in cooperation with the colony of Virginia, sent several exploring parties into the surrounding mountain areas. Before 1673, Wood cooperated with the colonial authorities in sending out two parties to explore the upper James and Roanoke Rivers. One of these parties, the Batts–Fallam expedition, reached the valley of the New River and beyond in 1671. Besides these largely private and commercial ventures, Governor William Berkeley of Virginia commissioned the German physician John Lederer to explore the Blue Ridge in 1669 and 1670. Lederer reported these expeditions in Latin and embellished them with exaggerations about impossible heights and fierce lions and tigers.

Perhaps the most interesting of the seventeenth-century exploration parties sent out by the English was one sent by Abraham Wood. In 1673, James Needham and Gabriel Arthur were dispatched into the Overhill Cherokee country of East Tennessee. Needham, a gentleman and head of the party, attempted to make direct commercial contact with the Overhill Cherokee in order to bypass the Ocaneechee Indians then serving as middlemen in the trade. The Needham–Arthur party did penetrate into the Overhill Cherokee areas; but Needham was murdered while returning, and the young Arthur was nearly killed, only to be saved by being adopted by a Cherokee chieftain. For his own safety, Arthur was sent with one of the chief's raiding parties and traveled during his year with the Cherokee to points as far south as western Florida and Port Royal, and as far north as the state of Ohio and the Kanawha Valley. Gabriel Arthur was likely the first European to be in West Virginia. The Virginia traders, however, were not the only English traders to penetrate the Southern Appalachians in the seventeenth century.

From the late 1670s through the 1690s the most significant explorations of Southern Appalachia were commissioned by the Charleston traders and the governing authorities of South Carolina. In fact, Dr. Henry Woodward had been sent on a series of explorations between 1670 and 1675, which took him several times to the Carolina Blue Ridge and the headwaters of the Chattahoochee River. James Moore and Cornelius Doherty were Carolinians who by 1690 regularly traded with the Cherokee. And in 1699 and 1700, the government of South Carolina commissioned Jean Coutre, a French *courier du bois*, to explore the Southern Appalachians as far north as Knoxville in the Tennessee Valley and the intervening country westward to the Mississippi River.

The Albany traders from 1692 to 1696 sent Arntot Cornelius Viele up the Mohawk River and from there over the New York Appalachians into the Delaware Valley and the Susquehanna. Continuing on, he went up the Juniata and over the mountains to the Allegheny River and the Ohio River. Thus, by the 1690s, the Appalachian Mountains were fairly well known by interested Englishmen.

The fur trade that drew the Europeans into the Appalachian forests was of growing significance throughout the seventeenth and eighteenth centuries. Despite the diseases, violence, and sharp practices of the traders, many Indian nations shared somewhat in the prosperity that this commerce brought. The Iroquois, for example, made large profits from this trade. And the Iroquois expected their tributary peoples to deal only through them; they in turn dealt largely at Fort Orange with the Dutch, then with the British after 1664.

The business of the fur trade in these years was mainly a traffic in excellent quality furs, such as beaver, fox, otter, and mink, and in various pelts, such as hides from buffalo and skins from deer and bear. Initially, the trade operated on a modest scale, which was fit into the existing trade system developed by the Indians. As time went on, however, vast European-owned fur trading companies, such as the Hudson's Bay Company and the North West Company, came to dominate the trade and to control large areas of the trade, especially in the north. In the mid-seventeenth century, "General" Abraham Wood was the dominant English entrepreneur, operating from his post at Fort Henry near present-day Richmond, Virginia. But by the 1690s, the easier access to the Indian source of fur supply led to the emergence of the Charleston traders and the enlarging importance of those trading from Charleston, South Carolina, which had a uniquely fortunate approach to both the Creeks and the Cherokee.

The colony of South Carolina was never able to successfully control the many fur traders who operated from Charleston into Creek and Cherokee lands, and even as far as the Choctaw and Chickasaw in the Mississippi country. These traders were mostly poor, illiterate men who were frequently caught in a desperate debt squeeze. Though many made comfortable lives for themselves living mainly in Indian society, the Indians hated most of the traders. A large number of these traders were unscrupulous enough to ply their Indian customers with rum before the trading began, and the Indians often became alcoholics. The Charleston trade was mostly in deerskins, averaging fifty-four thousand deerskins annually between 1699 and 1715. Indian slaves were also commonly traded before 1715, which increased tensions between tribes because such slaves were acquired by conquest.

In all, several thousand Europeans participated in the fur trade in eastern North America. Though most of them left no record of their experiences, the petty Charleston trader with a ten-mule train full of ironware and cutlery on his way to Cherokee country became a common sight during the eighteenth century. Many of these Charleston traders took Indian wives and frequently joined the tribe with which they traded. This "return to nature" had been first followed by the French *courier du bois,* who emerged during the first generation of the French in Quebec. The appearance of such names as McGillivary, Ross, Wiggin, Campbell, and Bunning among the Cherokee or Creek elite attests to the prevalence of this practice of the traders settling into the Indian tribes.

Thus, by the early eighteenth century, a brisk English fur trade from several points reached into the Appalachian area and was competing successfully with the more unified and more ancient French fur trade system through Quebec and Montreal. The British generally had the advantage of better products and usually offered better prices for the furs. Furthermore, since the Iroquois were able through political intimidation to channel a substantial portion of the trade through their hands, the English at Albany profited as well. The colonies to the south, too, developed fur trade connections, usually inducing specific Indian groups to turn to them for outlets to European markets. The Charleston traders, for example, depended largely on the Creeks and Cherokee, and the Pennsylvania traders, who appeared during the eighteenth century, depended upon the Mingo, Miami, and Shawnee in the Pennsylvania and West Virginia mountains and the Ohio Valley.

Before the emergence of the fur trade, the problem of boundaries between Indian nations was not particularly significant. Bear, beaver, buffalo, deer, mink, and fox were plentiful. The sparse Indian populations and their type of agriculture did not impose a heavy ecological demand upon the forests. But with the development of the fur trade, local game was frequently hunted or trapped into desperate scarcities. Indians often complained about Europeans trapping game on hunting grounds that had always been theirs, and disputes arose between Indian nations. The quest for the precious skins and furs stretched westward at an increasing rate. French, Carolinian, Virginian and, indeed, Iroquois imperial tentacles extended westward in a search for new forest grounds and a larger share of the market. For a time, the Appalachian forest had been virgin hunting ground, but by 1750, game in the Appalachian forest was not easily available. However, Daniel Boone and the "long hunters" attest to the continued richness of the game in the Kentucky's "reserve" of the Iroquois and the Cherokee, even as late as the 1770s.

Once the Indians entered into the fur trading system, they became vulnerable to the demands of the larger market and the political whim of those who supplied them with what they demanded. The basic commodities supplied to the Indians though the fur trade were guns, powder, and traps. While such goods gave the North American Indian a better military technology with which to stave off the invading Europeans, these products still made them dependent upon the very people who were threatening their continued freedom. Apart from the degrading influence of European whiskey and rum, the trade in slaves, and the weakening of the Indian by European-borne diseases, market dependence made it possible for eighteenth-century European powers to wield an immense influence upon the Indian nations, thus finally reducing them to political and economic dependence.

Trade rivalries on the southern frontier developed a bitterness that frequently flared into open warfare. The Spanish were firmly established in the Caribbean and in Florida, and during the seventeenth century, an ambitious Franciscan mission system of some thirty-eight mission points reached northward from St. Augustine, Florida, along the Atlantic coast. By 1655, these missions claimed some twenty-six thousand "Christianized" Indians. The French, initially focusing on the Quebec settlements after 1608, also established themselves at Mobile Bay in 1699, and then at New Orleans in 1718. All had a profound effect on the inland fur trade. The French challenged the British traders among the southern as well as northern Indians.

It is likely that the abuses of the Carolina traders were mainly responsible for both the Tuscarora War of 1711 and the Yamasee War of 1715. The Carolinians, of course, blamed French meddling when the Tuscarora rose up and attacked offending traders and colonists. An army of whites and Indians from South Carolina campaigned into the Tuscarora areas and destroyed them. More serious for the Carolinians was the Yamasee War of 1715–1717, which involved several other tribes beside the Yamasee—the Creeks, Choctaws, and some Cherokee. The British Indian agent for South Carolina, Thomas Nairne, was killed along with scores of traders caught in the Creek and Choctaw towns. For a time, Charleston itself was under a siege by the Indians. But in the end, the Cherokee were won to the English side, and a harsh peace was imposed upon the Creeks and the Yamasee. However, no major campaign was ever really launched against Yamasee during this war.

By 1730, the French influence was of particular concern to the British in Carolina. The colony of Georgia was established in 1733 in large part to protect Carolina interests from the Spanish and the French. And in the backcountry, great concern was shown for protecting the lucrative British fur trade with the Creeks and the Cherokee. In 1725, the British sent Colonel George Chicken into the Cherokee areas. He traveled to most of the major towns of the Cherokee, hearing complaints about traders and warning the Cherokee not to become too friendly with either the French or the Creeks. Then five years later, in 1730, Sir Alexander Cuming was sent among the Cherokee on an even more significant mission. Cuming's diplomacy proved to be immensely successful, ending with a trip to London by six Cherokee chiefs, where the Treaty of Whitehall was signed. By this treaty, the Cherokee agreed to fight against Britain's enemies and to trade only with the English. The Cherokee further agreed to allow only the British to build forts within their boundaries.

During these years of almost continual warfare between the British and the French, the French were never content to abandon any advantage in the southern Indian trade. Their diplomacy among southern Indians was a continual irritant to the British. For example, in 1736, the British sent a shrewd, ambitious German named Christian Priber among the Cherokee. But instead of encouraging British interests, Priber began to dream of a Cherokee empire and the special place he might have within it. Priber designated the Cherokee chief Moytoy as "Emperor" and chose the Cherokee town Great Tellico as the capital for the new Empire. Then Priber designated himself as "His Imperial Majesty's Principal Secretary." Suddenly, a great chill descended upon the British traders in Cherokee areas and the

English became alarmed. The French, of course, were most interested in these developments. The Carolina authorities sent two officers to arrest Priber, but they dared not move against him as long as he remained within the "Cherokee Empire." Priber received these officers cordially, saying cheerfully that he was working out an alliance with the French. After having his way for some seven years, Priber set out for the French strong point of Mobile in 1743 but was captured en route by the British. He was taken to Georgia for trial and died while still in prison.

Perhaps the most prominent figure in the great Appalachian fur trade era was an Irishman, George Croghan. Croghan arrived in Philadelphia in 1731 and immediately set about to build a trading empire that was to stretch across Pennsylvania into the Ohio Valley. He maintained a string of forts with resident agents reaching as far as the Miami and Shawnee in the Ohio country, with posts even on the Wabash River and Lake Erie. By 1750, Croghan was probably the most significant man on the Appalachian frontier. However, he spoke with more authority among the Indians than he did with the British colonial officials. The English were suspicious of his high-handedness and independence, although they frequently sought his favor when they desired his influence among the Indian nations. Croghan's fall was preceded in 1752 by a successful French attack on his trading post at Pickawillany in Ohio, which killed his agents and took his supplies. The French and Indian War of 1755–1764 ruined Croghan, and his whole enterprise collapsed as the frontier erupted into warfare. The ever-resourceful Croghan, however, returned to economic prominence as a partner in various frontier speculations in Appalachian Pennsylvania and New York. It was probably largely in response to Croghan's Ohio Valley fur trade enterprises that the French sent Celoron de Bienville on his journey down the Ohio River in 1749. During this journey, Bienville defiantly buried lead plates at each point where a river joined the Ohio, thus reasserting French claims to the upper Ohio.

When hostilities erupted into war between the French and the British in the 1750s, English fur trade west of the Appalachian Mountains collapsed. The British trade that had been so promising in 1750, only three years later was severely curtailed, and British subjects were moving into the area beyond the mountains at great risk to themselves.

During these middle decades of the eighteenth century, the Appalachian frontier changed drastically. The interest of the Europeans, particularly the British, became increasingly concerned with land title. This was manifest first with the growing interest of speculators in large western claims, then by numerous yeoman–settlers who began to occupy the more fertile fringe areas of the mountains. As the area attracted more settlers, the forest began to change. Small acreages were cleared, and the mountain valleys began to move toward a predominantly yeoman–farm economy and away from the Indian-dominated forest–fur economy.

In 1716, Virginia governor Alexander Spotswood conducted the earliest land speculation scheme in the Southern Appalachians. The governor led a large group of wealthy gentlemen into the wilderness of the Blue Ridge and the Shenandoah Valley. Elaborate camps were established at the end of each day's travel, and good fellowship accompanied good food and much drink. At the end of their journey, Governor Spotswood gave each of these gentlemen a golden horseshoe and knighted each of the men as a "Knight of the Golden Horseshoe," Virginia's new nobility. Many of the new "knights" did become interested in developing the Shenandoah Valley, and several were given generous grants.

Significant settlement of the Shenandoah followed quickly upon Virginia's decision in 1730 to change her land law and award speculators one thousand acres for each family they settled west of the Blue Ridge, so long as they recruited such settlers from outside Virginia. Already some Germans and Scotch–Irish had settled in the lower Shenandoah. In 1717, the Philadelphia Synod of the Presbyterian Church had a request from "Potomoke in Virginia" for a minister, and some Germans had settled the Shepherdstown area by 1727. But with the fear of increasing French activity in the mountains, Virginia's land laws were made more generous and a number of speculators obtained vast grants of ten thousand to one hundred thousand acres and more. The speculators brought settlers mainly recruited from among the Germans and Scotch–Irish in Pennsylvania. John and Isaac Van Meter, Alexander Ross, Morgan Bryan, John Lewis, William Gooch, Joist Hite, and Robert Beverley were such speculators. Gooch in 1727, Hite in 1733, and the Van Meters in 1730, were speculators who turned largely to the Germans for settlers. Robert Beverley, who obtained his grant in 1736, was probably the major speculator to recruit among Pennsylvania's Scotch–Irish.

Another way of recruiting settlers into the Shenandoah and the upper Potomac was developed within the vast domains of the Fairfax

SETTLEMENT CROSSES THE APPALACHIANS
(DURING THE CRUCIAL YEARS, 1730 - 1783)

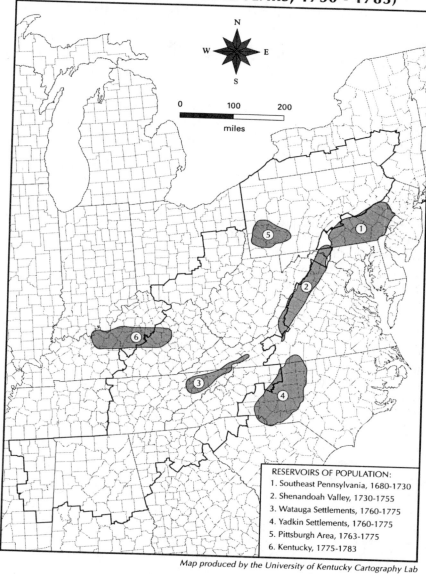

RESERVOIRS OF POPULATION:
1. Southeast Pennsylvania, 1680-1730
2. Shenandoah Valley, 1730-1755
3. Watauga Settlements, 1760-1775
4. Yadkin Settlements, 1760-1775
5. Pittsburgh Area, 1763-1775
6. Kentucky, 1775-1783

Map produced by the University of Kentucky Cartography Lab

proprietorship. Thomas, the sixth Lord Fairfax of the British nobility, was granted a patent in 1669 by Charles II, along with six other supporters of the royal family. By 1719 the Fairfax family had, either by purchase or by inheritance, come into the entire property. Their claim was to the whole area between the headwaters of the Rappahannock and the highest branches of the Potomac, an area of over 5.28 million acres.

In 1733, Lord Fairfax petitioned the crown to prohibit Virginia from making any further grants within his claim, and in 1745, this request was honored, though the claims already made by Virginia were not rescinded. Within his vast domains, Lord Fairfax attempted to introduce a neo-feudalism and organized vast manors such as the one at South Branch, which included fifty-five thousand acres, and at Patterson Creek, which was a manor of nine thousand acres. Many settlers were attracted to the lands within the Fairfax patent where they were able to obtain tracts of one hundred to three hundred acres, under a lease subject only to a down payment and a modest annual quitrent.

The area in which these speculators recruited most of the persons who came to settle Shenandoah lands in southeastern Pennsylvania. Within southeastern Pennsylvania between 1681 and 1730 a mosaic of cultures had developed. Considered by many in the Europe of the time as "the best poorman's country in the world," southeastern Pennsylvania became a mix primarily of English Quakers, Scotch–Irish and Germans. Attracted to William Penn's new colony by guarantees of religious freedom and a generous offer of land, subject only to a modest annual quitrent, many thousands of poor Europeans (generally from the Rhineland and Northern Ireland) came to southeastern Pennsylvania to establish themselves as yeoman farmers.

The Germans began arriving in Pennsylvania in 1683, settling first in the Germantown area just north of Philadelphia beyond the holdings of the original Quaker settlers. By 1727, there were some twenty thousand Germans in Pennsylvania, mostly in an area between the Lehigh Valley and Lancaster County and the Susquehanna River. These Germans spread into Maryland, founding Frederick, and then crossed the Potomac River to found Shepherdstown, (West) Virginia in 1727.

The Scotch–Irish, called "Protestant Irish" in the eighteenth century, were migrants from Northern Ireland. During the early seventeenth century, this group had migrated to Northern Ireland from many places in England and Lowland Scotland. In the initial migration into Northern Ireland, the Scotch–Irish were part of the English crown's scheme to pacify the Catholic Irish. During the course of the war-torn seventeenth century, many thousands of Protestants from all over England, but mostly from Lowland Scotland, were induced to migrate to Northern Ireland, where the confiscated estates of rebelling Irish nobility provided the basis for the offers of land made to them. Following the restoration of Charles II, and especially the Settlement of 1688, which placed London businessmen and a progressive agricultural gentry in command of Parliament, the offers to clear title to the land were betrayed in favor of the gentlemen speculators of England's southeast. Furthermore, the budding Irish linen industry found itself working against laws favoring weaving in England itself. The Northern Irelander's Presbyterianism even became an impediment to both his political activity and his security, when laws were passed after 1660 favoring the Church of England.

These staunchly Presbyterian Irishmen began coming to the American colonies late in the seventeenth century. The Scotch–Irish felt that they had been betrayed by the king and the English government and were easily induced into a second migration to North America. At first, it seemed that they would settle mainly in New England or New York, for Presbyterians were closely associated theologically with the Puritans of New England. But after 1715, they came overwhelmingly to New Jersey and Pennsylvania. They entered these colonies largely through the port of Philadelphia, as had the Germans. Here they found a Quaker-dominated colony and a large German population, neither of whom they had much in common with. The Germans and the Scotch–Irish were, in fact, very different people and tended to keep to their own communities, both on the Shenandoah frontier and in southeastern Pennsylvania. Indeed, the cultural balance between Scotch–Irish and German communities was already fairly well established by the time they migrated into Maryland and the Valley of Virginia.

Between 1715 and the American Revolution, it is estimated that 250 thousand Scotch–Irish made the journey to America. The German migration was nearly as large during approximately the same period. Such a large infusion of peoples could not help but have an immense influence upon the whole of American society and culture during these decades before the American Revolution.

The Scotch–Irish spoke a dialect in the eighteenth century that was then a version of a dialect "already old by the time of Elizabeth."

The reference to "magnificent Elizabethan swearing"; the love of the "r," as in fire (far), hair (har), and bear (bar); triphongs and quadrithongs, as "abaout" (for about) and "haious" (for house); the use of "h" for specific emphasis, as "hit" (it), "hain't (ain't)," and "hyander" (yonder); the double and triple negative for emphasis (as in Chaucer); and the omission of the "g" in "ing" endings, all attest to the ancient form of English established in the Appalachian Mountains in the late eighteenth century.

The Scotch–Irish provided the language norm for the backcountry dialect. Despite the numbers of Germans in backcountry culture and the remarkable persistence of the German language (Pennsylvania Dutch) in southeastern Pennsylvania, and for a number of years in the Valley of Virginia, the German language was gradually lost as they migrated into the valley sections of Virginia and the mountains beyond. German culture floated on such a vast sea of English speaking that German as a language of communication gradually lost out. But other distinctly German cultural traits came to be part of the Appalachian backcountry culture—such traits as the sectarian tendency in religion, certain characteristic ways of building, and farming practices.

Many Germans and Scotch–Irish came to America as individual indentured servants, though sometimes they crossed the Atlantic as families or whole congregations and settled in one place. A few migrants were criminals who agreed to deportation and indenture in lieu of prison time in England. And large numbers of "servants" were children and young people whom English society was glad to deport rather than take responsibility for. For a time, indentured servitude was the major source for labor on colonial plantations. Although Negro chattel slavery ultimately came to be thought of as a more dependable and controllable source of labor, indentured servitude was never abandoned during the colonial period. And not all indentured servants came voluntarily. However, the vast focus of frustration in Northern Ireland and Rhineland Germany insured that any time a shipmaster sought a cargo of servants in Belfast or Amsterdam, he would have an ample number of migrants for a profitable voyage to America.

Although the Germans and the Scotch–Irish made up the majority of the backcountry populations, a substantial portion of this population was considered "English." Perhaps as many as one-third of the Euro–Americans who came to the Appalachian frontier in the eighteenth century were of this miscellaneous group, drawn mostly from "come-outer" or dissenting elements or from those squeezed by overpopulation in the already established, low-country colonial society. Some were of English Quaker background, as the family of Daniel Boone, whose parents were thrown out of the Quaker Meeting for allowing their daughter to marry an outsider. Others were of French Huguenot background, such as the family of John Sevier. This miscellaneous so-called "English" group was a large one, and a high percentage of backcountry leadership came from it. However, this assorted English group lacked the cohesion and sense of group identity that both the Germans and the Scotch–Irish had. These so-called "English" frequently played a key role in mediating between the Scotch–Irish and the Germans, who often did not mix together well in backwoods society. The Scotch–Irish had a reputation for impulsiveness, were very politically active, and were fierce Indian fighters. The Germans, on the other hand, were sober and perhaps the best farmers in colonial America, but they were generally politically apathetic. The migration movement put these two groups into conflict with one another—first in southeastern Pennsylvania, then southwestward into the Shenandoah Valley, and westward into western Pennsylvania and the Southern Appalachian Mountains. The cultural tensions in the mountain society of the colonial backwoods were considerable as these two separate and very different groups attempted to find ways of living together.

Above these farmer–settlers, an aggressive mercantile elite placed itself in a frequently challenged domination. At first this group was quite small, but with time these persons with commercial and outside connections became stronger. Nevertheless, as late as 1770, this group was quite overwhelmed by the mass of settlers and squatters. Regardless of how important the speculator–mercantile elite became, the settler–pioneer was able to build a life pretty much to his own liking despite the plans and intentions of the great speculators. In fact, a substantial group of uncontrollable squatters flooded into the backwoods, paying neither taxes nor quitrents. One historian has called this contest between common settler and frontier planner "one of the enduring stories of the American frontier."

Another important group in backcountry society was the African population. Slavery was legal in each of the British colonies prior to the American Revolution, and the "peculiar institution" grew rapidly south of the Hudson River. The farther south one traveled, the larger the role of slavery became. Both colonial Pennsylvania and New York had a firmly established slave labor system. Although the mountain areas of the colonies proved more resistant to the slave system than the lowland areas, eventually slavery was frequently and profitably practiced in the more fertile valleys of the mountains.

Antislavery sentiment appeared early in the backcountry and was most commonly related to religious belief. The Quakers consistently opposed slavery as a sin, particularly after John Woolman agitated the issue in the 1740s in Quaker Meetings in Pennsylvania and areas in Virginia. Woolman's journeys took him into the Shenandoah Valley, and he nourished abolitionist sentiment there during the early eighteenth century. A strong antislavery sentiment also persisted among the Mennonites in the Shenandoah Valley. Furthermore, in East Tennessee in the 1780s, firm antislavery beliefs were established by Samuel Doak, Hezekiah Balch, and other founders of Presbyterianism in Tennessee.

During the years when the frontier of settlement penetrated the Appalachians, and Euro–American settlers made their way amid hostile Indian societies, a particular kind of society developed. It was a society besieged, for the Indian nations rightly perceived that the pioneer settler was a threat to their way of life. Fur traders might be thought of as possible allies and useful middlemen in a system that often seemed to bring benefit to the Indians as well. Though many traders were rogues and troublemakers, other traders were men of some character who married into Indian society, and Indians were glad to have such men among them. But the pioneer yeoman–farmer disrupted Indian hunting areas by establishing new clearings for mountain farms. Despite the fact that Indians were farmers also, Euro–American yeomen established scattered farms that took the place of the fur-producing forest. Furthermore, the century following 1689 saw years of continuing warfare between the French and the English and their respective Indian allies. Even before 1750 the continuing hostility of the French and British made backwoods life precarious and violent.

The Wars for Appalachia

THE FRENCH AND THE BRITISH were continuously at war, or in preparation for it, from 1689 until well into the nineteenth century. Fought partly in North America between 1689 and 1764, this series of wars is known collectively by American historians as the French and Indian Wars. The separate wars in America generally took the names of the reigning British monarch—King William's War (1689–1697), Queen Anne's War (1702–1713), and King George's War (1744–1748). The most decisive war was called the French and Indian War (1754–1763). This Seven Years' War of Europe was actually begun in Appalachian Pennsylvania, was fought on three continents, and became the crucial war for empire in India as well as in North America. Both the American Revolution (1775–1783) and the Wars of the French Revolution and Napoleon (1792–1815)—in America, the War of 1812—need also to be understood from this perspective of the British–French rivalry as a part of this continuing struggle.

In the 1730s and 1740s, the French in Quebec and the Mississippi Valley were still very powerful, but were feeling threatened by the expansion of New England, both on the Maine coast and on the Bay of Fundy, and other British colonies inland in the Ohio Valley. Another concern for the French was the challenge posed by the Iroquois Confederacy and their allied British traders at Albany. The French fur trade system depended primarily upon their relations with the many Algonquin-speaking Indian nations, and these Algonquin Indian nations were seriously challenged by the British-backed Iroquois Confederacy. When the French wooed the Iroquois into neutrality, the French gladly left the New York frontier undisturbed. But when the Iroquois actively allied themselves with the British, both the New York and New England frontiers, as well as the Iroquois themselves, became targets of Algonquin raids and frequent French operations.

The major collision points between the French and the British in the eighty years during which the Appalachian forest was fiercely contested—from 1730 to 1810—were mostly in the northern Appalachians in New York and Pennsylvania. But French pressure upon Indians to the south, in the lands of the Creeks and the Cherokee, also caused the Carolina and Virginia authorities great concern. Virginia's Land Law of 1730, which encouraged the settlement of the Shenandoah Valley, was in fact largely a measure aimed at the southern threat of the French. In New York, the areas of tension were centered on the Albany–Saratoga area and in the Mohawk River valley, the homeland of the Iroquois. In Pennsylvania and in the large areas of Appalachia claimed by Virginia, trade and land speculation interests pushed British interests into the Ohio Valley. It seemed as though wherever the English faced in North America, the French were there to contest with them. In fact, the specific flash point for the crucial war in the 1750s was in the upper Ohio Valley in Appalachian Pennsylvania. The climactic decade of collision between the French and the British came in the years between 1749 and 1759, when that area became one of the critical battlegrounds in a worldwide struggle for empire.

In 1749, the French sent a force of 230 Canadian militia commanded by Celoron de Bienville from Fort Otsego down the Allegheny and the Ohio Rivers to the mouth of the Miami River. At every major river confluence, Bienville buried a lead plate proclaiming the lands thus drained as the possessions of the French king. By 1753, the French had also built three new forts on the upper Allegheny River—at Le Boeuf, Venango, and Presque Isle—intended to reinforce the Bienville claims and to guarantee French control of the upper Ohio Valley.

Meanwhile, encouraged by Governor Dinwiddie, speculators in Virginia had developed land and settlement schemes also centering on the upper Ohio Valley. As she had done in the 1730s, Virginia during the mid-1740s turned to a policy of actively recruiting settlers to lands in the west. By 1754, Virginia had granted more than 2.5 million acres to various companies in and beyond the mountains. Three companies especially participated in these land schemes. The Greenbrier Company was the most modest, confining its activities to 100 thousand acres within the Greenbrier Valley. The Loyal Land Company, including among its investors Peter Jefferson, Joshua Fry, and Dr. Thomas Walker, sent Dr. Walker and five companions on the famous 1750 exploration through the Cumberland Gap into eastern Kentucky. Within the next four years, the Loyal Land Company settled some two hundred families on lands in southwestern Virginia. But the most influential and the most provocative to the French was the Ohio Land Company, which centered its interest on the upper Ohio Valley.

This company, including among its stockholders Thomas Lee, Lawrence Washington (George Washington's elder brother), George Fairfax, and Thomas Cresap, sent out explorers and a military party commanded by Colonels George Washington and William Trent to hold the lands the company believed they had been granted. Trent began construction of a fort at the Forks of the Ohio in February of 1754, only to have the French take the spot on April 17. Colonel Washington made a futile effort to retake what the French then called Fort Duquesne. In the end, Washington was driven away even from his hastily built strong point, Fort Necessity, on July 4, 1754.

Obviously, more than a handful of Virginia militia was needed to wrest the upper Ohio from the French. Thus, the British Crown was persuaded to send two regiments of regular troops and a Major General, Edward Braddock, to deal with the French threat. Braddock's impressive force of fifteen hundred regulars, plus militia and Indian allies—a very large force for the day—marched on Fort Duquesne, building a military road as it went from Wills Creek on the Potomac River toward the Forks of the Ohio. On July 9, 1755, within a few miles of Fort Duquesne, a much smaller force of French and Indians ambushed the troops and destroyed this formidable force. Braddock himself was killed, and British influence was thrown back along the entire Appalachian frontier. Large numbers of pioneer settlers in the Shenandoah Valley left their exposed farms for more secure areas in Pennsylvania, the Yadkin in North Carolina, or elsewhere. British fur traders quit the Ohio trade and concentrated instead upon safer and more settled areas. The crucial war with the French for control of the Appalachian forest began very unfavorably for the British.

To the north, in the mountains between Lake Champlain and the Hudson River, the French also swept the British from the key points. French General Louis Joseph Montcalm's capture of Fort William Henry in 1757 had a devastating effect on the northern Appalachian settlements of the British. But in 1758, the tide began to turn against the French. In London, William Pitt's emergence as Minister of War encouraged the rise of a remarkable group of younger generals—

Wolfe, Amherst, Forbes, Murray, Haveland, and Bradstreet. General John Forbes—with thirteen companies of Scottish Highlanders, four companies of Royal Americans, some Carolinians, two thousand Virginians, twenty-seven hundred Pennsylvanians, and a force of Catawba and Cherokee Indians—moved majestically toward Fort Duquesne at the Forks of the Ohio from eastern Pennsylvania. As they traveled, they built another military road, even as Braddock had done in 1755. On November 24, 1758, the French blew up Fort Duquesne and abandoned it. Forbes quickly rebuilt the fort, calling it Fort Pitt in honor of the great Secretary of War.

Seventeen fifty-nine was the year of disaster for the French in North America. Amherst captured Crown Point (Fort William Henry) and Fort Ticonderoga in the Hudson Highlands. And even Fort Niagara fell to the British. But the crucial blow was the fall of Quebec itself to General James Wolfe on September 17. Finally, Montreal fell to the gathering British forces in September of 1760. The French had been eliminated from North America "root and branch."

Another successful British campaign against the French and Indian threat was mounted in the south against the Cherokee in what was a major Cherokee War fought from 1759 to 1761. Unscrupulous Charleston traders had been the center of problems for years. In the 1750s, the Cherokee allowed the North Carolinians to build and garrison Fort Loudon in their midst—to protect them from the French and Spanish. As it worked out, the fort was a troublesome British presence to the Cherokee and became a focal point for difficulties that helped precipitate the war with the British.

The war was begun in 1759 with an incident between Virginia frontier militia and the Cherokee. In that year, an army of Scottish regulars and colonial militia under the command of Archibald Montgomery invaded Cherokee lands, destroying crops and orchards and wiping out the Lower Cherokee town of Keowee. But when Montgomery moved into the Overhill Cherokee country in an attempt to relieve the besieged garrison at Fort Loudon, he was soundly defeated in a bloody battle at Echoee. The Fort Loudon garrison was forced to surrender, and most of its soldiers were massacred. Montgomery's force, in fact, had great difficulty in fighting its way out of the Overhill areas and back to the safety of the Yadkin Valley.

In 1761, a much larger British force was assembled—regular British troops under Colonel James Grant, plus militia from Virginia and both Carolinas—in all, a force of some three thousand, by far the largest military force yet assembled in the southern mountains.

Grant's army entered the mountains in May through the Lower Cherokee lands near Keowee in western North Carolina. They were immediately attacked by a force of some six hundred Cherokee, who kept constant pressure on them as they proceeded through the mountains. In spite of much harassment, Grant moved on into Overhill areas only to find the towns deserted. After wholesale and systematic destruction of crops, orchards, and grain stores, as well as the towns themselves, the Cherokee were finally induced to sue for peace on November 19, 1761. Only then did Grant's army leave Cherokee territory.

With the collapse of the French power in North America, a new political situation emerged. Indian nations now faced only one European power. Those Indian nations traditionally allied with the French had to make the best arrangement they could in an obviously bad situation. Even those nations, such as the Iroquois and the Cherokee, who had been traditional friends of the British, were seriously weakened and had a dangerous new situation to face. With the French gone, the British had less need for Indian allies. And the British became less eager to present the Indians with gifts and ammunition. Furthermore, Forbes' force of seventy-five hundred that had marched on Fort Duquesne and Grant's army of three thousand that occupied the Overhill Cherokee areas were so massive that only the most naïve Indian leaders could feel that they might have a chance against an aroused British military power. Yet in 1763 came the first widespread Indian uprising in North American history.

Encouraged by the hollow assurances of the defeated French, Pontiac, an Ottawa chieftain living near Detroit, was able to obtain the help of most of the northern Indians in the first significant multination Indian uprising against Euro–American encroachment. However, only one group within the Iroquois Confederacy participated—the Senecas. Thanks in part to effective British diplomacy, none of the southern Indian nations became part of the "Pontiac Conspiracy."

In the spring of 1763, attacks were made on the frontier forts at Detroit, Miami, Pitt, Michilimackinac and elsewhere in the northwest. Forts Pitt and Detroit held out successfully, but not before several other strong points had been abandoned to the Indians. By the early spring of 1764, British regulars and colonial militia, coupled with a general Indian inability to coordinate such a large enterprise, brought the active uprising to an end.

If the long-run effect of Pontiac's Conspiracy was to leave the eastern Indians more to the mercies of British and their colonial forces, the immediate effect of the conspiracy was to frighten the authorities in London into a policy intended to conciliate the Indians. In October 1763, the British government issued the Proclamation of 1763, forbidding white migration and settlement beyond the crest of the Appalachians. This was, in fact, the British government's first effort at a systematic policy toward Indians. Issued hastily in the wake of Pontiac's Conspiracy, this was actually an initial establishment of a reservation policy, which became the approach later followed by the United States. In 1763, an immense reservation had been given the Indians.

The attitude of the British colonists toward this proclamation was universally and immediately hostile. To the Westerner—whether speculator, settler, hunter, or trader—the whole reason for the war with the French had been to win the trans-Appalachian area for themselves. Now that victory had been won, the action of the home government seemed to deny them the spoils of their success. Indeed, the Proclamation of 1763 can be considered as a first incident in a decade and a half of increasing misunderstandings between London and her colonial subjects that led the colonials to seek their independence from Great Britain.

Six of the British colonies had land grants extending to the Mississippi River—Virginia, North and South Carolina, Georgia, Connecticut, and Massachusetts. The rest of the British colonies, the so-called landless colonies, had more modest claims, at most extending to the mountains. Governors and legislatures of the landed colonies often made generous grants to individuals, but land titles were confused by grants made by other colonies or by the Crown itself. With the effective removal from control of the French and the Indians by 1763, the struggle for Appalachian lands narrowed to a contest between the various English claimants.

In the late 1760s, a group of so-called "Suffering Traders," Pennsylvanians with western ambitions but without colonial claims to base their speculations upon, bought the Iroquois claim to the Great Kanawha Valley and applied to the British Crown for confirmation. Many Englishmen of influence were brought into this Vandalia Project. In this scheme, a trans-Appalachian colony was projected roughly corresponding to the modern state of West Virginia. In the end, however, it collapsed. The Vandalia scheme matured at the wrong time. Despite powerful London allies—including Thomas Walpole, a leading banker; Lord Dartmouth, Secretary of State for the Southern Department; and even the Queen herself—by 1769, colonial and British attention came to be focused instead upon the Townshend Acts and the increasing friction between the colonies and Parliament. Named to honor the Queen, who claimed descent from the Vandals, the colony of Vandalia in 1765 was originally defined as a tract of some 2,862 square miles embracing an area south of the Ohio River between the Little Kanawha and the Monongahela. The Treaty of Fort Stanwix, negotiated with the Iroquois in 1768, cleared all Indian claims to the area, and by 1769 the colony was enlarged to include the area of the present West Virginia from the headwaters of the Potomac, including a portion of eastern Kentucky, to a line opposite the Scioto River.

Americans in this company included Benjamin Franklin, Sir William Johnson, George Croghan, and William Trent. Virginia, within whose claims the new colony was to be established, made vigorous protests. However, by then the frontier was so totally beyond the control of London that even with strong Pennsylvania and New York allies, the Vandalia Project came to nothing. Indeed, the whole western policy of the British government was greatly confused. From 1763 to 1774, the policy of London critically vacillated as the mother country and her colonies drifted into armed conflict. And contention for Appalachian and trans-Appalachian lands played a major part in this estrangement that ultimately led to the American Revolution.

Three Indian treaties negotiated in the 1760s and early 1770s extended the area of "legal settlement" beyond the line established by the Proclamation of 1763. In 1768, the Treaty of Fort Stanwix opened to settlement the Iroquois claim to the trans-Appalachian lands north of the Ohio River. In this same year, John Stuart, Britain's agent to the southern Indians, negotiated a treaty opening the lands in the Kanawha and Monongahela Valleys. In 1770, another treaty with the Cherokee, the Treaty of Lochaber, gained enough land so as to include the upper Holston in East Tennessee, where strong settlements already existed.

The British government decided in 1774 to attempt to control western settlement with strong restrictions. In that year, Parliament required that all land transfers be preceded by an authorized survey and that colonial governors were not to make any further land grants. Moreover, all surveyed parcels of land were to be sold at auction to the highest bidder. The Crown also transferred to the former French colony of Quebec control of all western lands north of the Ohio River from Virginia and other colonies with western claims. At first glance, and certainly to the English colonists at the time, this Quebec Act seemed to totally reverse the results of the French and Indian War. As a matter of fact, British agents close to London had moved into control of financial affairs in Montreal. Thus, the Quebec Act clearly seems to be a part of London's policy to control land speculation and to move toward an orderly distribution of western lands.

But by 1774, Virginia viewed her western position as desperate. In 1774, her vast claims north of the Ohio River had been transferred to London agents in Quebec, and Pennsylvania interests through the Vandalia Company threatened to take away the Kanawha region and perhaps even Kentucky. It was to strengthen her western claims that Virginia fought Lord Dunmore's War against the Shawnee and Mingo Indians.

The Shawnee were a particularly energetic and tenacious group of Algonquin Indians who split off from the Delaware after the defeat of the Delaware nation by the Iroquois in the seventeenth century. Most of the Delaware were "put in petticoats"—allowed by the Iroquois to continue to live in the Susquehanna country, but placed in a position of dependence. However, the Shawnee minority would accept no such restrictions, so a band of some two thousand people with never more than five hundred braves, split off and went south and westward to begin two centuries of wandering. They lived for a time in South Carolina, and then rendezvousing somewhere in western Virginia, the band found a home with Cherokee consent on the Cumberland River in the Nashville region. But the Chickasaw drove them from there to the upper Ohio Valley, where they found their uneasy home between contending Indian and British claims.

In the 1770s, British settlers from Virginia were edging out the beleaguered Shawnee from the Kanawha region. Lord Dunmore, the governor of Virginia, was induced into assertive action by various frontier incidents that goaded the usually pro-British Shawnee into "taking up the hatchet." The specific incident that triggered this war was the murder of the family of Chief Logan, a chief of the allied Mingo nation, a western branch of the Seneca nation of the Iroquois Confederacy. The Mingo and the Shawnee then joined forces under Cornstalk, the Shawnee chieftain, a military genius and one of the great figures of frontier America. With limited supplies and manpower, Cornstalk tested an army twice his strength. Then he divided his force in the face of the enemy and skillfully attacked one group of Virginians separately. But at the Battle of Point Pleasant on October 10, 1774, he found that he could not defeat even a part of the force sent against him. He immediately sued for peace, thus ending Lord Dunmore's War. The price of peace for the Mingo and the Shawnee was to surrender all claims south of the Ohio River, a claim contested in Kentucky during the American Revolution by some Shawnee, but never with Cornstalk's approval. As much as any single Indian nation, the Shawnee suffered at the hands of the Appalachian frontiersman. Cornstalk and his son were ultimately lynched in 1777 by a group of soldiers at Fort Henry (present-day Wheeling, West Virginia), while he was a guest at the fort and under the protection of a flag of truce.

During the decade prior to the outbreak of the American Revolution, more and more settlers made their way also into the upper Tennessee Valley. Significant settlement in the Watauga area and the upper Holston Valley had begun in 1768 after the Treaty of Hard Labor secured the area. Persons moving down the Great Valley of Virginia had built substantial settlements on the upper Holston by 1772. A number of those who came to the Watauga and upper Holston area were upcountry yeomen who had participated in the Regulator Movement, a protest movement of Yadkin-area farmers who had been defeated by North Carolina authorities at the Battle of Alamance in May of 1771.

From the Watauga area and the upper Yadkin came many adventurous men who, despite the nearby Cherokee, felt secure enough in the 1760s and early 1770s to proceed in small hunting parties into the rich Indian game preserves across the mountains in Kentucky and middle Tennessee. For a decade, these "Long Hunters" came in groups, sometimes as many as forty at a time, living for several years off the game that abounded in the forest and meadowland. After adventure spiced by danger, the Long Hunters returned to their homes, often laden with a fortune in furs. They hunted through the Tennessee, Cumberland, and Kentucky River Valleys, often ranging northward to the Ohio and westward as far as the Mississippi Rivers. At least thirty-five separate parties of Long Hunters, involving several hundred men, operated through the mountains and trans-Appalachian area in these years. The fact that by 1760 such parties could hunt in an Indian game preserve such as Kentucky with relative safety shows the weakness of the Cherokee and the once mighty Iroquois.

This is not to say that the Long Hunters did not have trouble with the Indians. They did! They were subject to attack from Indian raiding parties, and some were even killed. But any sizeable group of hunters could generally drive off these attacks. As members of these parties made their way back to the Watauga or the Yadkin settlements, laden with furs and skins, as often as not they were relieved of their burdens by the Indians, usually Cherokee, who considered all pelts from Kentucky—on or off animals—their property. One of the Long Hunters carved his sentiments on a tree after being robbed: "2300 deerskin lost, ruination by God."

The greatest of the Long Hunters was Daniel Boone. Boone was born of Quaker parents in 1734, not fifty miles from Philadelphia in Berks County, Pennsylvania. Rebelling against the settled life as well as the faith of his parents, young Daniel spent much of his time in the nearby wilderness exploring and learning forest skills. In 1750, Daniel's father was dismissed from Quaker Meeting in Berks County for allowing his children to "marry out of Meeting." Whereupon the Boones left eastern Pennsylvania and, by slow stages, made their way down the Shenandoah into the Yadkin Valley of North Carolina. In 1755, when he was twenty-one, Daniel served as a wagoner under Braddock in that disastrous campaign into western Pennsylvania. While with Braddock's army, Boone met John Finley, an adventurous trader of some experience, who filled the young Boone with dreams about Kentucky.

With the Pennsylvania–Virginia frontier pacified and the French power destroyed by 1759, Boone along with hundreds of others returned home to the Yadkin Valley, where he bought a farm. But farming, even in the backwoods Yadkin country, was too tame for him. In 1760, he began making hunting trips into the mountains and beyond, frequently being away from his wife and family for two years at a time. Sometimes he hunted in company, sometimes alone. First he went into East Tennessee. Then in 1769, in company with Finley and four others, Boone crossed the Cumberland Gap into Kentucky. When Boone returned to the Yadkin Valley in 1771, his mind was fired with Kentucky, his consuming passion for the next seventeen years. In the end, however, Boone proved a far better dreamer and pioneer leader than investor and careful husbandman. In 1788, he lost his land in Kentucky, whereupon he migrated into the Kanawha Valley. After settling first near the mouth of the Kanawha close by Point Pleasant, in 1791 he moved to a point near Charleston, West Virginia. Then in 1795, the ever-restless Boone, now sixty-one years of age, moved to Missouri to an area somewhat west of St. Louis, where he lived the last thirty-five years of his life.

But the most significant years for Boone were between 1775 and 1781, when he led his own and six other families from the Yadkin and Watauga settlements up the Wilderness Road into the Bluegrass region of Kentucky. Then, as the leader of one of the three trans-Appalachian patriot strong points, he held out against the British and their Indian allies during the American Revolution.

The American Revolution probably had more effect on the Appalachian area than any other war, even the French and Indian War or even the Civil War ninety years later. The American Revolution began far from the Appalachians in coastal Massachusetts. Yet the issue of Appalachian and trans-Appalachian lands played a major role in dividing the colonists from their mother country. Once the war was joined, the bulk of the fighting was done in the seaboard region. In fact, Britain's best chance of victory lay in remaining close to the sea, where her naval supremacy could be used to advantage. Ultimately, at Yorktown near the Virginia coast, that naval supremacy was temporarily lost, thus forcing the surrender of an army, the third she had lost in America. Before Cornwallis's surrender at Yorktown, however, Britain had lost two other armies, both on the edges of the Appalachian Mountains.

In October 1777, Britain lost her first army at Saratoga, New York, on the edge of the northern Appalachians when an exhausted British army faced a vast gathering of militia and American Continentals fully three times its size. Saratoga was the turning point of the American Revolution, for following this patriot victory the French decided that success of the American cause was possible and entered the war as an active ally in 1778. Without French help Yorktown would not have been possible.

After the collapse of the British strategy at Saratoga, to bring the colonies to their knees by severing rebellious New England from the main body of the colonies, the British shifted their hopes to a "southern strategy." This began in the overwhelmingly Loyalist colonies of Georgia and South Carolina and attempted to roll up the southern colonies one by one. This strategy was initiated with the capture of Savannah on December 29, 1778, and seemed well on its way toward success with the decisive British victory in central South Carolina at Camden in August 1780. To secure his western flank, the British general in the south, Lord Charles Cornwallis, sent an army of a thousand men toward the mountains under one of his ablest commanders, Major Patrick Ferguson. With the traditional friendship of the British with the Cherokee and the Cherokee apprehensive about the frontier settlements in the Tennessee Valley, the chances of success for Ferguson's mission were excellent. But as at Saratoga almost three years before, a British army marched to the edge of the Appalachians through communities of firm patriot sentiment, and the move again spelled disaster for British arms.

Early in 1780, word of the British activity in South Carolina and of Ferguson's move toward the mountains reached Colonel Charles McDowell, commander of a small American militia force in Burke County in western North Carolina. Fearful that he did not have strength enough to cope with Ferguson, McDowell appealed to the "Over-Mountain Men" in the Watauga settlements in East Tennessee, who were under the command of Isaac Shelby and John Sevier.

After the British victory at Camden in central South Carolina, Ferguson was perhaps overconfident, for he wrote a strong warning to the pioneers in the Watauga region threatening that unless they returned to their allegiance to George III, he would invade their region and destroy their homes. The response of the Wataugans was immediate. Assembling first at Sycamore Shoals, the militia army of some three hundred Over-Mountain Men passed under Roan Mountain and through Gillespie's Gap to Quaker Meadows on the Catawba River. There they picked up McDowell's command from Burke County and proceeded on toward the British force. By the time they found Ferguson drawn up on the top of one of the smaller "balds," Kings Mountain on the North Carolina–South Carolina border, their numbers had grown to nine hundred. Upon arrival, they immediately rushed into battle, and after an hour and a half of fierce fighting, the American militia was completely triumphant. At least 150 British soldiers died, among them Ferguson, and the rest of the army of nearly one thousand was taken captive. The Americans, fighting "Indian fashion" from ambuscade and sheltered, lost only twenty-eight men. Nearly a year later, in early January 1781, some thirty miles westward from Kings Mountain, a portion of Nathaniel Greene's American army under General Daniel Morgan, badly mauled a contingent of Cornwallis's army under Banastre Tarleton in the fierce Battle of Cowpens. Thus, these two American victories secured the southern flank of the Appalachians for the patriot cause and played a crucial role in frustrating the southern strategy of the British. In the process, the British in effect had lost a second army in the vastness of the Southern Appalachian forest.

A major result of the American Revolution in Appalachia was the further deterioration of both the Cherokee and the Iroquois as significant political powers. It was understandable that both of these Indian nations would sympathize with the British and even be led to take up arms against the rebellious colonists. Both nations had been traditional friends of the British. The Cherokee, in fact, were still ruled by some of the same chiefs who had been feted in London in 1730. And the Iroquois were heavily influenced by the Mohawk chief, Joseph Brant, a Dartmouth graduate who was the adopted son of Sir William Johnson, His Majesty's representative to the northern Indians. Furthermore, the growing settlements of the Americans represented a major and obvious threat to the Indians. The settler disrupted their hunting grounds, and the yeoman–settler–militiaman represented a menacing and effective military threat. It is not in the least surprising that when the war came, most Indians responded favorably to British overtures.

At the time of the American Revolution, at least five significant Indian groupings still played important roles in the power politics of eastern North America. Most significant was the Iroquois Confederacy, now the Six Nations since the Tuscarora had joined the original Five Nations during the early eighteenth century. The Iroquois still dominated the northern Appalachians and upstate New York. Below Fort Pitt on the Ohio were the Delaware, Shawnee, and Mingo, who lived in an uneasy truce with the Iroquois, backed by the many tribes in the upper Mississippi Valley and the Ohio country. To the south were the Cherokee in their southern mountain home and the Creek on the coastal plain of Alabama. Beyond the mountains to the west were the Wyandot, Ottawa, and various Wabash and Illinois tribes. In the southwest along the lower Mississippi were the Choctaw and the Chickasaw. The years of the American Revolution can be viewed as the last real chance for these Indians to unite and make a serious contest of the struggle for eastern North America—a chance that was missed!

During the early years of the American Revolution, both the Americans and British counseled neutrality to the Indians under their influence. The British southern superintendent, John Stuart, consistently urged the Cherokee to remain neutral, fearing the effect of their hostility on the frontier settlements, which to that point might have remained loyal to the Crown. But there were British Loyalists who urged upon the British government a policy of inciting the Indians into frontier raids. Governor Dunmore of Virginia was one of these, as were Lord Dartmouth and Greg Johnson in New York, the son of Sir William. Furthermore, there were always Indian chiefs who were easily incited to act against the pioneer settlements that they saw as threatening to them. Dragging Canoe of the seceding Cherokee group that came to be known as the Chickamauga was one of these, as was Joseph Brant, the Mohawk chief.

Despite the predominant advice of the British, the war party among the Cherokee led that nation into a war in 1776 in an operation designed to wipe out the Watauga settlements in East Tennessee. But the news of this attack was leaked to the Wataugans by Nancy Ward, a prominent Cherokee leader. Attacks were widespread from the Watauga country to Rutherford County, North Carolina, and the adjacent areas of South Carolina. The patriot retaliation was immediate. Captain Thomas Howard led a small force of Carolina militia into the mountains, surprised a sizeable Cherokee band, and completely destroyed it. The major force was launched by the four colonies of Virginia, both Carolinas, and Georgia, and was placed under the command of General Griffith Rutherford. Beginning on September 1, Rutherford led some two thousand colonial militia (some sources claim five thousand) and several hundred Catawba Indians, through Swannanoa Gap into Cherokee country. The Cherokee retreated before this vast army, as the invaders systematically destroyed every dwelling and the growing crops, as well as all the stored grain they could find. Nothing was spared as the invaders made their way through the Upper and Valley Cherokee lands into the Overhill areas. There were many skirmishes, but no real pitched battles. The Cherokee merely abandoned their towns to the invaders. In all, some sixty-six Cherokee towns and villages were destroyed before a treaty was signed in May of 1777, in which the Cherokee surrendered sizeable portions of their nation to North and South Carolina.

To the north and west, meanwhile, the year of "the three sevens" was Kentucky's bloodiest year, and 1778 saw the completion of two American forts beyond Fort Pitt in the Ohio country. An American plan was originally supposed to move cautiously on the British at Niagara and Detroit, but the surprise Iroquois raids on the Wyoming Valley in northern Pennsylvania and Cherry Valley in New York brought a change. Settled primarily by Connecticut Yankees because of the land claims that Connecticut had to the area, the Wyoming Valley in Appalachian Pennsylvania was left defenseless when all of its male population volunteered for the patriot army. When the Mohawk descended upon the valley in 1778, there was little resistance, and the settlement was totally wiped out.

The patriot answer to this attack was two expeditions into the Iroquois country in the summer of 1779, which completely defeated the mighty Six Nation Confederacy. In August from the west, Colonel Daniel Brodhead with six hundred men moved from Fort Pitt up the Allegheny River and surprised a Seneca party at the mouth of French Creek, but met no other opposition. Brodhead found the upper Seneca towns deserted, and he destroyed eight of them.

To the east, Generals John Sullivan and James Clinton moved up the Susquehanna toward Iroquois country in May of 1779. Theirs was a massive army of five thousand, including three brigades of Continental soldiers with supporting light infantry, light riflemen, and artillery. Cautiously, Sullivan moved this vast army farther into the mountains and into Iroquois country. In late August, forty-four hundred of Sullivan's forces met eight hundred Loyalists and Iroquois. This uneven Battle of Newton was the only open battle of this campaign. After the Tory–Iroquois force was defeated, the whole land of the Seneca, Mohawk, Cayuga, and Onondaga was devastated. Forty villages were destroyed and immeasurable acreages of orchards and cornfields were laid to waste. It was estimated that the equivalent of 160 thousand bushels of corn was destroyed in these raids.

Though the Iroquoian grainery of the British was destroyed in this campaign of 1779 and in the process, the myth of Iroquoian invincibility destroyed as well, the British were able to hold on in the west. Niagara and Detroit were not seriously threatened before 1780, nor did the devastation of the Iroquois heartland stop further Indian border raids into Kentucky and elsewhere. Even after 1780, the Iroquois repeatedly raided the Pennsylvania and New York frontiers. Between February and September 1780, fifty-nine Indian war parties killed 142, captured 160, and destroyed four frontier forts.

Despite the fairly close support of Cornwallis's massive British army in the south by a small force of Chickamauga Indians, the bulk of the Cherokee were not well prepared for the hostilities in the south in 1780. Immediately after the Battle of Kings Mountain, the leader of the Wataugans, John Sevier, selected two hundred and fifty of his best men and led them by forced marches across the Blue Ridge into the central settlements of the Overhill Cherokee. Even the sacred city of Echota was destroyed by this sudden, ruthless campaign. The Overhill Cherokee were unresisting and astonished, for they supposed that Sevier was moving against the offending Chickamauga farther south down the Tennessee River. The governor of Virginia, Thomas Jefferson, initiated this war on the Cherokee, hoping to strike at the Chickamauga and define a new boundary.

The American Revolution had the effect of passing control of the Appalachian frontier to the new government of the United States.

First, Lord Dunmore's War in 1774 had pushed the formidable Mingo, Shawnee, and the Ohio Indians from the area of West Virginia. Then the Cherokee had been pacified by the massive campaign of Griffith Rutherford in 1776. Finally, even the mighty Iroquois were defeated by the Sullivan–Clinton campaign of 1779. Yet the Ohio Indians— the Wyandot, Shawnee, Mingo, Delaware, and others—remained as a significant force in the area north of the Ohio River. Even though the dramatic winter 1777–1778 campaign of George Rogers Clark and his Kentuckians into the area of the Old Northwest resulted in victories over the British and their allies at Kaskaskia and Vincennes, Indian power north of the Ohio River was considerable. In June 1782, the Wyandot defeated a colonial militia of some five hundred near Sandusky, Ohio; and in September, a force of about three hundred British and Indians laid siege unsuccessfully to Fort Henry on the south side of the Ohio River in (West) Virginia. But at Blue Licks in Kentucky, in the last large-scale battle of the American Revolution, the Indians—mainly Shawnee—were stunningly successful against a patriot party that included Daniel Boone.

The Indian stronghold in eastern America was not totally broken by the events of the American Revolution. A base of power still remained to the Indians north of the Ohio River, and this was not broken until Anthony Wayne's campaign into northern Ohio, climaxed by the Battle of Fallen Timbers in 1794. Other bases of significant Indian power remained in the South prior to 1812, especially in Creek areas and in Florida. But these Indians were successfully neutralized for a time after the American Revolution. Thus, the effective Indian challenge to the occupation of the Appalachian area was removed. With the British also removed as a factor in the drama of western settlement, the story of the Appalachian Mountains became wholly related to the history of the United States of America.

Part 2

The New Nation and the Appalachian Backwoods

After the United States gained control of almost all of the Appalachian Mountain area, a somewhat different and frequently discriminated-against society emerged in the nation's backwoods. When a divisive Civil War came to the United States, this mountainous area was much fought over and tragically divided. In the War's aftermath, the region became known by mainline Americans in quite stereotypical ways.

Backwoods-Cohee Society

THE COASTAL AREAS of the British colonies were settled by English migrants, who often came as rather well-positioned individuals and groups, but who happened to be out-of-favor during England's revolutionary period, 1640–1688. After the so-called Settlement of 1688, those who migrated from England, and from Germany, tended to be persons "left out of the settlement" and these people generally settled in backwoods areas that approached and even entered the Appalachian Mountains.

Tensions between the earlier-arriving tidewater elite and the eighteenth century latecomers, who tended to settle in the backwoods, sometimes broke into open violence. Even before the eighteenth century, Bacon's Rebellion in Virginia took place in 1676. British colonial history, in fact, is full of east–west conflicts, including Culpepper's Rebellion in Virginia (1677–1680) and the various rebellions in Massachusetts, Virginia, and New York associated with the Glorious Revolution in 1688. Leisler's Rebellion in New York, the Quitrent Riots in New Jersey, and especially the Regulator Movement in North and South Carolina continued this tradition of colonial backcountry revolt against the eastern elite before the American Revolution.

The Regulator Movement (1767–1771) was particularly closely associated with Appalachian settlement, for it was the Scotch–Irish and German settlers who had migrated down the Valley of Virginia and then out of the mountains down the Roanoke River into the Yadkin country who formed the backbone of the Regulators. In the Yadkin country, these frontier yeomen found themselves in conflict with the tax policies of "easterners" in control of the governments of both North and South Carolina. These taxes were levied in cash at a time when the Carolina frontier economy was without specie and was largely a self-sufficient economy dependent on barter. When officials began collecting taxes in kind and taking away the farmer's cattle, hogs, and implements, the yeomanesque frontier erupted into violence. The newcomers considered such measures repressive. They organized themselves into Regulator groups and attacked sheriffs and tax collectors, thus challenging the authority of the colony. Governor William Tryon of North Carolina raised an army of more than a thousand and moved against a Regulator Army that outnumbered his but lacked the discipline of his colonial troops. One great battle, the Battle of Alamance in May 1771, where two hundred Regulators were killed, broke up the movement. Tensions remained high for years, however, and Regulator issues were important through the time of the American Revolution.

Unlike Virginia land laws that quite specifically encouraged speculation in order to recruit settlers for frontier protection, North Carolina's laws concerning the settlement of her western lands during the colonial and early national period made quite modest acreages available through a "headright system." Free "headrights" of one hundred acres were available for any head of family who settled in North Carolina, though substantial grants were available through purchase as well. North Carolina's system, of course, extended into areas that later became Tennessee.

The yeoman ideal—the hope of having land of one's own—impelled most Appalachian settlers to take up mountain farms as soon as the region was reasonably secure from Indian attack. The French and Indian War of 1755–1763, and then the American Revolution of 1775–1783, drove most Indian nations beyond the mountains. For veterans of the American Revolution, large tracts were made available where veterans might receive their severance pay from a grateful government, especially from the new states of Virginia and North Carolina.

Of course, speculators were always an integral part of backwoods land ownership and settlement patterns. In fact, it took the speculative schemes of Governor Spotswood and other Virginians to open the settlement of the Shenandoah. And the backwoods farmer seemed always in conflict with absentee speculators. In fact, squatters and "would-be yeomen without clear title" were also part of this conflict.

Confusion concerning legal title to the land has been a curse in the Appalachian area since the earliest European settlement. The Virginia Land Law of 1770 allowed the claims to western land that were later granted for military service during the Revolutionary War to be sold and transferred. This enabled speculators to buy up millions of acres from veterans, often for a mere pittance. Added to the confusion of conflicting claims of the various states and old English grants, the result was constant litigation. Consequently, a virtual army of lawyers and a wild traffic in land ultimately left much of the best land in the hands of absentee owners.

As the new government of the United States emerged in the 1780s, its western boundary was set at the Mississippi River, thus including essentially all of the Appalachian area within the boundaries of the new nation. The fortunes of those who came to settle in Appalachia were inextricably bound to the fortunes of the United States and its constituent states. Nine of the original thirteen states had areas that included parts of the Appalachian Mountains. And the next three states to join the Union also included Appalachian areas—Vermont, Kentucky, and Tennessee.

A great post–Revolutionary War migration of people flooded into the Appalachian Mountain area and suddenly changed the society of the mountains. Whereas before 1775 the presence of powerful Indian nations made Euro–American settlement precarious, after the American Revolution, Euro–Americans with their African slaves came into the newly secured region in large numbers. Sons and daughters of the American Revolution, whether veterans, "sunshine patriots," Loyalists, Negroes, German, Scotch–Irish, or English, came into the mountains by the thousands to take up farms.

In 1770 the Cherokee, the largest Indian nation in the southern mountains, probably outnumbered the Euro–Americans and their African slaves within the southern mountain area by about ten thousand. But by 1790, the year of the first U.S. census, slaves and Euro–Americans in the mountain area from Pennsylvania southward totaled nearly 180 thousand, while the Indians in the region could never have exceeded 50 thousand. The Appalachian Mountains had suddenly become a "white man's country."

There were large areas in Appalachia that became quite rich agriculturally, especially in the Ridge and Valley section in Virginia and East Tennessee. But in the vast, truncated highlands of eastern Kentucky and West Virginia, where many pleasant valleys were drained by streams that then ran pure and were full of fish, the soil was thin and had only limited agricultural potential. But game—squirrels, deer, bear, mountain lions, even bison—filled the forests, and a man could build his cabin in some wide valley and be master of all he could see, whether landowner or squatter. The land was beautiful and the rainfall abundant, and one's well or spring appeared never to run dry or offer bad water. A good spring was especially valued. Such forest agriculture could lead to major success in hog or cattle raising, and this kind of "ranching," especially in the high Virginia mountains, was preferred to spending one's efforts in clearing the forest in order to raise a garden or corn.

Many came in these early years as squatters with no clear title. If things didn't work out, such people easily moved on. But some squatters remained, particularly if they were content to stay on the remote lands of speculators who chose to let their lands lie idle and wait for better times. Remote Appalachian land could in fact be purchased for just a few dollars per acre even as late as the mid-twentieth century.

A most interesting political story within Appalachia during the 1780s was the story of the rise and fall of a potentially wholly Appalachian state, the State of Franklin. The Watauga settlements in East Tennessee had developed a considerable population, probably as many as twenty thousand people, between the late 1760s and the end of the American Revolution. Realizing that they were in areas within North Carolina and beyond Virginia's western claims, the settlers, mostly from Virginia, formed themselves into the "Watauga Association" in May of 1772. It was this same spirit of frontier self-government that later led them to attempt to found the State of Franklin.

In the year that the American Revolution ended, 1783, the North Carolina legislature, under the influence of William Blount and other speculators, passed what became known as "the Land Grab Act." In the tradition of North Carolina's headright policy, this act offered land in the Tennessee country in parcels of one hundred acres for the price of ten pounds each. Exceptions were made for lands still within the Cherokee nation and those lands set aside as military reservations in the Cumberland River valley. But before North Carolina could move toward an orderly control of the region, then made up mainly of migrants from Virginia, a movement toward a separate state for Eastern Tennessee developed.

Delegates from three counties met in the small frontier city of Jonesboro (Tennessee) in August of 1784, elected the leader of the Watauga community and Kings Mountain hero, John Sevier, as governor of the new State of Franklin, and invited the neighboring counties in Virginia and the trans-Appalachian counties of North Carolina to join them. A second convention met in November 1784, and finally a third convention early the next year formally established the "State of Franklin." Although North Carolina had responded with a friendly cession law in November of 1784, North Carolina later took a hostile attitude toward the new state. She specifically organized the area as the Washington district of North Carolina and designated separate officials for this district, even though a separate and parallel set of officers had been selected by the State of Franklin.

Thus, the Franklin project was thrown into direct opposition to North Carolina. John Sevier had been initially drawn into the Franklin scheme with some reluctance. But he was quickly pushed into its leadership when he was elected governor of Franklin. Certain enemies of Sevier, John Tipton principally, used their influence to turn North Carolina against the new state. For a time during 1785, this mountain area had two complete sets of officers, judges, and local governments, neither recognizing the authority of the other. At one point, Governor Sevier was declared a traitor to the State of North Carolina, was tried and convicted at Morganton, only to escape on a horse saddled just outside the courtroom window, moments after the verdict was read.

In 1787, the Franklin project collapsed. The Federal Constitution of that year established the principal that no state could be divided without its consent. And Sevier was systematically wooed away from the Franklin project. By the spring of 1788, support for Franklin had almost died out. Sevier and other leading "Franklinites" were brought into the government of the Washington District and the emerging state of Tennessee. Sevier, in fact, became Tennessee's first governor when it was admitted to the Union in 1796.

In Kentucky, another unusual local governmental scheme—the Transylvania Company—rose in the 1770s, only to collapse in the early 1780s. Transylvania, much of whose area was within Appalachia, was a bold frontier speculative project that came fairly close to success because of the charisma of two of its leaders—Richard Henderson and Daniel Boone. Henderson, the guiding light of the project, was the North Carolina judge who masterminded the project, based on a title to lands between the Kentucky and Cumberland Rivers "bought" from the Cherokee. Even in Indian times, the Cherokee did not have a clear title to these lands, for they shared them with the Iroquois. Henderson recruited Boone to guide settlers to the far side of this claim on the Kentucky River, and in 1774 founded Boonesboro. Boonesboro became one of three patriot strong points in central Kentucky to hold out against British and Indian attacks during the American Revolution. After the war, however, the Virginians, led by George Rogers Clark, moved toward statehood for a state called Kentucky based upon Virginia law and land claims. The Transylvania scheme lost out entirely.

As Kentucky County, Virginia, the Kentucky project had emerged in the Bluegrass region around Harrodsburg and Danville. In Kentucky, the move toward statehood was basically a Bluegrass and Ohio River Valley matter. Eastern or Appalachian Kentucky did not play a particularly significant role in the emergence of Kentucky as the fifteenth state in 1792.

During the years following the British defeat in the Revolutionary War, those who were moving into the Appalachian Mountain area were largely absorbed in local issues. Yet great events were moving toward important conclusions on the eastern seaboard. A new national government was taking shape as delegates met in Philadelphia in the spring of 1787 to draw up a new constitution.

The constitutional revolution of 1787–1789 was largely a product of the eastern seaboard. No western leader was prominent in the constitutional debates in Philadelphia. In fact, the nearest thing to a spokesman for the west at that time, Patrick Henry from Henrico County, Virginia, refused to attend the Philadelphia sessions even though he was elected as a delegate from Virginia.

The debate over ratification of the Constitution was most critical in Virginia, New York, and Massachusetts. North Carolina was opposed to the new Constitution for a "more perfect Union," preferring instead the older Articles of Confederation. North Carolina had representatives at the Philadelphia Convention, but none of her representatives were willing to sign the final document. South Carolina and Georgia were swept swiftly into ratification by well-organized, downstate interests friendly to the new document. But the crucial three states—Virginia, New York, and Massachusetts—had closely fought battles over ratification. Had any one of those three failed to ratify, the new Constitution could not have been easily implemented.

It was largely the western and mountain representation at these three critical ratification conventions who opposed the new Constitution, though the picture was a mixed one. Despite their strong support of the Revolution in the previous decade, most of the mountain areas seem to have approached the possibility of a stronger national government with much suspicion. The old government under the Articles of Confederation seemed satisfactory to most mountaineers.

Though it was weak, in their view a limited government seemed preferable to one with too much power.

The political culture of the people who shared a yeomanesque "mentality" would indeed place them in opposition to a strong constitutional government. With the yeoman's approach to liberty as a staunch libertarian, with his equalitarian beliefs and his willingness to let government remain as remote as possible, his general preference for the loosely structured Articles of Confederation can be understood.

In the Virginia ratification convention, the representatives from Kentucky's areas generally shared a negative view toward the new document, as did those from western New York and western Massachusetts. And of course North Carolina never ratified the Constitution of 1787 until after the new government was a functioning reality. But those representatives from the West Virginia areas at Virginia's convention generally favored the stronger government, because they believed that a stronger government might better deal with the Indian "menace" north of the Ohio River and negotiate a more secure control of the Mississippi River. As the new Federal government began, first with its capital city in New York City, then in Philadelphia, from the view of most western and mountain persons, the government of the new Union began under a shadow of substantial suspicion.

The group that had constructed the Constitution of 1787, a combination styled "the Federalist Party," was given responsibility for governing the new nation during the first twelve years under the new Constitution. Usually local leaders were the community's "better element," and the more common people—particularly from remote backwoods areas—seldom showed much interest in national matters. Such lesser men tended to defer to their patrons and superiors, despite the substantial democratizing influence of the American Revolution. This was especially true when property qualifications disqualified many. Prior to the 1820s, in fact, there were significant limitations on the privilege of voting in most states.

The policies of the new government mostly followed the advice of the new Secretary of Treasury, Alexander Hamilton, and reflected the view that prosperity could best be assured for the new nation if conditions were created supportive of the mercantile and business groups then emerging. Hamilton's policy to establish the full credit of the United States with the twin programs of "Assumption" and "Funding"—to have the U.S. assume the debts of the states and to fund those debts at par—had the effect of sending scores of bond buyers into the remote rural areas of the country to buy up the bonds at bargain prices. In the uninformed backwoods, many persons believed that such bonds "weren't worth a Continental," and were purchased by these speculators at an assured profit. However, the high point of Appalachian disaffection over Federalist policies was reached in the 1790s during the Whiskey Rebellion in Appalachian Pennsylvania.

The Whiskey Rebellion was the result of Hamilton's program to establish a source of revenue in order to pay for his various national initiatives. Hamilton's first revenue measure had been an import tariff, a measure that passed with little opposition. But his second revenue measure in 1791 involved an excise tax levied on distilled whiskey.

About one-fourth of the total national distilling industry at the time was located in four counties in Appalachian Pennsylvania. There, some twelve hundred separate distillers provided a valuable product that was used in this frontier area as much as a medium of exchange as for consumption. There was little cash in the area. The farmers there believed that the tax on their principal manufacture, made from products that they produced themselves, was unfair and discriminatory. When Federal customs officials attempted to collect the tax in 1794, local mobs interfered, tarred and feathered some agents, and escorted others out of the area by force.

Hamilton and the Federalists eagerly accepted the challenge and took the opportunity to respond with an overwhelming force to support law and order. Despite the opposition of Pennsylvania's governor, Thomas Mifflin, Hamilton himself led a Federal force of fifteen thousand militiamen westward. President Washington even accompanied the army as far as Carlisle, Pennsylvania. Of course, the rebellion collapsed. As large as the American army at Yorktown, this vast force scarcely found any rebels at all, although a few were jailed.

Furthermore, the different policies of the Washington Administration regarding Indian policies of the Northwest Territory and the Southwest Territory were also controversial in the South and had the effect of turning many in the Southern Appalachians against the Federalists. President Washington, Hamilton, and Henry Knox, the Secretary of War, concluded that the new government could carry on a vigorous anti-Indian campaign against only one concentration of Indian power. Washington and Knox decided that the government would move against the Indians of Ohio. Three successive campaigns were launched against the Miami/Shawnee/Mingo concentration in northern Ohio in the early 1790s. Meanwhile in the southwest, efforts against the Creeks and Choctaws were left entirely to the states involved, while the Federalist government carried on a policy of accommodation toward the southern Indians. In fact, so sparse were the federal efforts in support of southwest frontier, that most of the leaders in the southwest in those years flirted seriously with Spanish offers for help.

The political fallout from the Federalist policies in both western Pennsylvania and the southwest was serious. Hamilton's overreaction in the case of the Whiskey Rebellion had the effect of making western Pennsylvania, and indeed most of the western and Appalachian country, firm supporters of the party opposing Hamilton. This Democratic Republican party—the party of Thomas Jefferson and James Madison—won the west overwhelmingly in the election of 1800 and swept the Federalists from office. Significantly, Jefferson's Secretary of the Treasury (Hamilton's old office) was the congressman from Pennsylvania's "Whiskey Rebel district," Albert Gallatin.

It would be misleading, however, to suggest that Federalist policies from 1789 to 1801 were universally unpopular in Appalachia. The Federalists had many supporters in Appalachia. Backwoodsmen, particularly in western Virginia, applauded President Washington's determination to destroy the power of the Ohio Indians. Three successive and expensive invasions were launched against them: the first, under Josiah Harmar in 1790, a second commanded by Arthur St. Clair in 1791, and a third under Anthony Wayne in 1794. The first two ended in bloody disaster, but General Wayne's decisive victory at Fallen Timbers over some two thousand braves of the Wyandot, Miami, Mingo, Shawnee, and Delaware Nations secured the safety of the frontier from Kentucky northward for many years. Furthermore, the diplomacy of the Federalists, which resulted in Jay's Treaty with England (1794) and Pinckney's Treaty with Spain (1795), removed the British from the Northwest forts, opened the Mississippi River to navigation, and guaranteed a safe place to deposit goods shipped to New Orleans. But the Indian resistance remained strong west of Ohio. There was great ferment developing among the Indians, as shown in the rising millennial Indian faith that encouraged all Indians to stand and fight in "these last days." During Jefferson's administration, the Shawnee chieftain Tecumseh's dream of a massive Indian coalition to stand against the white onslaught began to take on somber reality.

By 1800 quite a different European-derived society had developed along the Appalachian frontier in the backwoods of the new nation. In Pennsylvania and in the mountain South, slavery developed a firm foothold, especially in the richer agricultural areas. None of America's coastal cities in the North or the South developed a real interest in its backcountry hinterland, and eastern elite groups tended to view the backcountry as uncomfortably boorish, though offering a useful buffer against possible Indian attack.

From Virginia and Maryland southward, a slave-owning, plantation elite dominated southern life, and this planter elite took a generally hostile attitude toward their backwoods, which they came to regard as a threat to their continued control. The interests of the backwoods hunter or fur trader, and even the backwoods yeomen, were largely ignored by each of the states. And those in this "different" society even gave themselves a name to signify this difference. They called themselves "Cohees." In Virginia, they called those from the east—the elite who dominated the state—"Tuckahoes," after the name of one of the Randolph's plantations, one of the great families in Virginia's east. The New York writer James Kirke Paulding visited western Virginia in 1817 and noted that "the mountain called the Blue Ridge not only forms the natural but the political division of Virginia . . . The east and west sections of these States are continually at sixes and sevens . . . This snug little rivalry is beginning to build vigorously . . . The people of whom I am now writing call those east of the mountain Tuckahoes, and their country Old Virginia. They themselves are the Cohees, and the country New Virginia."

Another writer in the early National Period who noticed this same division was the southern feminist Anne Newport Royall, editor of the Baltimore-based magazine *The Huntress*. She noted in 1826 that, "On the bosom of this vast mass of mountains . . . of Virginia . . . there is as much difference between the people of the western states and those in the east as there is between any two people in the union . . . these present a district republic of their own, every way different from any people."

This backwoods or "Cohee" culture that developed in the Appalachian backwoods during the early National Period had several characteristics. Economically, this culture was a diversified one, though a yeoman-style agriculture dominated. Anthropologist John S. Otto has described this kind of rural culture, which developed from Delaware to Texas, as "the Plain Folk Agriculture of the Old South." Otto suggests that this kind of agriculture was characterized by 1) a grazing, farmland economy, with cattle and hog grazing on an "open range" in the forests, but with "patch farming" in the cleared portions of the forests; 2) a life where families lived on isolated farmsteads in dispersed rural neighborhoods; and 3) county seat towns or neighborhood churches and school houses serving as the centers of community concern, interest, and recreation.

Traditionally historians of the American frontier have seen the plain-folk farming as a stage that preceded a later type of commercial farming. But there is good evidence to suggest that this kind of yeoman farming was not a stage, but rather quite a different approach to farming. Indeed, it was a way of life quite separate from capitalistically oriented agriculture. This yeomanesque approach to farming probably reached its apogee symbolically with the election of Andrew Jackson in 1828, but declined in significance after that time.

The large literature that has developed in recent years called "the New Social History," focuses on the lives of ordinary people of the early Republic, using quantitative techniques made possible by the use of computer analysis of masses of data. Such New Social Historians have examined census schedules, county land records, wills, and other documents that purport to expose the life of the common people. These historians present a picture of a rural population concerned about family survival and not with a focus on the accumulation of wealth. This kind of yeomanesque, pre-capitalist farming appears to have predominated in the nation's rural areas in the New Republic's early days, and it certainly dominated the more remote areas of Appalachia until well into the twentieth century.

Several New Social Historians have turned their attention to areas within the Appalachian region. Such scholars are Robert D. Mitchell and Warren R. Hofstra, who have looked particularly at the Shenandoah Valley, Tyrel G. Moore and Mary Beth Pudup who have looked at eastern Kentucky, Tyler Blethen and Curtis Wood who have studied western North Carolina. In addition, David Hsiung and Durwood Dunn have looked particularly at East Tennessee, and Wilma A. Dunaway has applied this approach to the region as a whole.

These studies claim to revise the traditional view associated with isolated rural societies in general and with Appalachian society in particular. Some have shown that agrarian capitalist tendencies appeared early and laid the basis for much of modern industrial capitalism in the generations well before the Civil War. Though some have emphasized the attitude or "mentality" of rural people as they moved in states from self-sufficiency and neighborhood trade to a wider involvement in grain or livestock markets, others have insisted that even during the colonial and early national periods the farmers were really capitalists all along, and their isolation was not nearly so great as has been supposed.

Such studies remind us that even an apparently simple Appalachian economy was really quite complex. Capitalist tendencies clearly existed in Appalachia's preindustrial agriculture, as speculators, town merchants, planters, and even small entrepreneurial farmers and ranchers participated in an emerging regional market economy early on. Actually, the records that New Social Historians analyze with such care—the land records, titles, wills, and even census records— are themselves records that an entrepreneurial society produces. Those with a yeomanesque "mentality" often did not bother with such technicalities as land title or a will.

In truth, the Southern Appalachian economy was quite diversified by the pre–Civil War period. The yeomanesque approach to farming was clearly in decline by 1830 as large families put pressure on land availability, while the broader market system was attracting tens of thousands of mountain-raised animals to the major coastal cities. Furthermore, markets were emerging in each isolated county seat town. The stores of these towns sold foodstuffs, dry goods, tobacco, and slaves. Beginnings also were made in some manufactures. In Maryland, Virginia, and Pennsylvania, foundries developed prior to the Civil War based on the close proximity of ores and fuel, both charcoal and coal. And in these early days, a salt mining industry developed in mountain areas where that resource was found. The two principal areas of Appalachian salt mining were in Virginia—in the southwest in the area of Saltville, and in the Kanawha Valley in the area of modern Charleston.

Before the 1850s, important beginnings were made toward coal mining in parts of Appalachian Maryland, Virginia, and Kentucky. During this period, mining for gold also developed significantly in northern Georgia and western North Carolina. Though as early as 1750 lead and zinc were mined in Wythe County, Virginia, and copper was both mined and smelted in Polk County, Tennessee, gold mining was the most colorful and influential of all the mining developments in Appalachia before 1840.

Two major Appalachian gold fields developed. The first gold mined in Appalachia was found in 1799, when a wave of prospectors came into western North Carolina in Lincoln, Rutherford, Burke, and Wilkes Counties. By 1825, Rutherford County had become the center of the young nation's most extensive gold mining. Several thousand men ultimately produced some $9 million in gold, most of which was sent to the Philadelphia mint.

However, the major gold strike before the great California gold rush of 1849 was in 1828 along Yahoola Creek in what is now Lumpkin County in north Georgia. Gainesville became the major supply base for this gold field, which was then within the boundaries of the Cherokee Nation and thus a major factor in the increasing tensions between the Cherokee and the state of Georgia. As a result of this Yahoola rush, Dahlonega (first called New Mexico) and Knucklesville developed as major camps. The former had a boom population of about five thousand, while the latter was at one time a tent and shack city of three thousand. In the years of its operation, some $40 million worth of gold was extracted from this field, and for a time a U.S. mint was located at Dahlonega.

Women's roles on yeoman farms during the Cohee period were also varied and complex. On some farms, the "Goody" or "Goodwife" had an exalted place, with the expectation that she would bear many children and see to their proper raising; i.e., the yeoman's labor force. This has led some writers to conclude that she was much exploited by a traditional paternalistic society. Yet some traditional feminist scholarship holds that women on essentially subsistence farms were more equal to men simply because neither received a cash wage. Generally a gender-based dividing line of farm work set aside the "inside work" as women's work, and "outside work" as men's work. Inside work included cooking, housework, spinning, weaving, washing, and usually the care of the garden and poultry. Outside work included plowing, seeding the fields, harvesting, care of cattle and hogs, as well as whatever long-range trading was done.

Historian Wilma Dunaway's treatment of regional farmwomen in the eighteenth and early nineteenth century emphasizes the poorer, harsher situations they found themselves in. She claims a kind of "last colony thesis" for them, which places women at the bottom of exploited peoples, as the World System of capitalism slowly moved to dominate the area.

The remarkable profile of Tennessee Civil War veterans shows that the mothers of those soldiers from ordinary yeomanesque background did all kinds of housework, cooking, carding, and the making of clothes for the many children. More comfortable households might have a few slaves, so that supervising slave labor and organizing the clothes making and maintenance would be included in the woman's role. On the death of a husband, a widow might turn to certain specialized skills such as needlework, weaving, or clothesmaking. This Tennessee Civil War Veterans Survey reminds us of the immense time women spent on textile arts in preindustrial days. The miles that women walked each day using a "Scottish Wheel," or the backbreaking labor spent working her loom, leads us to realize the eagerness with which the Cohee wife welcomed an opportunity to acquire ready-made cloth.

Concerning the religious life of the Cohee/backwoods culture in the early nineteenth century, these years witnessed the development of a revivalistic and highly sectarian kind of Protestant Christianity. The Scotch–Irish had come to North America under the general guidance and leadership of the Presbyterian clergy. The Presbyterian Church seemed set to become the church that would grow most dramatically after the American Revolution as populations spread westward. But the small band of frontier, seminary-trained Presbyterian ministers—probably never more than fifty men—was not nearly large enough to provide the religious leadership that such a massive movement required. Instead it was the popular, revivalistic churches of the eighteenth century, especially the Methodists and Baptists that had sprung to strength during the Great Revivals, that mainly nourished backcountry religion.

Already non-establishmentarian churches—the Baptists, Methodists, Mennonite, and various Reformed churches—had combined with some rationalists, such as Benjamin Franklin and Thomas Jefferson, during the Revolution, to produce the "Religious Settlement" of the American Revolution. This settlement insisted upon a separation of church and state and a voluntary church built on a predominantly Protestant base. With the growing numbers of Baptists and Methodists during the Second Great Awakening (1790–1820), the religious identification of the backwoods changed dramatically. Unlike the Presbyterians, the Baptists ordained any man whom a local congregation deemed worthy. And the Methodists sent neophytes, often with little education or training, among their rapidly expanding societies, equipping them with a plan of study that would lead them toward full ordination. For the Baptists and Methodists and other mass-based, revivalistic churches, the major requirement for ordination was a proper faith and an open heart.

A recent study of Appalachian religion makes a compelling case for the emergence of a distinctive regional religious culture. Based upon the old "anti-missionary Baptists" and the camp-meeting revivals of the nineteenth century, this culture is still an integral part of much of modern Appalachian life.

If as Protestants have long held, "every man is his own priest" and the Bible is the proper guide to faith, it is easy to understand how many Christian denominations and sects developed in Appalachia. Many of the churches that the German immigrants to Appalachia had brought with them were strongly sectarian and reflective of the free, even sectarian, church tradition. However, as Germans moved beyond the Shenandoah Valley and into the further reaches of the Appalachians, other aspects of the German tradition were lost. For example, family names were changed, as Schmidt and Muller became Smith and Miller, and the use of the German language slowly died out.

Most of the characteristic Appalachian speech patterns that have dominated the area were built on an essentially Scotch–Irish base. The Scotch–Irish spoke a form of English already old at the time of their eighteenth-century migration to North America. The English spoken today in the Appalachian Mountains is indeed one of the most ancient forms of living English spoken in the world. Here we see such archaic usages as double, triple, quadruple, and even quintuple negatives for emphasis, and the use of "h" before vowels, also for emphasis. Long forgotten words in the language, such as "disremember" for "forget," are still in common usage in modern Appalachian speech. The remarkable retention of traditional British ballads, broadsides, and folk songs is closely associated with the language memory of even modern Appalachians.

Political concerns were also a significant part of Cohee life, especially for the Scotch–Irish. The Germans tended to be essentially apolitical and to concentrate their energies on farming. But the Scotch–Irish had been interested in political matters since the sixteenth century, when Presbyterianism and the Reformation galvanized their interest in politics while still in Scotland. In fact, H.H. Brackenridge, an early American novelist of some renown and himself a Pennsylvania politician, noticed this political activism of the Scotch–Irish of the Appalachian backwoods as early as 1792.

In national politics it was the Jeffersonians from 1801 to 1825 who began building a strong and abiding identification between the people of the Appalachian backwoods and the government of the United States. Jefferson had a clear vision of the importance of the West and its place in the future of the United States. Jefferson built his home, Monticello, on one of the easternmost of the Appalachian Mountains, and he faced his home westward. Some of his neighbors were mountaineers, and his successors, Madison and Monroe, lived in the same Albemarle County neighborhood on the edge of the Appalachian Mountains.

The policies of the Jeffersonians were generally popular with mountaineers. Although he was a planter, Jefferson had idealized the yeoman-farmer, and the major achievement of his first administration was the 1803 purchase of the Louisiana Territory. This was an act of wide popularity and established the United States firmly in the heart of the continent. Not only was the nation greatly enlarged by this purchase, but it also secured control of the whole Mississippi Valley.

The War of 1812 was a generally popular action in the West and in the Appalachian backwoods. The United States surely did not "win" this war; its capitol building was burned, and its navy was swept from the seas. But the U.S. again avoided being defeated by the world's greatest naval power. Against England the United States had proven that its earlier victory during the American Revolution had been no accident. After this war, national pride soared, and the loyalty to the United States—especially in the Appalachian backwoods—was to be sorely tested in the years ahead as divisive issues tore section from section.

Like the American Revolution, a series of Indian wars also accompanied the War of 1812. During the War of 1812 period, there were three Indian wars—"Tecumseh's Conspiracy," which was destroyed in 1811, the Creek War of 1813, and the First Seminole War of 1818. All had the effect of further diminishing Indian power in eastern America.

Tecumseh was a remarkable leader and political genius, probably the greatest Indian statesman since the Mohawk Hiawatha. A Shawnee chieftain, but with family ties to both northern and southern Indian nations, and in whose veins ran both Iroquoian and Algonquin blood, Tecumseh understood that if the Indian was to survive politically, he had to unite against the growing power of the United States. Tecumseh most likely came upon the scene too late, for the tide of Euro–American settlement and power had become irresistible by his time. But his analysis of events and his strategy for dealing with the power of the United States was probably the only feasible way for Indian nations who desired to remain independent. Tecumseh saw the danger posed by the United States, but counseled caution and restraint until Indian plans were fully matured. He refused to be drawn into a premature confrontation with the United States despite much provocation. His plan was either to meet his enemy on his own terms, or if it was determined that no other alternative was left except to fight and die, to do just that. But many of his followers were not as patient. His own brother, a mystic called "The Prophet," was drawn into such a premature battle during Tecumseh's absence, and his "Conspiracy" was badly wounded in the great battle at Tippecanoe, Indiana, in 1811. Thereafter, Tecumseh could do little but seek success for his cause as an officer in the British Army during the War of 1812, a war he did not survive.

The Creeks, the major remaining Indian power unconquered in eastern America in 1812, were destroyed in a brilliant and ruthless campaign led by Andrew Jackson in 1813. Jackson's Creek Campaign was totally successful as he marched through the seats of Creek power in central Alabama. And in 1818, Jackson led a similar campaign against the Seminoles, a branch of the Creek Confederacy. As a general commanding the Tennessee and other militias, he defeated these Florida Indians, driving them into submission or into the swamps of the Everglades.

Thus, by 1820 the United States and its constituent states had emerged as the sole effective claimant to sovereignty in the whole of the Appalachians and its neighboring areas. Though Indian nations still existed in parts of Appalachia—especially the Cherokee, who were then enjoying a dramatic cultural renaissance—they remained there at the sufferance of the dominant white society. If another conflict came, the eastern Indian societies would be no match for the power of the United States.

In the post–War of 1812 period, so successful were the Jeffersonians politically that the partisan struggle was confined within the Democratic Republican Party of Jefferson and Madison. But this one-party pattern did not last long. A new party system emerged in the years following the controversial election of 1824, and this new arrangement set the basic political patterns for the region and the nation until the Civil War.

In this new political era, the central political figure was Andrew Jackson, the hero of the War of 1812, and himself a Scotch–Irishman and son of the backwoods. Though he lived within the Appalachian area only briefly in Jonesboro, Tennessee, Jackson traveled frequently in the region and had many political allies throughout the mountains. Jackson was the first Scotch–Irishman to be elected president and the first "outsider" to be elected to that office. All former presidents of the United States had been members of the elite of the American Revolution era, and all had either been Virginia planters or New Englanders from Massachusetts. Most mountaineers thought of Jackson as one of their own.

Yet Jackson had bitter opponents in the mountains, too. Tennessee politics, for example, had always been frightfully personal, as Jackson had risen to importance as a leader of the Blount Faction, a group opposed to Tennessee's first governor and frontier hero, John Sevier. And the national politics in the 1820s became unusually personal as well. In the presidential election of 1824, though Jackson carried most of the Appalachian area, significant sections of Appalachia supported Henry Clay of Kentucky. In Tennessee, Jackson also had to contend with the personal political strength of Davy Crockett and John Bell, both of whom represented a long tradition of anti-Jackson partisanship in Tennessee. The party that grew up as an opposition party to "King Andrew," designated itself the Whig Party. The Whigs, in fact, became the majority party in both Virginia and Kentucky.

One of the major issues that concerned Cohee populations in the southern mountains in the 1820s and 1830s was Indian removal. Cherokee lands in northern Georgia, western North Carolina, and East Tennessee attracted ambitious persons from the surrounding white-dominated areas. This was especially true when gold was discovered within the Cherokee boundary in northern Georgia in the mid-1820s. White pressure to acquire Indian lands became immense, and this pressure inaugurated the first of the gold rushes of the nineteenth century—a phenomenon that was to be repeated in 1849 in California, in 1876 in South Dakota, and in 1898 in the Yukon.

The gold discoveries were within boundaries guaranteed to the Cherokee by a treaty with the United States. It was an awkward situation to have a "foreign nation" existing within the jurisdiction of the Federal Union that was, as it was supposed, a vehicle of the several sovereign states making up that Union. The continued presence of a "foreign" Cherokee Nation represented a substantial dilemma for the three sovereign states within whose boundaries the Cherokee Nation existed: Georgia, North Carolina, and Tennessee. Georgia took the lead in challenging the existence of this internal foreign nation, with Tennessee and North Carolina lagging at various distances but never opposing Georgia's initiatives.

From 1810 to 1835, the Cherokee enjoyed a dramatic cultural renaissance. They had taken President Thomas Jefferson's advice to follow the white man's ways and to "civilize" themselves. The Cherokee adopted a constitution patterned on the 1787 U.S. Constitution, invented a system of writing, and published a newspaper, *The Phoenix*, written in the Cherokee language. They experienced an active poetic and literary renaissance and even adopted slavery on the southern pattern. But when the Cherokee's white neighbors demanded their lands and that they submit to the laws of the states that surrounded them, they refused. Most mountaineers in the southern states agreed that the Cherokee must either leave for lands in the West if they insisted on keeping their separate national existence, or amalgamate into white society and submit to the laws of the states concerned. As president of the United States after 1829, Andrew Jackson reflected this general opinion.

An opposing view among some American citizens, mostly from states in the northeast, held that a treaty was a sacred obligation and that to continue in the tradition of broken Indian treaties any longer was not honorable. Thus, Cherokee claims to their national territories should be recognized. However, few Cohees in the southern mountains took this view, though there were some who did. One such was Davy Crockett, born in the mountains of East Tennessee and who by the 1830s represented a West Tennessee constituency in the U.S. Congress. Davy Crockett was a mountain frontiersman par excellence and a bitter political rival of Andrew Jackson. But on the Cherokee issue he fought a losing battle. His opposition to the so-called "Ridge Treaty,"—the treaty made with a minority faction of the Cherokee who agreed to removal—cost him his position in Congress and led to his migration and later heroic martyrdom at the Alamo in Texas.

Despite their refusal to accept removal by the majority faction among the Cherokee, led by Chief John Ross, the Cherokee were ultimately removed from the Southern Appalachians. Some have criticized Ross's stubborn opposition as refusing to recognize the inevitable, but others see his determined opposition as a heroic defense of the right and honorable position.

The literature on Cherokee Removal is large and controversial. Even Thomas Jefferson had been involved, for as president he set the alternatives to the Cherokee of becoming "civilized" or suffering removal. For Jefferson, the choice was up to the Indians. For Henry Clay and many westerners, it was clear that the "savages" were inferior, thus removal was the only alternative if whites wanted the land. In the case of Andrew Jackson, who was president at the crucial time, he had no hesitation. Jackson believed that removal was the only policy available if the Indians were to be protected from what he termed "annihilation" as a separate nation.

Despite his early opposition to Jackson's aggressive policy of removal, John Ridge with his father, Major Ridge, both principal chiefs of the Cherokee, ultimately agreed with Jackson's belief that removal was inevitable if the Cherokee were to survive as a separate nation. Thurman Wilkins, the major historian who has studied the Ridge faction, takes the view that Chief John Ross refused to face reality and allowed himself to be swept up in the popular Cherokee view that they should "stay at all costs." The Ross–Ridge split became bitter, and even after the Ridge faction signed the Removal Treaty in 1836 and the Cherokees were removed, this division persisted. It ultimately led to the public murders of both Ridges in Oklahoma in 1839 and to the tragic division within the Cherokee that nearly destroyed them.

The removal program was carried out in 1838 and 1839 by the United States Army. This resulted in a "Trail of Tears" between East Tennessee and Oklahoma, during which some five thousand Cherokee died, or one-fourth of the nearly twenty thousand Cherokee who were rounded up and forced to migrate to the west during that terrible year. Private John Burnett, who served as an interpreter in the U.S. Army under General Winfield Scott, noted many years later that the operation carried out "the most brutal order in the History of American Warfare. I saw helpless Cherokees arrested and dragged from their homes, and driven at bayonet point into the stockades . . . I saw them loaded like cattle and sheep into six hundred and forty-five wagons and started toward the west as the tragic trek began in November . . . The long painful journey to the west ended March 26th, 1839, with four-thousand silent graves reaching from the hills of the Smokey Mountains to what is known as Indian Territory in [the] West."

Several hundred Cherokee avoided removal by retreating into the wilderness of the Great Smokies during that winter of 1838–1839. The larger group of these refugees was led by Chief Utsela, but a smaller group included the family of a minor chief, Tsali, called "Charlie" by the Americans. According to the prevailing story, Tsali's group was captured but then escaped as they were being accompanied to one of the stockades. Two soldiers were killed in the confusion surrounding their escape. The killing of U.S. Army soldiers represented a statement of resistance to General Scott, and he did not dare tolerate it. So an entire regiment was detached to hunt out and punish the murderers. Tsali and several of his brothers and sons were persuaded to surrender and were quickly executed. With these executions, the Army gave up its efforts to round up the Cherokee eastern remnant under Chief Utsela. Tsali and his kin passed into Cherokee legend, and the sizeable group of the Eastern Band of the Cherokee was allowed to continue its existence in the remote mountains of western North Carolina. With Cherokee Removal the last vestige of Indian control of any significant parts of the Appalachian Mountains ended.

The Challenge to Cohee Society, 1820–1860

IN RECENT YEARS, a substantial literature has emerged exploring the nature of antebellum Southern society that particularly probes the question of why the relatively poorer, non-slaveholding whites largely supported secession. In the early 1940s, Thomas Jefferson Wertenbaker even suggested the question of why what he called "Cohee Civilization" did not stop the spread of plantation America before a bloody war was necessary. More recently, some scholars in the tradition of the New Social History claim to see a class struggle developing within the Old South, between the substantial yeomen and the paternalistic, plantation elite. Yet there are others who claim that although the loyalty of non-slaveholders passed through a period of political confusion, in the end, their ultimate loyalty was to the planter elite, who did indeed speak for the whole white South. Surely a careful look at the life and society in the southern mountains should prove useful.

A sense of backcountry or of Cohee separateness, whether sectional or class-based, did in fact develop within the slave states, and their opposition to the tidewater planters seems to have been quite firmly established by 1830. There were clear differences between the two. Planter society was essentially aristocratic, and its aims and values were derivative of the way of life of the English country gentlemen. Cohee society, on the other hand, was much more democratic and took its clues from the yeoman tradition in Europe. In America, a substantial difference in economic interests and values emerged. Though both were agricultural, planter society was tied to slave-produced crops such as tobacco and cotton, and both of these products were geared to capitalistic production to be sold on a world market. The Cohee economy, on the other hand, produced a diversity of crops, such as corn, animals, and wheat, and geared its production mainly to home or local needs. When the yeoman farmers did produce for a market, it was usually hogs, chickens, and other livestock, and was sold seasonally on long drives to southern cities.

Planter society in the Old South supported "establishment" institutions such as formerly state-supported churches, the Presbyterians, and the Anglicans. This society also supported the existing power balance that was then in place in Southern state governments. Cohee citizens in Southern states supported dissenter and sectarian churches, such as the Baptists, Methodists, or Brethren, and found themselves frequently at theological odds with Southern planters during the years between 1820 and 1860.

The small, pre-capitalist farmer of the antebellum period generally shared a yeomanesque mentality, which contrasted with the market-oriented approach to agriculture that the slave-owning, plantation elite possessed. The planters also took part in the existing power balance put in place by the constitutional compromises, which counted slaves for purposes of legislative representation but denied blacks the right to vote.

In 1829–1831, for example, "Trans-Allegheny Virginia"—then relatively the more prosperous and more populous section of the state if only white populations were counted, the area with most of the state's newspapers, and an area where the population grew most rapidly between 1800 and 1830—began bringing pressure for constitutional revision concerning representation in the state legislature. Under different circumstances, eastern Virginia might have continued to make legislative concessions to the faster-growing areas in the mountainous west. But Tidewater Virginia was then caught in a deep depression, because its older tobacco lands were giving out. Furthermore, in the heat of late August 1831, the Nat Turner Insurrection, the Old South's largest slave revolt, resulted in the death of sixty-one whites and an unknown number of blacks.

When the Legislature reconvened in 1831 to consider the new State Constitution, the Old South witnessed its last full-blown debate on the slavery issue. The westerners argued strongly for some scheme of emancipation that would end slavery in Virginia, noting that the presence of a large number of slaves gave whites in the Tidewater areas what they considered unwarranted strength in the Legislature. Slaves did not have the vote, of course, but were counted for representation purposes. Furthermore, the hysteria caused by Nat Turner's Insurrection had the initial effect of causing a temporary revulsion against slavery. After a remarkably full and free debate, the legislature voted by only 73 to 58 to reject emancipation and to retain chattel slavery indefinitely. The antislavery votes had come mainly from western Virginia, and a shift of a mere seven votes would have placed the state on the road toward emancipation in the 1830s.

Another South clearly challenged the Old South of the planter elite in the days before the Civil War. The Germans and Quakers within Cohee society tended to take an especially strong antislavery position. Within this largely mountain-centered challenge to slavery, Hinton R. Helper, author of the strongly antislavery and influential *The Impending Crisis of the South* (1857), reflected the views of the Germans of the up-country South. And Southern Quakers maintained their quiet and consistent witness against slavery in the Shenandoah Valley of Virginia and in the North Carolina up-country.

In Appalachia, as in the Old South generally, slavery was a complex institution. Slave conditions in Appalachia varied from those counties where the plantation system was fully developed—as in Madison County and other Tennessee Valley counties in northern Alabama, or Floyd County (Rome), Georgia—to a county (Mcdowell, in what was to eventually become West Virginia) that had absolutely no blacks at all in 1860. Madison County, Alabama, was the only Appalachian county with a more than 50 percent black population in 1860. Furthermore, the mountain South presented the remarkable presence of a large, multicounty area inside the Old South in which blacks were almost entirely absent. The seven-county area around Parkersburg, (West) Virginia—an area twice the area of Rhode Island at some fifty miles wide and one hundred miles long—had a population in 1860 less than one percent black. The Appalachian South also enjoyed certain important Underground Railway routes, though the scope of the Underground Railway there remains murky. However, Harriet Tubman used a mountain route for most of her escapes.

There is no reason to believe that slavery was particularly mild in Appalachia as compared with other areas in the Old South. Probably slavery was harshest in the lower reaches of the Mississippi River simply because the work in sugar-growing areas was much more difficult. Slaves certainly feared being sold "downriver," thus indicating a recognition of slavery's harshness there. But a few stories of slavery in Appalachia should suffice to offer an idea of slavery's harshness even in the southern mountains.

Sophia Ward was born a slave in 1837 in Clay County, Kentucky. Clay County reported a slave population of 349, with 262 free blacks and 6,041 whites in the county in 1860. She said of their life in eastern Kentucky:

> "I wuz a slave nineteen yeahs and nine months, but somehow or nuther I didn't belong to a real mean pet of people. The white folks said I was the meanest nigger that ever wuz. One day my mistress Lydia called for me to come in the house, but no, I wouldn't go. She walks out an says she gwaine make me go. Then I grab that white woman when she turn her back, and shook her until she begged for mercy. When the master comes in, I wuz given a terrible beating with a whip but I didn't care for I gave that mistress a good 'un too."

Aunt Sophia, who was interviewed in her ninety-ninth year continued,

> "We lived off to the back of the master's house in a little log cabin that had one winder on the side. We live tobly well and didn't starve for we had enough to eat. We didn't have as good as the master and mistress had. We would slip into the house after the master and mistress wuz sleeping and cook to suit ourselves. . . .
>
> "My master wuzn't as mean as most masters. Hugh White wuz so mean to his slaves that I know two gals that kilt themselfs. . . . One nigger gal . . . he whipped . . . most to death for fergittin to put onions in the stew. Next day she went down to the river and drowned herself."

The conditions under which slaves lived varied greatly. Not only were there "good" masters and "mean" masters, but the economic situation of the slaves varied according to the wealth of their master. In previously Cherokee areas of Appalachian Georgia, prosperous plantations emerged with communities of one hundred or more slaves, such as the place where Callie Elder lived in Floyd County near Rome. The plantation house was a "whoppin big place," and there were "too many slaves on that plantation for me to count." The slaves lived in log cabins daubed with mud inside and furnished only with beds held together by cords. Food was largely "cornbread, and meat with plenty of vegetables." Sundays, she remembered, they had "wheatbread." Her master was "just as good to us as could be," but the men had to be in the fields at sunrise and the women by 8:00 A.M.

Amelia Jones of Clay and Laurel Counties, Kentucky, was owned by a small planter named Daw White. "He was a Southern Republican and was elected as a congressman . . . from Manchester, Kentucky. . . . Master White was good to his slaves. He fed us well and had good places for us to sleep, and didn't whip, only when it was necessary. But he didn't hesitate to sell his slaves. He said, 'You all belong to me, and if you don't like it, I'll put you in my pocket,' meaning of course that he would sell that slave and put the money in his pocket."

Mrs. Jones continued, "The day that he was to sell the children from their mother, he would tell that mother to go to some other place to do some work, and in her absence he would sell the children. It was the same way when he would sell a man's wife. . . . when he returned his wife would be gone. The master only said, 'Don't worry, you can get another one.'"

Slaves could be sold at any gathering of people, but regular slave markets existed throughout the southern mountains. Slave markets operated in Winchester, Staunton, Lexington, and Bristol in Virginia, and in Tennessee at Knoxville, Chattanooga, and Jonesboro. Even in the much poorer Cumberland Mountains of Kentucky, regular slave auctions were held in London, Pikeville, and Manchester. Of the Manchester slave market, Mrs. Amelia Jones noted that her father was sold at auction there. "There was a long line of slaves to be sold and a good price was paid for each. They were handcuffed and marched away South."

The auction block in Manchester was built in an open space from "rough made lumber" and had a few steps, then a platform on which the slave stood. "He would look at the crowd as the auctioneer would give a general description of the ability and the physical standing of the man. He heard the bids as they came, wondering what his new master would be like."

Nor were many of the barbaric aspects of the slave trade absent from Southern Appalachia. An observer traveling in 1833 reported that he

was at Rowley's Tavern, 12 miles west of Lewisburg, Greenbrier Co., [West] Virginia. A drove of 50 or 60 negroes stopped at the same place that night. They usually camp out! But as it was excessively muddy, they were permitted to come into the house. So far as knowledge extends, droves on their way to the south eat twice a day, early in the morning and at night. Their supper was a compound of potatoes and meal and was without exception the dirtiest, blackest-looking mess I ever saw.

They slept on the floor of the room which they were permitted to occupy, lying in every form imaginable, males and females. . . . There were three drovers. . . . Each of the latter took a female from the drove to lodge with him, as is the common practice of the drovers. . . . Six or eight in the drove were chained. . . .

In the autumn of the same year, I saw a drove of upwards of a hundred, between 40 and 50 of them were fastened to one chain, the links being made of iron rods, as thick in diameter as a man's little finger . . . They generally appear extremely dejected. I have seen in the course of five years, on the road where I reside, 12 or 15 droves at least, passing to the south. They would average 40 in each drove.

By all indications slavery was enlarging in Appalachia even as it was in the Old South up until the Civil War. In Burke County, North Carolina, the percentage of slaves in the county population rose from 7 percent in 1790 to 27 percent in 1850, and 26 percent in 1860. The number of heads of families owning no slaves in 1790 was 1,091, and in 1860 was down to 1,007. The number of heads of families owning one to ten slaves was 152 in 1790 and 153 in 1860. The number of heads of families owning more than ten slaves was 12 in 1790, but rose to 60 in 1860. The population of Burke County, on the eastern edge of Appalachian North Carolina, grew only slightly from 8,110 in 1790 to 9,239 in 1860, though the area of the county was much smaller in 1860 than it had been in 1790. Such data seem to suggest that a larger number of slaves were being held by a small but growing elite. In Burke County, a strong nine-family slaveholding elite had developed, and most of these families had English and Scotch–Irish names.

The information available on Appalachian slavery and slave-owning elites indicated that slave-owning and pro-slavery sentiments in the region were firmly established. The principal study of the Appalachian slave-holding elite is John Inscoe's *Mountain Masters, Slavery, and the Sectional Crisis in Western North Carolina*. Inscoe finds a professional and business-based group of large landowners in Appalachian Carolina who were well connected by marriage as well as by political and economic ties to the slave-owing elite in the rest of the South. In fact, some of this mountain elite, particularly U.S. senator Thomas Clingman and the influential William H. Thomas, were passionate Southerners and early champions of secession.

Slave owning was a symbol of status in Southern society, and in a typical Southern Appalachian county, the local elite leaders typically owned several slaves. In Jackson County, North Carolina, the Cherokee's friend, William H. Thomas, is a classic example of the mountain elite. He was the county's foremost slave-owner and a leading merchant, with several stores in the county. He also owned a tannery and carried on a significant trade with the "Cherokee remanent" in the state. In Jackson County, only six other men owned more than ten slaves.

A slave-owning elite developed in almost every Appalachian county where slavery was legal. Persons able to accumulate wealth in such a society invested some of their wealth in slaves, probably much as successful farmers today invest in machinery. And as agricultural success continued in a favorable market for Southern-grown commodities such as cotton, tobacco, hemp, and livestock, further profits were frequently invested in country stores and town businesses as well as in slaves. Even though the black population may have been small in these counties, powerful elites with important statewide connections strongly supported the slave-owning system.

In fact, in the 1850s, pro-slavery made substantial inroads in the mountains of southwest Virginia and the Shenandoah Valley. The increasing pro-slavery sentiment of the Shenandoah can be seen in part as reflecting the area's agricultural prosperity and the apprehensions about the ease of slave escape in an area so exposed to Northern antislavery propaganda. But southwest Virginia's increasing pro-slavery sentiment appears to have been due largely to the building of the Virginia and Tennessee Railroad in the 1850s. The railroad brought in a Virginia elite that was responsible for the building and the running of the railroad in the towns in the Roanoke, New, and upper Holston Valleys. Close ties developed with Lynchburg, Petersburg, and other eastern Virginia cities, and with a railroad-oriented elite from these towns.

Although Appalachian slaveholders perpetuated many injustices, it can also be said that the American antislavery movement was in large part born within the Southern Appalachians. Prior to 1830, in fact, the majority of antislavery societies in the United States were in the mountain South. In 1827, of the 1,130 antislavery societies in the nation as a whole, 1,106 of these were in the South, and most of these were in the southern mountains. Antislavery advocates in the South were, after all, much more immediately offended by the realities of slavery than were persons in the North, where the effects of the American Revolution had led to the removal of slavery. By 1820, each state north of the Mason–Dixon Line, the boundary between Pennsylvania and Maryland, had either abolished slavery outright or had set in motion a scheme for the gradual emancipation of the slaves within the state.

For a time it seemed that the spread of support for emancipation might reach southward, even into Virginia, Kentucky, and Tennessee. Virginia seriously debated emancipation as late as 1830–1831. In Kentucky, antislavery advocates were hopeful that slavery could be done away with in the first constitutional convention in 1792, and until the convention in 1849, a constitutional prohibition against slavery in Kentucky seemed possible. But all antislavery moves were countered by strong pro-slavery pressures. In Tennessee, which never seriously attempted to abolish slavery statewide, there was a serious effort in the 1840s to separate East Tennessee from the other portions of the state. Furthermore, the eastern mountain portion of that state for a time became the nation's center of antislavery activity.

Until 1830, East Tennessee was the major center for antislavery activities within the United States. The antislavery base in East Tennessee had been laid by the founders of Presbyterianism in that state— Samuel Doak, Hezekiah Balch, Samuel Carrick, and others. Most of these early Presbyterian ministers preached a "New Light" gospel of a socially aware Evangelicalism. Several of these ministers were prominent in the establishment of the State of Franklin, and in the late eighteenth century they established the roots of the antislavery movement in East Tennessee. The mountainous areas of Virginia, now mostly West Virginia and the Shenandoah Valley, also had strong antislavery groups. But in Virginia, the antislavery sentiments were mainly aimed at either sustaining a minority antislavery witness, as with the Mennonites in the Shenandoah Valley, or in support of the movement that reached its near success in the constitutional debates of 1830–1831. With the failure of the antislavery efforts in 1830–1831, the antislavery movement subsided in Virginia and trailed off into sectionalism, which led ultimately to the birth of West Virginia during the Civil War.

In East Tennessee, the religious base for antislavery built by Doak, Balch, and others attracted several abolitionist Quakers who along with other antislavery advocates had been driven from the Piedmont of North Carolina because of increasing persecution by pro-slavery persons in that area. Thus, in the 1820s for a time, Jonesboro, Tennessee, became the capital of the nation's antislavery crusade.

Jonesboro was a most interesting Tennessee Valley town. It had been the seat of the State of Franklin and was one of the first laid out towns in the "West," serving briefly as the capital of Tennessee. Jonesboro was also the home of Martin Academy, an early "log cabin" Presbyterian school, and it had a strong Presbyterian church. It became the county seat of Washington County. And from 1821 to 1825, it was home to an antislavery printing establishment that for a time published the nation's leading antislavery journal, Benjamin Lundy's *Genius of Universal Emancipation*. During some of these years, the publication included on its staff the young William Lloyd Garrison. More important perhaps was the *Emancipator*, a paper in Jonesboro edited by the iron manufacturer and Quaker, Elihu Embree, the first periodical published in the United Statesthat took an open and clear abolitionist position.

More important to the antislavery movement than this temporary journalistic bastion within the Southern Appalachians was the antislavery educational system initiated by Samuel Doak and other pioneer Presbyterian ministers. The "log cabin colleges" in Tennessee—schools built alongside Presbyterian churches, both being served by the same seminary-trained minister—almost always taught a strong antislavery doctrine. When it became too dangerous to continue to teach and preach antislavery in the slave state of Tennessee, these ministers and their students migrated into the Midwest and the West where they became important abolitionist leaders. Such persons were: John Rankin, one of the major forces in the Underground Railway and an aggressive abolitionist, living in Ripley, Ohio after the 1830s; Gideon Blackburn, president of Centre College, and later minister in Illinois; and others, such as David Nelson, James and William Dickey, and Samuel Carothers.

During the 1850s, a corner of Appalachian Kentucky also became the locale for a "radical abolitionist witness." This was the witness established by John G. Fee in Madison County, Kentucky. Fee had been invited into the area by Cassius M. Clay, a Kentucky aristocrat who had been converted to emancipationism while a student at Yale University. Clay had heard antislavery advocate William Lloyd Garrison speak and returned to Kentucky to try to build a political career on an antislavery base. He ran for the state legislature on several occasions, winning only during his earliest tries. He ran once for governor of Kentucky in 1851, but he gained only a little over thirty-five hundred votes of the one hundred thousand cast. He developed a small but loyal constituency, largely in Kentucky's mountain areas, and became one of the founders of the Republican Party in the state.

Fee was also a Kentuckian from the Ohio River county of Bracken, and had been schooled first at Augusta College in Bracken County, and then at Miami University in Ohio. He became a Presbyterian minister and was trained at Lane Seminary in Cincinnati. While at Lane, he became an abolitionist and pledged to return to Kentucky to preach the abolitionist doctrine in his home state. This led to his removal from Kentucky's pro-slavery Presbytery and his support by the Northern abolitionist society, the American Missionary Association. He was a dedicated abolitionist, and on Clay's invitation came to "the interior of slavery" in southern Madison County to establish a community, which he named Berea (see Acts 17: 10–11). Here he instituted several antislavery churches as well as a school. When the excitement of John Brown's raid in Appalachian Virginia at Harper's Ferry led to a great fear in Madison County and the belief that the abolitionists of the county were about to encourage a slave insurrection, representatives of the pro-slavery majority of the county and its leading citizens rode to Berea and insisted that the Bereans leave the state. They were able to return only fitfully until the issues of the Civil War were well settled in 1863. After the Civil War, Berea became a major force in linking Northern evangelical ex-abolitionist persons with the post–Civil War Mountain Mission.

Most citizens of Coheedom, however, did not take an antislavery position. A small elite in almost every mountain community owned slaves. But a majority of the mountain population, especially in Appalachian Kentucky and Tennessee, and in (West) Virginia probably was antislavery. Frederick Law Olmsted, while traveling through western North Carolina just before the war, said of one of his hosts in that area:

> I asked him if the people here preferred Iowa and Indiana to Missouri at all because they were free states. "I reckon," he replied, "they don't have no allusion to that. Slavery is a great

cuss, though, I think, the greatest there is in these United States.

"There ain' no account of slaves up here in the West, but down in the east part of the State about Fayetteville, there's as many as in South Carolina. That's the reason the West and the East don't agree in this State. People out here hates the eastern people."

The sectionalism that emerged in the mountain area of each Southern state appears to have had, at least in part, an antislavery base. Through the 1830s, 1840s, and 1850s, slave society had become more and more sensitive in its defense of its "peculiar institution." From a "necessary evil," which was the position taken by most apologists for slavery in the days of Jefferson and Madison, Southerners increasingly took the position that slavery was a "positive good." The phrase was John C. Calhoun's, himself born and raised on the fringes of Appalachia in South Carolina.

As Southern society sold itself on slavery's morality, it became increasingly insistent upon a uniformity of opinion within its border. Thus, in North Carolina, Tennessee, Kentucky, Georgia, and Virginia, where substantial antislavery sentiment existed, particularly in the mountain sections of these states, antislavery sentiments were either driven from the state or hushed into silence. In the mountain town of Barbourville, Kentucky, for example, such a solid citizen as Dr. Samuel Freeman Miller was induced to leave the state following the failure of Kentucky's antislavery constitutional debates of 1849. An antislavery man, Miller left for the free state of Iowa, where he became its first governor. He was later appointed by President Lincoln to the United States Supreme Court, where he served with unusual distinction from 1862 to 1890. By 1845, slavery was not a debatable subject inside the slave states, and any significant group within the slave states held their antislavery sentiments at great peril to themselves.

Cohee political leadership was divided, even as the nation was in these years prior to the Civil War. Some mountain leaders such as Senator Thomas Clingman of North Carolina and William H. Thomas of Jackson County, North Carolina, were aggressive Southern nationalists, and both supported secession and slavery as an institution. Yet other mountain leaders were much less sure about the drift of their states toward secession. In Tennessee, both the Whig leader, William G. Brownlow, and the Democrat, Senator Andrew Johnson, bitterly opposed Tennessee's separation from the Union. Yet neither believed in antislavery, and both seemed to believe that slavery was best protected by remaining within the Union. In Kentucky, the admirers of Henry Clay largely transferred their loyalties to John J. Crittenden, who was particularly well-known for his many efforts to compromise the issues that were dividing the Union. In Kentucky, too, many mountaineers were admirers of Cassius Clay, one of the founders of the Republican Party in that state. Yet many Kentuckians admired John Breckinridge and Humphrey Marshall, both of whom supported the Confederate cause despite the failure of secession in Kentucky.

Politically most Appalachians, then as now, seemed to have been content to be left alone by government and were concerned more with local issues than with national ones. Since before the American Revolution, the tradition of patron–client politics had been firmly implanted in North Carolina, Virginia, and their frontier offspring. In such a system, things were done politically because of whom you knew, what patron you looked to, and how he looked after you. Roads were built, teachers hired, and justice obtained according to a network of patron–client arrangements that stretched from the national capital to state government and down to the county seat. It did matter "who you knew, and who you were." Those with the most powerful patrons were the ones who exercised the most power in local matters. "It had always been this way," it was said.

Family and clan loyalties were easily incorporated into this system. The politics in the mountain areas of the slave states, in fact, remained essentially personal politics. It was really not Democrats vs. Whigs, but "Jackson men" vs. "Clay men." Parties tended to be collections of families who were loyal to some national or state leader.

The party system that emerged after Andrew Jackson was elected president in 1828, divided pro-Jackson Democrats from their opponents who took the name "Whig." Most Jacksonian policies were in harmony with what Appalachian Americans generally desired: 1) a spoils system of appointing persons to government office; 2) Cherokee Removal; 3) the destruction of the "money power" of the Second National Bank, which the Jacksonians saw as a defense of the little man against the manipulators of credit; and 4) the extension of the franchise. Yet the Whigs had a surprisingly strong Appalachian following thanks to the personal popularity of Henry and Cassius Clay, Davy Crockett, Alexander H. Stephens, and "Parson" William G. Brownlow. In fact, Jackson's opponents were able on occasion to present themselves as more democratic than the Democrats, as in 1840 when the Whigs presented their own "log cabin" candidate, William Henry Harrison, who was opposed to the "dandy," the Democratic candidate for president, Martin Van Buren.

Finally an issue did break through the personalism of post-Jackson polities: slavery. Or rather, the issue of the status of slavery in the newly conquered territories in the Trans-Mississippi West. This issue split apart the Whig Party in the1850s. Despite the Whig's majority status in Kentucky, Tennessee, and North Carolina by 1840, Northern "conscience Whigs" became increasingly antislavery after 1850. Meanwhile, the Southern Whig party came more and more to represent the planter elite. The Whigs had probably been more responsible for the "Great Compromise" of 1850 than the Democrats. This "Great Compromise" was supposed to settle once and for all the question of slavery in the Federal territories in the West. But events in the 1850s slowly tore this settlement apart: Harriet Beecher Stowe's popular *Uncle Tom's Cabin* (1852) and Hinton R. Helper's *Impending Crisis* (1857); the Kansas–Nebraska Bill (1854); a civil war in Kansas (1855–1857); the rise of the Republican Party after 1854; the Dred Scott Decision (1856); John Brown's raid upon the Appalachian town of Harper's Ferry (1859); and finally the election of 1860.

As the planter elite in the South became convinced that it could not stay linked to a Union determined to limit the spread of slavery, the people of the southern mountains found themselves confronted with an increasingly uncomfortable situation. The danger of secession had been averted in 1850 in the midst of a bitter congressional battle that centered on the admission of California. But in 1860, a presidential campaign played out in such a way that the secession of seven states, three of them with Appalachian areas, was a fact before the new president was inaugurated. Yet as the clouds of sectional division swept the nation into war, hardly anyone saw the dimensions of the disaster that was coming.

The Civil War Era, 1860–1877

SO THE WAR CAME! During the Civil War in Appalachia, most small farmers in East Tennessee, northern Georgia, West Virginia, and eastern Kentucky usually identified more strongly with the Federal Union than they did with the seceding state governments. In southwestern Virginia and western North Carolina, however, most people were initially sympathetic with, even enthusiastic about, secession. Still, many Appalachian Southerners tended to be both pro-slavery and pro-Confederate, particularly the elite among them in the rich valleys and mountain county-seat towns. In the southern mountains, class identification was the most dependable guide as to how a person or family identified during the Civil War, rather than how close the area was to states loyal to the Union. Elites tended to be pro-Confederate, and common farmers tended to be pro-Union.

Many mountaineers, however, had migrated westward in the expansionist years before the Civil War. They found similar mountain lands in the Ozarks of Arkansas and Missouri, and in even larger numbers they made their way into Texas. Along with Davy Crockett and Sam Houston, they helped build the Texas Republic. In the Mexican War, a war bitterly opposed by the antislavery Northeast, the Appalachian areas were strongly supportive. East Tennessee, in fact, gave the "Volunteer State" its reputation during the Mexican War when its sons rushed to the colors in support of this war of westward expansion. The wartime president, James K. Polk, was a Tennessean and the heir to Andrew Jackson's mountain political constituency. In fact, the Mexican War probably had the effect of cementing Cohee identification with the Union.

As the Union drifted into bitter division, this growing rift was generally not well understood in the mountain portions of the east-

ern United States. Though Cohee society may have been largely antislavery, it had made its peace with slave society. Conflicts there
particularly existed on the state level. But to some Cohee leaders, the
idea of a war over slavery that might disrupt the Union was unthink-
able. The Union was an effective agency that had allowed the United
States to fight a most successful war with Mexico, its only real rival
in North America. To the Appalachian lover of the Union, one should
not tamper with an institution that was so successful. Yet other mountaineers seemed more concerned with the security of the institution
of slavery and strongly supported secession when it came.

The situation in the mountain area of the South during the Civil
War era can best be understood if the area is seen as a part of the
nation's vast borderland as opposed to the "extreme sections"—the
Deep South and the Deep North, South Carolina, and Massachusetts,
where a united sentiment made the war a genuine "War Between the
States." In the "borderland" areas of the Union, a divided sentiment
made for a most vicious kind of war—a true Civil War. In areas that
remained loyal to the Union, this borderland included southern Illinois, southern Indiana, southern Ohio, much of New York and Pennsylvania, as well as the four border states—the four slave states that
did not secede: Delaware, Maryland, Kentucky, and Missouri. And
in the seceding states, the whole of the mountain area must also be
considered a borderland area, where the Civil War was a war between neighbor and neighbor, father and son, and a time often characterized by guerrilla violence.

In most of the mountain areas of the South, a strong antislavery
and pro-Union sentiment was sufficient to create large enclaves of
"treason" within mountainous sections of the seceding states. The
centers of Union strength within the Confederacy are seen most
clearly in West Virginia, which ultimately was able to secede from
seceding Virginia, and in East Tennessee, which had to be occupied
for nearly two years by the Confederate Army until "liberated" in
September of 1863. In north Georgia and north Alabama, pro-Union
sentiment was strong enough that many areas were beyond the effective control of the Confederate authorities. In these mountainous
Confederate borderlands, the effects of the war were particularly destructive. Not only was society divided, but much of the area was
fought over and fought through by major armies. Though the burned-
out cities of the Confederacy in the Deep South suffered in the War's
last months, the fought-over districts of East Tennessee, the
Shenandoah, and other mountain districts within the Confederacy

were probably more viciously decimated and across a much longer period of time.

As the various Southern states moved toward secession, all of them faced Unionist sentiment in one degree or another. Even Alabama and Georgia faced significant mountain area minorities that did not ever fully accept secession. A spirit of local independence emerged that led some to talk of the "Independent States" of Dade in Georgia and Winston in Alabama. Even strong sentiment for a new, independent "State of Nickajack" emerged late in the war. Particularly in northwestern Virginia and in East Tennessee, a clear and widespread pro-Unionism made these major areas troublesome to the emerging Confederacy. East Tennessee's pro-Unionism indeed led to a rejection of Tennessee's first vote on secession in February 1861. However, a second vote in early June reversed the earlier result, though East Tennessee still voted against secession on June 8, 1861, by a vote of 32,923 to 14,780.

The Appalachian Mountains played an important strategic role in the Civil War. On the eastern front—the front along the Potomac, Rappahannock, and York Rivers between the two capitals in Washington and Richmond—the major battles were in the tidewater sections of Virginia. But the nearby Shenandoah Valley played a crucial role in this eastern theater, especially in Confederate strategy. The Confederates invaded the North twice—in 1862 into Maryland, and in 1863 into Pennsylvania—and in both cases the Confederacy used the protection of the Shenandoah Valley as one avenue for its invasions. The Blue Ridge Mountains provided sufficient shield so that the Confederate sympathy of the Shenandoah Valley folk turned the Valley into an important asset for the Confederacy. T.J. "Stonewall" Jackson, himself an Appalachian Virginian who knew the area well, fought his classic Valley Campaign there in May of 1862. With some sixteen thousand troops, Jackson defeated four separate Union commands representing a combined force of forty-five thousand men. A few months later, this same valley helped carry Lee's invasion into Maryland. And in June and July 1863, it was the avenue for the great Confederate invasion into Pennsylvania. It also carried Lee's battered army back safely into southern Virginia after the defeat at Gettysburg. Later, the Confederate army of Jubal Early was even able to threaten Washington, D.C., directly in a foray from the Shenandoah Valley.

A crucial part of Grant's ultimate victory for the Union in the eastern theatre was his decision in 1864 to send General Philip

SOUTHERN APPALACHIA IN THE CIVIL WAR

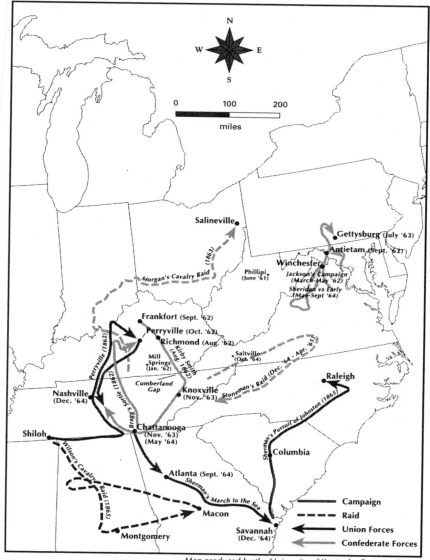

Map produced by the University of Kentucky Cartography Lab

Sheridan to pacify the Shenandoah and neutralize both General Jubal Early's Confederate army and the economic and strategic advantage that the Valley's support gave the Confederacy. Sheridan's triumphs in the winter and early spring of 1865 were crucial to the ultimate defeat of the Confederate armies before Richmond in April of the same year.

In the West, the vast area in and beyond the Appalachians, the Union was generally victorious. Aside from the Battle of Richmond in Kentucky in late August 1862 and the Battle of Chickamauga in September of 1863, all the significant battles in the West were Union victories—New Orleans, Forts Henry and Donelson, Shiloh, Mobile Bay, Stone's River, Lookout Mountain and Missionary Ridge, Atlanta, and Nashville. The two major concentrations of mountaineer loyalists in northeastern Virginia and East Tennessee in large part drove much of the early major military actions for the Union. The separatist effort that led to the Wheeling Convention in reaction to Virginia's Secessionist Convention was quickly supported by the intervention of Ohio troops under George B. McClellan.

West Virginia Unionists had begun to plan their move for a separate state long before Virginia actually seceded on April 17, 1861. An initial formal meeting was held in Charleston on April 11, calling for a convention to assemble in Wheeling on the Ohio River in case Virginia actually seceded. This "Wheeling Convention Movement" was far enough advanced by June of 1861 when McClellan moved his army into the state, that the quick Union victories at Philippi on June 3 and at Rich Mountain on June 11 insured success for the new state. These victories were much emphasized in the Northern press, for they were the Union's only early successes to balance the losses then being suffered in northern Virginia. It was on the basis of these early victories that McClellan was brought eastward by President Lincoln to command the Army of the Potomac, the major Union army in the eastern theater.

The impetus to "rescue," or tie to the East Tennessee Unionists, in part explains major Union Army efforts in the West. The various battles for control of Tennessee from early 1862 until General Burnside's occupation of Knoxville in September of 1863 explain much of the Union strategy in the West. Indeed, the final battle for Tennessee ended with the destruction of Hood's Confederate army by General George H. Thomas's Army of the Cumberland at Nashville in mid-December 1864. The whole Civil War career of General Thomas, in fact, demonstrates a central concern of Union efforts in the West and its essentially Appalachian dimension. George Thomas, arguably the most effective of the Union generals as the only Union general to completely destroy a Confederate army in the field—a feat he accomplished twice—operated in and through Appalachian Kentucky, Tennessee, and Georgia, thus demonstrating the general flow of major Union operations in the West. Part of the impetus for this focus seems to have been prompted by the opportunity to operate in support of the strong Union sentiment in East Tennessee.

Thomas's first major action against the Confederacy was against the journalist-general, Felix Zollicoffer. Zollicoffer was a pro-Confederate Nashville editor who had the misfortune to command the Middle Tennessee forces, which tried to carry out the aggressive Confederate policies in the Tennessee/Kentucky Cumberlands that Zollicoffer himself had called for. Zollicoffer's forces invaded Kentucky to try to prevent the recruitment of Union troops from that state and Tennessee's mountain areas, but only succeeded in joining in a battle far beyond his ability for either supply or support. He was killed while leading his troops into a complete defeat that destroyed his army at Mill Spring, Kentucky, in January of 1862.

Meanwhile, East Tennessee was falling into increasing violence. The East Tennessee Presbyterian minister, William Blount Carter, led an effort in November 1861 to burn as many as nine railroad bridges in the area. Six of them were indeed destroyed, but a massive invasion of Confederate troops snuffed out any possibility of an uprising, and the bridges were quickly replaced. But this effort induced the Confederacy into a troublesome occupation of East Tennessee. An alternately harsh, then accomodationist, policy under various Confederate generals only made the Unionists of the area more hostile and its young men eager to escape into Kentucky to join the Union Army. When General Kirby Smith was the Confederate official in charge for over nine months in 1862, he referred to East Tennessee as "Traitordom."

After the fall of Vicksburg in July of 1863, which cut the Confederacy for the first time by giving the Union control of the entire Mississippi River, the key to the Union's attack upon the remaining Confederacy focused on Chattanooga, in the heart of the mountain South. This was a crucial geopolitical position, and an important key to the control of the Confederacy east of the Mississippi.

Northern strategists saw the importance of Chattanooga early on, and soon after Vicksburg a concentration of Union forces descended upon this spot—Sherman from Vicksburg, Hooker from the eastern front, joining with the already formidable Army of the Cumberland under Thomas. The Confederates had already recognized Chattanooga's importance, for Longstreet's corps had been transferred there earlier from the East and had given the Confederate commander, Braxton Bragg, a temporary predominance, thus in part explaining the Confederate victory of Chickamauga in September of 1863. Following Chickamauga, the Union hurried forces to Chattanooga, and Sherman and Hooker joined Thomas to give the Union a superb fighting force.

In late November, Chattanooga, a river city controlled by high ridges on its outskirts, was made secure for the Union by the "Battles of the Sky"—the Battle of Lookout Mountain and the Battle of Missionary Ridge. When the Confederates broke and ran from their commanding heights, and with Chattanooga securely within Union hands, it became only a matter of time before the Confederacy was smashed. With the Chattanooga key in Union hands, the Confederacy could be sliced any way the Union decided—through Alabama to Mobile, or through Georgia from Atlanta to the sea. The Atlanta campaign that followed the next spring, and the March to the Sea by Christmas Day 1864, were but the logical results coming from the control of Chattanooga, which was won by Thanksgiving Day 1863.

The Union liberation of East Tennessee occurred when General Ambrose Burnside, in command of an army of twelve thousand, moved into the area from Kentucky. Confederate control was already much weakened in an area "bleeding at every pore." In early September of 1863, Burnside occupied Knoxville, but soon after the Confederate victory at the Battle of Chickamauga on September 20, much of lower East Tennessee returned to Confederate influence. All that fall Burnside's small army provided a tempting target for the Confederacy's massive strength then gathered around Chattanooga. Finally, Longstreet's corps was dispatched from Bragg's Confederate army, which was attempting a siege of the Union army in Chattanooga. But Burnside's army proved perfectly capable of holding his fortified position at Knoxville when Longstreet attacked in late November 1863. Meanwhile, as already noted, the Union had concentrated sufficient strength at Chattanooga to dramatically break Bragg's siege. Thus, in late November of 1863, a total of some seventy-two thousand Union troops and at least fifty thousand Confederate troops were then contesting the Tennessee mountains at Knoxville and Chattanooga.

The movement of major armies through Appalachia was not the

region's only experience with wartime violence and destruction. An interesting contrast to the story of separation of northwestern Virginia from the Old Dominion was the story of southwestern Virginia during the Civil War. As northwestern Virginia remained loyal to the Union, southwestern Virginia was enthusiastic for secession, at least initially. But as the war progressed, its vital Virginia and Tennessee Railroad became a continuing target for Union campaigns. By the end of the war, the area was torn to pieces by internal tensions and four successful and destructive Union raids between 1863 and 1865.

A mountain campaign of quite limited strategic effect was launched into eastern Kentucky up the Big Sandy River in December of 1861 and January of 1862. A unique aspect of this campaign was that the Union forces were commanded by an Ohio Congressman and future president of the United States, James A. Garfield. Garfield's pre-Congressional background was as a Disciples of Christ minister and college president. What does the U.S. Army do with a Congressman who resigns his seat to join the Army with great patriotic fervor? He was given a commission as a Major General and placed in command of a seemingly harmless army filled with recruits from his home state of Ohio. Opposing Garfield's army was Humphrey Gilbert, a West Point graduate and well-known politician with an army drawn from several states, including Kentucky. The armies facing each other were about the same size, and both were filled with raw recruits. But Garfield had had so little traditional military training that he believed that once one was given an army to command, one should use it and invade the area at his front. He launched his army full speed up the Big Sandy Valley, into a part of a state that never seceded, and toward the upriver villages of Paintsville and Pikeville. Garfield was entirely successful in a very aggressive campaign, but the long-run effects of this campaign were not significant. After his conquest, Garfield's army was withdrawn. Kentucky never seceded, yet the upper Big Sandy remained essentially a contested area throughout the war.

Confederate control of East Tennessee was lost in late November 1863. However, even after East Tennessee came under Union control, various Confederate raiders, John Hunt Morgan among them, operated in and through the area with some regularity. General John Hunt Morgan was the Confederacy's most dramatic raider. A Bluegrass Kentucky aristocrat in command of a dramatic handful of Confederates, Morgan raided across a vast area in the Cumberlands and in the Tennessee Valley as well as into Kentucky. He raided the Bluegrass of Kentucky frequently and made one spectacular foray across the Ohio River into Indiana and Ohio. He was ultimately killed in East Tennessee.

More significant than the Morgan raids in the overall military balance, though less publicized, was the raid of thirteen thousand Union troops across north Alabama and north Georgia commanded by General James H. Wilson in early 1865. By that time in the last months of the war, all semblance of systematic Confederate resistance was collapsing. This massive force tore up railways, destroyed as it chose, and finally captured the fleeing Jefferson Davis in Middle Georgia as he attempted to escape from the dying Confederacy. Wilson's raid inflicted the war's principal damage upon Alabama, and he captured Montgomery, the cradle of the Confederacy, without firing a shot.

After sporadic fighting in southwest Virginia, a major battle developed in early May of 1864 when a Union army attacked the long bridge over the New River near Dublin. Some nine thousand troops on both sides collided in a fierce battle lasting only a little over one hour, and brought twelve hundred casualties. Four months later, a particularly tragic mountain campaign was the badly mishandled Union campaign against Saltville in southwest Virginia, under the command of Brigadier General Stephen G. Burbridge. Burbridge was the unpopular commander of the District of Kentucky, and he decided in September 1864 to launch a campaign against the South's chief saltworks in Smyth County, Virginia. The area was then lightly defended, though the Virginia and Tennessee Railway was nearby. The saltworks themselves were on the upper Holston River, thus transportation lines were convenient for Saltville's defense.

Burbridges's superiors questioned this campaign from the first, but in the end it was allowed. It began on September 19 as the Union forces moved out of central Kentucky and struck out across the eastern Kentucky mountains. The destination of the attack was quickly ascertained by the Confederates, who began gathering troops drawn from Virginia and Tennessee, as well as groups of nearby Confederate guerrillas. Burbridge's army of over five thousand was constantly harassed as it passed through the nearly two hundred miles of mountainous territory between Mt. Sterling, Kentucky, and Saltville. By the time the Union force arrived in the Saltville area, the Confederates were able to gather about twenty-eight hundred men.

The advantages other than numbers lay with the Confederates, and on October 2 the forces met in an all-day battle near Saltville.

Negro troops in the Union force were particularly decimated in that day's fighting, and when Burbridge retreated that night, he left his wounded on the field. On the morning of the third, Confederate forces without command went about the field of battle systematically murdering probably several hundred blacks and others that had fallen. The ranking Confederate general in the area, John Breckinridge, commanded that the massacre stop as soon as he learned about it. But the Confederate bushwhacker Champ Ferguson probably personally and cold-bloodedly killed fourteen persons that day. One authority on the Civil War claims that Saltville, even more than Fort Pillow, deserves to be called a true massacre.

Destructive as the war was physically and psychologically to Southerners, it may have been even more destructive of the cultural environment and institutional structures of the southern mountaineers. On the civilian side, the Civil War totally disrupted life. Schools were closed and trade was interrupted. Agricultural life was devastated as raiding parties destroyed grain and animals. Neighbor feuded with neighbor. Whichever side wished to destroy the other could get some "legitimizing authority" willing to sanctify any level of depredation. It was guerrilla warfare pure and simple.

Historian Gordon McKinney points out that early in the war, western North Carolina became a haven for slaveholders and their slaves as they fled the more exposed coastal areas of the Confederacy. For a time, this movement involved an influx of thousands who were "flying from our Eastern Counties with their slaves to the centre . . . to devour the very short crops." Western Carolina seems to have enjoyed only a brief time of favorable fortune before the pressures of the war brought a virtual institutional collapse. Neither the yeomanesque farmers of Carolina nor the mountain masters of the area were up to the challenge of the war's destructive effects.

Furthermore, though far from Union lines, many of the people in western North Carolina, were pro-Union, and over five thousand men from the area left for the North—most to join the Union Army. Divisions in western Carolina were bitter and usually drawn along class lines. The county-seat elite were usually Confederate, while rural folk were more often sympathetic to the Union. To the rural yeoman, "riff-raff and abolitionists" to their enemies, their opponents were seen as "monarchists who wanted to enslave independent common people."

As the war progressed, yeoman farmer recruits from western North Carolina, southwestern Virginia, and other mountainous areas across the Confederacy, began deserting in large numbers. In January of 1863, apparently desperate for supplies, a group of some fifty deserters from a North Carolina regiment attacked and ransacked Marshall, the county seat of Madison County, North Carolina. A remote valley of that county, Shelton Laurel, had protected deserters before and did so again. The Confederates in the area felt that they could not allow this incident to remain unpunished, so they sent an entire legion supported by some two hundred Indians, mostly Cherokee, into Shelton Laurel. Several of the hollow folk were killed in the battle, and fifteen men and boys ages thirteen to sixty were taken prisoner. In an open space, thirteen of these prisoners were systematically shot as an example to the surrounding countryside.

In all the war's years, the southern mountains as a whole were subject to a vast influx of deserters from both armies. The relative isolation of the mountains and its central location to the war itself made Appalachia a deserter's haven. In fact, the military authorities from both sides were faced with a massive problem. For the first time in its history, the United States had to resort to a military draft. By 1863 both sides had conscription laws, and the draft was unpopular on both sides. In the North, New York City was completely beyond the control of its local authorities for a full week at the time of the Battle of Gettysburg because of antidraft riots. Many of the new immigrants in that city were not willing to risk their lives in a war to free the slaves—the Emancipation Proclamation had been issued on January 1, 1863, and this clearly enlarged the purpose of the war.

The Confederate draft law was more chaotic and ill-drawn than the Union's law and with time more flagrantly violated. The Confederate law allowed for the exemption of persons who owned large numbers of slaves, which gave support to the feeling among many non-slaveholding whites, particularly mountaineers, that the war was a "rich man's war, but a poor man's fight." Even in the heady, early days of the war, desertion was a problem in the Confederate Army. As the rebel cause became more and more desperate, the problem became endemic. By Christmas 1864, more than half of the Confederate Army had deserted. Some deserters fled westward, but the vast majority of these deserters made their way into the nearby mountains and added their concerns and fears to the fractured society already suffering there.

The war in north Georgia took a unique turn, as a kind of sub-war was fought, not so much between independent guerrilla groups as between local surrogate groups representing the two sides. Historian Jonathan Sarris has written convincingly of the war around Dahlonega led by a pro-Confederate Lieutenant, James Jefferson Findley. Findley left the Confederate service to fight what he saw as the "real war" against the Unionist in Fannin and Gilmer Counties and other remote counties to Dahlonega's north.

It was a time out of joint generally! This was true for the nation at large, but it was especially true of the Appalachian South. Constituted authority had collapsed. And in the region, an area in part seceded from secession, authority was twice removed from stability. And when authority collapses, those most willing to resort to violence are those most likely to control matters. "When the pot boils, the scum rises," it was said. These were the appalling conditions that dominated the Appalachian area in the era of the Civil War and for some years following the war—an era referred to in the region as "the time of the Bushwhackers."

The bushwhackers included native ruffians, banditti, deserters, guerrillas, and desperate people generally who dominated large areas of the Appalachian Mountains from early 1862 until at least 1870, and even later in some places. In literally every mountain area within the ex-slave states, informal bands—bushwhackers—terrorized whole districts. Despite the venality of their terrorism, all of them could find some authority to sanction their depredations. If a pro-Union group terrorized the rebels of one district, a home guard or other group with Confederate leanings could be gathered to protect the good rebel citizens and drive the "damnyankees" or "Tories" out. Home Guard units were more or less officially recognized informal forces, whether approved by pro-Union or pro-Confederate local governments.

West Virginia suffered at least twelve gangs of bushwhackers, including the "One Arm" Berry Gang, the Black Striped Company, and the somewhat official Confederate raider, John S. Mosby. In North Carolina, the One-Eyed Battallion operated in the areas of western North Carolina not subject to Harvey Bingham or "Captain" Price. North Georgia had its Doc Morse Gang, Jordon's Gang, and at least three other groups. Northern Alabama was terrorized by a pro-Union group called the Destroying Angels. And in East Tennessee, the Confederate occupation had to confront William Blount Carter's Raiders, the East Tennessee Relief Association, and the Doc Morse Gang, which foraged into Tennessee from north Georgia. Kentucky suffered under two separate governments, one pro-Union in Frankfort and another at Bowling Green that sent representatives to Richmond. And each government supported rival bushwhacking gangs and Home Guard groups. The most famous of Kentucky's bushwhackers were Champ Ferguson, Sue Mundy (Marcellus J. Clark), and William C. Quantrill's Raiders from Missouri. Besides his infamous "Sack of Lawrence, Kansas" in August of 1863, Quantrill operated mainly in the Ozarks and in western Kentucky but also made some raids into eastern Kentucky.

Because Appalachia was so central to the operations of a nation at war with itself, it is not surprising that during this period several native sons of Appalachia played particularly significant roles in the nation at large. Appalachia provided its only president of the United States, Andrew Johnson of Greeneville, Tennessee, during these years. Johnson had risen from the grassroots of Tennessee politics. A tailor, taught to read by his wife, he entered political life as a Jackson Democrat on the local level in the position of city councilman, then as mayor of Greeneville. Later he rose to the state's lower house, then to the Tennessee Senate, and then the governorship. In 1861, he was the only U.S. senator from a seceding state to remain in the U.S. Senate. He was appointed by Lincoln to be military governor of Tennessee in 1863. When it came time for the Republican Party to choose a running mate for Lincoln in the election of 1864, Lincoln's original vice president, the abolitionist Hannibal Hamlin, seemed a political liability. The Republicans had won the election of 1860 with only 42 percent of the popular vote, and in 1864 it was thought more politic to enlarge the appeal of the ticket with a loyal Democrat such as Johnson as vice president. Clearly it was a ticket-balancing exercise. Thus, an ex-Democrat but loyal Southern politician was chosen as Lincoln's running mate.

When Lincoln was assassinated only one month into his second term, Johnson was thrust into a position for which he had little preparation. It is problematical that Lincoln, even with his prestige as the president who had won the war, could have guided the process of Reconstruction with the moderation he desired. Certainly, though he attempted to carry on essentially the same policies that Lincoln had begun, Andrew Johnson was no match for the "Radical Republicans." These "Radicals"—Charles Sumner, Thaddeus Stevens, Ben Wade, et al.—launched a campaign against Johnson of personal vituperation seldom paralleled in American politics. President Johnson was drawn into an undignified mud-slinging campaign during the Congressional elections of 1866. In Tennessee stump-fashion, Johnson responded to the heckling that accompanied his speeches and "acted in a way no President should act." He succeeded only in electing an overwhelmingly Radical Congress determined to make the South pay for its sins and accept responsibility for the past war.

Andrew Johnson perceived that his life had been "one desperate, upward struggle out of poverty." He had become the spokesman for Tennessee's tradesmen and small farmers, and the representative of the "honest yeoman." He had thundered against the "slaveocracy," then against secession. In the Reconstruction period he carried on his struggle, but this time it was against those who did not hold his view on race. Johnson held definite prejudices concerning Negroes. Even as he denounced slavery in earlier times, he condemned the institution for promoting miscegenation. He believed blacks were inherently inferior, persons who possessed "less capacity for government than any other race of people."

The Radicals in Congress rejected the moderate policy of reconstructing Southern state governments that Johnson was trying to implement, which essentially followed Lincoln's program. In its place, a new Radical-dominated Congress in 1867 divided the ex-Confederate areas (minus Tennessee, which already had a Radical Republican government) into five military districts, and the major general in charge was instructed to oversee the development of properly constituted governments; i.e. Republican-controlled state governments supported by the newly enfranchised blacks. Johnson vetoed these new Reconstruction Acts, but his vetoes were overridden by the large Radical majorities then in both houses of the U.S. Congress.

The so-called "moderate" governments of the South, which Johnson had attempted to get Congress to accept, failed to recognize the determination of the victorious North to have the South change in several important ways. When these "moderate" governments sent to the U.S. Congress senators and representatives who had been prominent in the Confederate government, including the Confederacy's vice president, and when they enacted "Black Codes" that placed blacks in a condition not far from slavery, most Northerners supported the Radical Republicans. By 1867, the Radicals were determined to remold the South in keeping with Northern expectations.

Johnson's last two years in the Presidency were miserable. Not only were his vetoes overridden, but he was impeached for dismissing one of the members of his own cabinet. Conviction failed by only one vote in the Senate. In the process, Johnson's power was destroyed and the "Radical" Congress made policy despite his wishes. The Republican Party bypassed him as their nominee in 1868 and chose instead the war's major hero, Ulysses S. Grant. Johnson returned to Tennessee but was elected again to the U.S. Senate in 1875, just months before his death.

By the 1870s, in fact, the hopes of the Radical Republicans were generally frustrated by the determined opposition of the ex-Confederates in all the states of the South, now including Kentucky. Though slavery was abolished and the market economy expanded with its Gilded Age enthusiasm, African American hopes for really different social arrangements were still frustrated. White mountain farmers generally accepted the new patterns of racial segregation, and non-elite groups generally accepted the negative results of the war for them. By 1876, the old elites had again assumed control, though some of the old leading politicians, such as Thomas L. Clingman in western North Carolina, were forced into political exile.

Another eastern Tennessean of considerable prominence during these years was Johnson's rival, "Parson" William G. Brownlow. Brownlow, a Methodist minister turned editor and Whig politician, was one of the region's most vituperative and colorful politicians. His pen was pure poison, and when Tennessee voted to join the Confederacy in June of 1861 after rejecting a similar act the previous January, Brownlow moved up and down East Tennessee preaching opposition to the illegal government of the Confederacy. He welcomed the Carter invaders, but when the Confederate Army reconquered East Tennessee and imposed its occupation, Brownlow was jailed. However, his jail cell became the source of a stream of bitter letters telling of his mistreatment and Confederate barbarity. Uncertain just what to do with him, the Confederates finally banished Brownlow to the North. But there he went on the lecture circuit, telling of his mistreatment and of Tennessee's "loyal mountaineers" awaiting salvation by an invading Union army. In 1862, he wrote one of the nation's best-sellers, *Sketches of the Rise, Progress and Decline of Secession*, which further detailed Confederate duplicity and barbarity, his views of secession, and the virtues of the loyal mountaineers. The whole North was reading "Parson Brownlow's Book," as it was more commonly known.

After the war and the final pacification of Tennessee, a pro-Union government was reestablished in Tennessee in late 1865, with Brownlow as governor. The government he presided over was loyally Radical and Republican and corrupt besides, though it is clear that Brownlow did not profit personally. Such corruption was typical of these postwar years, however, for corruption was generally rife in American government, both on the national and state levels. Brownlow's government in Tennessee was acceptable to the Radicals in Congress, and because of it Tennessee escaped the military occupation of the South established by the Reconstruction Acts of 1867 for the other ten states of the ex-Confederacy.

In two other Confederate states, Civil War governors were sons of Appalachia. Joseph E. Brown was Georgia's first non-planter governor. This son of north Georgia was jealous of Georgia's "states rights" during the war in the face of the growing Southern nationalism of Jefferson Davis's government. Brown's career after the war was even more interesting, because he had a genius for changing sides and remaining on top no matter what the circumstances were. No sooner was the war over than he joined the Radicals and was appointed by the Republican governor to a position on Georgia's supreme court. Just before the Radicals fell from power in Georgia, Brown made an alliance with the key Bourbon Democratic "Redeemers" in Georgia, John B. Gordon and Alfred H. Colquitt. These three remained the ruling triumvirate in Georgia politics until the 1890s.

If Joseph E. Brown made his political career as a successful chameleon, Zebulon Vance, North Carolina's Civil War governor, was a colorful politician of great principle and personal magnetism. Vance was from Asheville and opposed secession until Lincoln's call for seventy-five thousand troops in April of 1861. The story is told that Vance was making a political speech against secession, and with hand upraised he was told of President Lincoln's call for the troops in order to put the rebellion down. His hand came down from that gesture, he said, "on the side of the Confederacy." As wartime governor, Vance's opposition to Confederate nationalism was as clear as was Brown's, but he was clear in his opposition to the Republican Radicals during Reconstruction, and was again elected governor of North Carolina in 1868 as a Democrat. Vance was a great stump orator and storyteller and remained a significant force in North Carolina politics for many years.

Unlike the effect upon the South and most of the Appalachian South, the effect of the war on the North and on many areas in northern Appalachia was to stimulate the economy greatly. By 1890, the industrial boom that accompanied the Civil War in the North helped move the United States to become the world's largest industrial producer. This was the war's effect on much of Appalachian New York, Pennsylvania, Maryland, and parts of West Virginia. Pittsburgh became one of the major industrial centers of the nation, and various smaller Appalachian cities in the North became thriving centers as well—Johnstown, Altoona, Scranton, and Bethlehem in Pennsylvania, and Wheeling in West Virginia. To the southward, this wartime industrial development spilled over into certain mountain cities fortunate enough to be near established lines of transport. Where the Union Army used rail lines to supply the invading armies, capable engineering placed key lines in excellent repair. The Louisville and Nashville line, for example, was placed in such fine shape as far as Chattanooga that Chattanooga's success after the war was assured. And key Shenandoah Valley towns were placed in a position to profit quickly in the postwar years by excellent rail conditions—such towns as Bristol in Tennessee and Covington and Staunton in Virginia.

But there were vast sections of Appalachia that ceased to have significant contact with mainline American developments, a condition that persisted in some areas for more than a generation. So complete was this retreat from national awareness that Horace Kephart would write on the eve of the First World War, with some truth, that the "Southern highlands . . . are a mysterious realm."

A remarkable isolation did seem to settle upon vast areas of Southern Appalachia following the Civil War. To the remoteness of mountain regions far from adequate transportation was added a reinforcing stereotype about a "strange and peculiar people." A frequent stereotype of the time was that of the mountaineer's violence, especially as related to the feuds, or "family wars." The post–Civil War period did mark the era of the feuds, for recognized authority had evaporated during the Civil War, and it took many years to reestablish adequate trust in government. In the interim, the family and its kin networks stepped in and provided structures for law, order, and justice.

Yet the continuing vendetta associated with Appalachian feuds can be found in only part of the Appalachian region. Though violence and continuing Civil War divisions were characteristic of the Great Smoky area, the ongoing vendetta or feud tradition did not develop there as it did in eastern Kentucky. There were incidents of individual violence in the Tennessee–North Carolina border area, as with the case of the murder of a student–veteran at Mars Hill College after he had told of a wartime experience. It developed that one of his listeners had been one of his victims but had survived. But in the Smokies, violence was not continued as a vendetta. In the Cumberland–Allegheny area, however, vendettas were set in motion in part by wartime action, which inflamed eastern Kentucky and the areas of West Virginia and Tennessee that bordered on Kentucky.

Furthermore, some experts on mountain feuds believe that the Civil War had less to do with the mountain violence than the willingness of outside mineral and timber interests to acquire mountain wealth no matter the cost.

Actually, the feud spirit had its earliest roots before the war. In Kentucky, some feuds were already active before the Civil War; for example, the Baker–White feud in Clay County, which had begun in the 1840s. Yet the war created a situation where the state not only retreated from its responsibilities for providing local law and order, but the violence of the Bushwhacker Era created situations that inflated the level of violence.

Family wars and clan violence emerged in many counties in Appalachia during and after the Civil War. In Rowan County, Kentucky, five feuds flared at one time or another. Other Kentucky counties that were especially caught in the violence of one family network or another were Clay, Breathitt, and Menifee. In Pike County, the conditions of the time and the place spawned the most celebrated of all mountain family wars: the Hatfield–McCoy Feud.

This particular feud has been much studied, partly because of the attention paid it in the national media and partly because of its dramatic nature. The incident of its beginning was minor—a dispute over a pig. But violence escalated when it was perceived that justice miscarried as well as on election day, when possession of local courts was contested. This feud included a romantic dimension when Roseanna McCoy fell in love with Johnse Hatfield. The numbers of deaths caused by this ongoing vendetta is unclear, but probably was no more than twenty. One wholly unique aspect of the Hatfield–McCoy feud was the involvement of two separate state governments, prompted by the fact that the Hatfields were prominent in Mingo and Logan Counties, West Virginia, and the McCoys were a Pike County, Kentucky, family. Only the Louisa Fork separates the states in that area.

Historian Altina Waller has made a particularly careful study of the Hatfield–McCoy Feud, and she contends that "Devil Anse" (Anderson) Hatfield was its central figure. Though a violent and aggressive man, he became in Waller's view, a kind of folk hero as he tried to make his way against the rising tide of commercialism that was penetrating the mountains. As Waller tells the story, though it began as a rather modest family feud, as a result of the intervention of a Pikeville commercial elite in alliance with the government of Kentucky, this feud became a celebrated campaign to hunt down the

Hatfields. The major violence, Waller insists, was not produced by mountain society, but came as a result of outside commercial interference, especially from railway building and coal mine companies. Though recognizing the general tenor of the post–Civil War era that encouraged the violence, Waller is at pains to play down the significance of the war as causing the worst aspects of this feud. Both "Devil Anse" Hatfield and Randolph McCoy, the principals, had been Confederate sympathizers. And this feud did not become serious until the 1880s, over twenty years after the war.

After the Civil War, a remarkably similar way of life developed in Appalachia's most isolated sections. Without significant contact with one another, quite a similar culture persisted in western North Carolina and the adjoining sections of East Tennessee and north Georgia on the one hand, and the Cumberland–Allegheny Highlands of eastern Kentucky, southwestern Virginia, and West Virginia on the other. One result of the Civil War had been to increase the isolation in both areas, and this in turn made possible the development of a traditional and remarkably similar Appalachian culture in both of these two widely separated areas in the Southern Appalachians.

The Civil War ended the Cohee Era in Appalachia. The destruction of farm animals wiped out a substantial herdsman economic base east of the Mississippi River, and cattle growing shifted dramatically westward. In fact, many of the West's ranchers and cowboys were former mountain Cohees who had been engaged in Appalachian stock growing before the Civil War. Many ambitious farmers from Coheedom found it useful to migrate westward after the war, for the collapse of authority in the mountains coupled with the thinness of the soil on mountain farms added to Appalachia's declining agricultural status that had been in process since 1830.

Those who stayed in Appalachia's valleys and mountain ridges found life more difficult than it had been before the war. Many institutions had been physically destroyed—schools, churches, and towns. Furthermore, bushwhacker bands, who had gained control of large areas during the war, maintained their control for some years following 1865. In many parts of Appalachia, the family was the only institution with stability enough to wrest control from the bushwhackers. Approached this way, the emergence of the family as the unit of control casts important new light into understanding the so-called "Feud Era."

Violence and feuding aside, familism and family loyalties have been forces that have dominated Appalachian life and politics following the Civil War. Furthermore, war issues cemented partisan loyalties to such an extent that political affiliation came to be determined by birth. In Appalachia, the Republican Party inherited those families who had been strong for the Union, and the Democrats for the most part, those who had sympathized with the Confederacy. In many areas of Appalachia, the Republican Party became dominant. In fact, today probably the six most Republican-dominated counties in the nation are in Appalachia. Perhaps the *most* Republican county in the United States is Jackson County in eastern Kentucky, which habitually votes Republican by seven to one. Yet Jackson is one of the poorest counties in the nation.

The Reconstruction Period following the Civil War has been portrayed as an Age of Hate. For the South and the Southern Appalachians during this period, a picture has emerged painted largely by a Southern Democratic rhetoric of "damnyankees" who came South and imposed their will through the Republican Party upon the defeated section. This scenario says that the military occupation of the South and the enfranchising of the former slaves so enhanced Republican votes that the Radicals took over. According to this rhetoric, the Radicals were led by "carpetbagger" politicians from the North as they attempted to bring about a racial revolution to do away with "the Southern Way of Life." Yet in all this tragic period, according to this Democratic story, the worst offenders of all were those Southerners who betrayed their section by voting Republican—the "scalawags."

The ex-Confederates, so this Southern Democratic picture suggests, could do little for themselves as long as the U.S. Army remained in occupation of the South. But in time, thanks to Democratic Party heroes such as Wade Hampton in South Carolina and John B. Gordon in Georgia, leaders of the Ku Klux Klan, and other defenders of the "Southern way of life," the South was "redeemed" from the ex-slaves, the scalawags, and carpetbaggers. By 1877 this "redemption" was complete.

Since the 1940s, a revisionist view of Reconstruction has risen to dominate with what most historians believe to be a more accurate picture. Many of the Radical Reconstruction governments in the South, it is admitted, were corrupt. But these revisionist historians remind us that this corruption was no worse than that of the nation as a whole, or indeed, of the "redeemer" governments in the South which followed them. The Reconstruction period did indeed make a real effort to revise American race relations, as blacks and their Northern ex-abolitionist friends tried to redefine Southern race relations. But this experiment had failed by 1870. In fact, one recent scholar claims that the Republicans proved to be so tepid that, except for the end of slavery, no real change came to Southern society as a result of the Civil War.

The scalawags, those native Southerners who cooperated with the Reconstruction governments and voted loyally Republican, were in fact mostly southern mountaineers. Early on, the term "Republican" was too much for even Southerners who opposed the war to carry. So such titles as "Constitutional," "Unionist," or "Conservative" were used until the late 1870s. But most southern mountaineers who were Unionists became Republicans. Though mountaineers provided few of the statewide leaders of the Republican Party during Reconstruction, most of the votes from white Southerners that supported the Republicans during the Reconstruction period came from the mountain South.

An especially interesting Appalachian political leader in the Reconstruction years, and a leading scalawag as well, was Roderick R. Butler of Wytheville, Virginia, and Mountain City, Tennessee. Butler served in the Union Army and became a Tennessee State Circuit Judge and Congressman, where he served with considerable distinction. Another mountain scalawag was Horace Maynard, a Massachusetts man who came south in 1839 to be an instructor of mathematics at what was then the "University of East Tennessee" in Knoxville. He entered politics as a Whig and finally as a champion of the Union, then became a Republican. He was Tennessee's Attorney General during the war from 1863 to 1865 and served five terms in the U.S. House of Representatives after 1866. "Parson" William G. Brownlow was frequently called a scalawag. The "corruption" for which the Democrats in Tennessee damned him involved questionable evidence that turned up only after he died in 1877, which claimed that he had received five thousand dollars as a result of a friend's speculation in his name.

Another mountain scalawag was the Virginian James W. Hunnicut, "who stood for full legal and social equality for Negroes and whites" in the United States in the 1860s. Archibald Campbell of Wheeling, West Virginia, was perhaps the region's most prominent Republican scalawag. Editor of the Wheeling *Intelligencer* and nephew of the Reverend Alexander Campbell, the founder of the Disciples Church, Archibald Campbell was frequently called a "Black Republican." This free-spirited ex-abolitionist was a "genius of the editorial page" and was for years the Radical Republicans' most effective spokesman in West Virginia.

Finally, there was Christopher C. Sheets from the hill country of northern Alabama, who helped organize the Republican Party in Alabama. He was one of the most vocal native white voices during the Radical Constitutional Convention in 1867. One scholar has noted that Alabama scalawags endorsed the Fourteenth Amendment in 1867 in a convention where the "hill and mountain white people" predominated, an endorsement that preceded the enfranchisement of Alabama blacks. Sheets was the leader of this group of Alabama hill people.

As elsewhere in the South, the newly emancipated freedmen in Appalachia hoped to rise to an independent yeoman status. But this dream was largely frustrated by the determined opposition of the old elites and President Johnson's pardoning of the ex-slaveholders. As early as President Johnson's proclamation of May 1865, which promised full restoration of property for ex-Confederates except for their slaves, the freedmen's dream of a farm arrived stillborn. Instead, after a brief effort to control black labor through the Black Codes, the ultimate answer, generally acceptable to the freedmen, was the sharecrop agreements negotiated. By 1880 only 7.9 percent of blacks throughout the South owned their farms, though that figure was 18.1 percent among East Tennessee blacks. Once the ex-slaves had accepted the fact that they would have to struggle toward land ownership as independent farmers, their success as independent farm owners rose to encouraging levels, especially in Appalachia.

The return of Democratic Party control in the South was completed state-by-state between 1868 and 1877. In some states, such as Virginia and Georgia, Radical Republican control lasted for only a matter of months before the Democrats returned to power. In other states, Radical "Black and Tan" Republican governments governed for several years, as in Alabama from 1868 to 1874 and in Tennessee from 1866 to 1869. All federal troops were withdrawn from the South in 1877, and the Southern states then fell under the control of the redeemer-style, conservative "Bourbon Democrats," who dominated most Southern states until well into the twentieth century.

Because of the bitterness left by the Civil War and the Reconstruction, those Southerners who had supported first the Union, and then the Radical Republican governments—mostly the ex-slaves and the mountaineers—were in a very precarious position. As the solid Democratic South emerged after 1880, the troublesome black and mountaineer constituencies in the South were pointedly left out of the New South's political equation. And this was true not only in state politics, but in national politics as well. To a remarkable degree, the Appalachian American came out of the whole Civil War experience a forgotten and isolated group.

Part 3

Modern Appalachia

The triumph of modern corporate capitalism was apparent by the late nineteenth century. The Appalachian region fit into corporate America's plans mainly as a producer of fossil fuels. However, significant non-capitalist attitudes persisted in Appalachia, and the region's experience seemed to question much of the morality and justice of American corporate capitalism.

The "Discovery" of Appalachia

APPALACHIA HAS ALWAYS BEEN a complex area. From the first settlement of the region, elite speculators and a few merchants mixed with the larger number of pioneer settlers who were seeking to build yeoman farms. As transportation corridors developed, strips of commerce and mainline culture merged in the region's towns. Also, some areas in Appalachia, notably in the Ridge and Valley province of the region—in the Valley of Virginia and the Tennessee River Valley—rich soils supported a prosperous agriculture. In the 1950s, Cratis D. Williams, often referred to as the "Dean of Appalachian Studies," recognized this continuing complex social division in Appalachia when he insisted that there have been three quite different groups of people within Appalachia. The first he called the commercial, town-oriented elite, which has been little different from a similar class in the rest of the nation. The second type of person in Appalachia was a large group of prosperous farmers located in the regional areas most suited to agriculture. And finally, there was the group Williams called "Branchwater Mountaineers," a very large group within the region from settlement until about 1920, but by the time Williams wrote, a definite minority in the region. It is about this third group, Williams said, that the region's various stereotypes have been developed.

Because the traditional Branchwater Mountaineer developed a society along largely non-literate lines, to understand this part of Appalachian society, we have had to depend upon observations by persons from outside the region who have studied the area. A recent study of the background of Appalachian stereotyping, however, suggests that the initial source of the image of the backward, rural and antiprogressive mountaineer, was begun by the region's own commercial, town-oriented elite.

The earliest explorers of the Appalachian area primarily described the Indian societies that dominated the region. Later, the backwoods society was described by many literary figures, including William Byrd (1728), John Filson (1782–1784), H.H. Brackenridge (1792), James Kirk Paulding (1816), Anne Newport Royall (1824), James Fenimore Cooper (1823–1841), and William Gilmore Simms (1850). And various religious observers left generally pessimistic accounts of the state of mountaineer faith, such as the Reverend Hugh Jones (1724), the Reverend Francis Asbury (1771–1815), Philip Vickers Fithian (1775–1776), the Reverend Elias Cornelius (1817), the Reverend Jeremiah Evarts (1826), and the Reverend Henry Ruffner (1838). Various governmental officials and diplomats also left written accounts, from George Chicken (1725) and George Washington (1747–1754) to Benjamin Hawkins (1797) and Thomas L. McKenney (1827). Furthermore, a number of scientists wrote about various aspects of the region, as the geographer Thomas Pawnall (1755–1770), the geologist Elisha Mitchell (1827–1828), and the naturalists John Bricknell (1730), William Bartram (1773–1778), and Andre Michaux (1785–1799). Just before the Civil War, several travelers explored the status of slavery in the South and observed mountain society. The abolitionist writers were the Englishman James S. Buckingham (1839), Harriet Martineau (1834–1836), Frederick Law Olmsted (1854), and James Sterling (1856–1857). There were, in fact, at least one hundred accounts written by travelers during the pre–Civil War period, and some claimed that they had discovered a new region.

During the Civil War, one of the most widely read books of the time was William G. Brownlow's *Sketches of the Rise, Progress and Decline of Secession* (1862), a polemic which pled the case of the "loyal mountaineers of East Tennessee" caught in the Confederacy. "Parson Brownlow's Book" was read widely in the North and had an effect upon President Lincoln.

Despite the vague awareness of loyal mountaineers, to most post–Civil War Northerners the South was an area full of plantations, "pickaninnies," poor whites, and a romantic but violent elite. When Northerners traveled south from Cincinnati in those days, they were genuinely surprised to find mountains, and seemed relieved when their view of the South appeared to be verified in the Atlanta area and southward, even though the miles through Old South plantation areas were much fewer than through mountainous terrain. As for those who lived in these "hidden mountains of the South," the poor white stereotype—largely the creation of abolitionist writers interested in demonstrating the debilitating effects of slavery—reinforced the already developed backward stereotypes and for many years seemed adequate to explain those who lived in mountain cabins with families that were much too large.

The word "hillbilly" did not appear until 1900, when a New York *Journal* reporter defined such people as "free and untrammelled white" citizens living "in the hills" with "no means to speak of," who "dresses as he can," drinks whiskey, and "fires off his revolver as fancy takes him." On the other hand, a romantic and positive image had already emerged about the Southern mountain folk in such books as Davy Crockett's *Autobiography* (1834) and the historical novels of William Gilmore Simms. But most literate Northerners after the Civil War were essentially unaware of those who lived in the Appalachian South. The postwar literary "discoverers" of the region, the so-called Local Color writers who used Appalachian materials, painted pictures of such curious people in the region that clear and lasting regional stereotypes began to emerge in the Northern consciousness.

The many writers who described this "peculiar and discreet people" in the decades after the Civil War were of three quite different yet occasionally overlapping types. Probably the earliest were the missionaries who came to save the Appalachian soul and bring these "forgotten Americans" into the American Protestant mainstream. Then there were the popular writers of the Local Color School, who produced a widely read stream of short stories and novels designed to meet the demands of a reading public fascinated by the various kinds of people living in the United States. The last type of writer was the business promoter, who was mostly concerned with industrial development, thus persons interested in the possibilities of Appalachian labor and mineral resources.

Probably the earliest writers to deal with the Appalachian people as a distinct group were certain abolitionists who, even before the Civil War, saw these predominantly non-slaveholding whites as possible allies in the struggle against slavery. In the mid-1850s, John G. Fee, a Kentucky abolitionist, and his colleague in the founding of Berea College, John A.R. Rogers, a Connecticut man educated at Oberlin College, developed a vision of the antislavery mountaineer, thus reinforcing a view earlier suggested by Cassius M. Clay in the 1840s and underlined in Hinton R. Helper's *Impending Crisis* (1857).

From the 1860s to the early 1890s, Fee's fragile mission in the midst of a slave state, but on the edge of a perceived antislavery, mountainous Kentucky, became an aggressive, biracial witness to equality. This mission to Appalachia spread from Berea to several areas in the mountains under the sponsorship of the American Missionary Association (AMA), the nation's principal antislavery mission society.

By the late 1870s, other denominational agencies had joined the AMA in an enlarging mountain mission. The Presbyterians, who had first been in the mountains as the church of the Scotch–Irish, began their post–Civil War mountain mission in the early 1870s in North Carolina with the Dorland Mission. The Southern Presbyterian joined the mountain work, which they saw largely through the vision of E.O. Guerrant's Soul Winner's Society. Then came the Methodists, Brethren, Dutch Reformed, Baptists, and other denominations. By 1920, some seventeen Protestant denominations supported over two hundred mission schools and numerous preaching posts as well as at least five hundred missionaries who toiled in the Appalachian South. A massive promotional literature emerged to sustain these missionaries and their churches, school, hospitals, and service agencies.

Much of this denominational literature served purely sectarian purposes, and much of it reflected a view of the Appalachian mountaineer, though already Protestant, as a person different from mainline Protestants in both lifestyle and values. The Appalachian mountaineer was seen by these missionaries as a worthy person, as witnessed to by his pro-Unionism and his Republicanism, but with crucial deficiencies, such as grinding poverty, a "feud temper," ignorance, and a lack of "practical Christianity." Clearly the answer to the mountaineer's predicament was a proper education carried out under missionary guidance.

Many were those who responded to the challenge in this great missionary century. William G. Frost, for example, was called from Oberlin College to the presidency of Berea College in 1892. For thirty years, Berea had been a unique experiment in biracial education, but the presence of large numbers of blacks on campus discouraged the attendance of many southern mountaineers. During Frost's first decade as Berea's president, he developed a vision for the college as a principal vehicle for Appalachian advance.

It was probably in 1894 that Frost met in Washington, D.C., with a former student, C.W. Hayes, then employed by the U.S. Geological Survey. Together they mapped out "the Mountain Region of the South," a 194–county area, "the backyards of eight states" that Frost termed "Appalachian America." His forays into the mountains—"explorations of discovery" he called them—began in 1893. The Appalachian Mountains, Frost found, were "not snow-capped and sublime, but rather picturesque and hard to travel." The explorer, Frost said of himself, "soon realized that he was riding into the last century." Frost made his fullest evaluation of "Our Contemporary Ancestors" in an article in *Atlantic* in 1899, and here established many of the stereotypes about mountaineers: of a technology of the log cabin and the long rifle, where the jackals of civilization were destroying an Arcadian rural simplicity.

The seeds of the Local Color School of literary writers were sewn well before the Civil War, with such writing as Davy Crockett's (1834), and those of the Georgia backcountry, as depicted by the Reverend Augustus B. Longstreet in *Georgia Scenes* (1835). By the time of the Civil War, the Appalachians had already provided something of a field for literary craftsmen. The war itself produced several significant novels by successful and unsuccessful writers. For example, Charles O. Kirk, about whom little is known, wrote a book with the title *Wooing and Warring in the Wilderness*, published in 1860. A more prolific and financially successful author was Emma Southwork, a Washington, D.C., lady who wrote sentimental romances. Mrs. Southwork wrote *Fallen Pink, or a Mountain Girl's Love* in 1868.

George Washington Harris's hard-hitting *Sut Lovingood's Yarns* appeared just after the Civil War in 1867. Harris was a Knoxville man, a farmer, riverboat captain, ardent Confederate, railroad engineer, and literary genius. His literary creation, Sut Lovingood, was a violent, "dern-fool mountain man" whose rough language and cruel humor was turned against pretentiousness. *Sut Lovingood's Yarns* never became popular, but its influence, especially upon Mark Twain, was considerable.

The Local Color School was a unique part of the impact of the Civil War upon American literature. The war had underscored the great variety of American life, and now that the Union had been saved, literate, middle-class, urban Northerners wanted to learn more about the nation's different peoples. Thus "Local Color writers" emerged to tell the story of the various groups (minorities) that then made up the United States. These were such writers as Mark Twain and Bret Harte, who wrote about the West; George Washington Cable, who wrote of the Cajuns of Louisiana; and Hamlin Garland and Willa Cather, who wrote about the Great Plains. With such a different group in the heart of eastern America as the Appalachian Mountain people, it was inevitable that the mountaineer should be discovered for literary purposes.

The first author to attempt to market the Appalachian mountaineer in a strictly Local Color novel was Katherine Sherwood MacDowell, who wrote under the name Sherwood Bonner. Mrs. MacDowell was a Mississippi-born woman who came east and served as Longfellow's secretary. She appears to have written the first novel using what she perceived to be Appalachian materials for the purposes of local color. Her book *Like Unto Like* (1878) is a tale set in the Civil War and Reconstruction periods and is unconvincing both in dialect and characterization. She clearly did not know mountaineers, though she struggled mightily.

The earliest successful Local Color writer using Appalachian materials was Charles Egbert Craddock, the pen name for Mary Noalles Murfree, a middle-Tennessee daughter of an aristocratic and doting father. Miss Murfree was in a better position to know about mountain folk than Mrs. MacDowell had been, for she had spent many happy summers at her family's resort cottage at Beersheba Springs in the Tennessee Cumberlands in Grundy County. When in her twenties she found herself easing into a writing career, it was natural that she turned to the mountains for her material. She had shared evenings in the wide hall at Beersheba Springs with mountain men, women, and children, exchanging talk for the impromptu concerns she gave for them. Unconsciously she was learning their ways and their dialects.

Mary Murfree became the nineteenth century's most successful writer to use Appalachian materials. Over twenty volumes appeared, beginning with *In the Tennessee Mountains* in 1884 and continuing until the eve of World War I. Though she published her first mountain story in 1876, her literary reputation was not secure until the 1880s, when the Appalachians became her recognized "literary terrain." To the literate world, Miss Murfree's characterizations were then the major source for understanding the Appalachian American. Her pages are full of elaborate prose, which admired the scenery while emphasizing an unusual, violent, and uncouth people.

Mary N. Murfree's books, though widely read, never reached the top of the best-seller lists. But twice, John Fox Jr., with *Little Shepherd of Kingdom Come* and *The Trail of the Lonesome Pine*, wrote books on Appalachian subjects that reached that summit of literary success. John Fox was a Bluegrass Kentuckian, Harvard educated, the younger brother of a family involved in various business enterprises in the mountains. But John Fox was not successful in business. As a timekeeper in his brother's coal mine in Whitley County, Kentucky, he became enamored with the folk he met there. He became very close to several mountaineers: Uncle Tommie, Uncle Billy and Old Hon, and a Milk Maid who shared his love. For a time, these plain mountain people became closer to Fox than his own family, and they taught him much about life. After two years in his native Bluegrass, during which he was occupied in "being ill," he returned to the mountains and each evening visited Uncle Tommie, Old Hon, and the Milk Maid, studying their speech, habits, and customs.

Fox's stories emphasize the unusual and the sentimental. Only a fair student of character, his heroic mountain figures tend to be misplaced Bluegrass aristocrats. In addition to writing his novels, Fox went on the lecture circuit to tell Americans about mountaineers, about their feuds, violent ways, and their fierce "simple meanness."

There were dozens of other writers who sought to use Appalachian materials, but none were as widely read as Murfree or Fox. Some were in certain ways more effective, and certainly many were more sympathetic to their mountain characters. Lucy Furman, for example, whose novels span the same thirty-year period during which Fox was writing, came to the mountains as a missionary "schoolmarm," and her appreciation for mountaineers was considerable. But few native Appalachians wrote of their region before the 1930s.

Perhaps the only one of all the several hundred writers during the Local Color era who could speak as an "insider," was a woman from near Chattanooga, Tennessee, trapped in a marriage to a very limited mountain man. Emma Bell Miles, the daughter of a teacher, received an uncertain schooling, but was a voracious reader, talented painter, and writer who was supported by patrons to a brief exposure to an art school in St. Louis. Then she returned to Walden Ridge near Chattanooga to marry Frank Miles and accept the hard routine of a poor mountain woman with four children. Despite tremendous handicaps, she struggled to write and did produce a book, *The Spirit of the Mountains* (1905). This book is full of appreciation for the mountain people as survivors, their simple, satisfying lives, and their values. The people in her pages are seen whole and realistically, not presented with condescension or pity, or with prejudice or sentimentality. Yet her book appeared without notice from any of the nation's major literary magazines.

The third type of writing after the Civil War in which mountaineers were widely discussed was that produced by business promoters. For the most part, this business literature was very deprecating of those who either lived atop the mineral resources these promoters wished to exploit or those who would provide the labor base for the new Southern industry they were championing. The Appalachian people were generally presented in such a way by these business promoters that, although they were to be ruthlessly shoved from their land or recruited into low-paying jobs, little concern was shown for them. Industry was seen as an avenue to allow them to escape their limited lives.

Some business promotional writing about Appalachia, such as Edward King's *Great South* (1873), tended to see the coal, timber, tourist, and business potential of the area in almost wholly geographic-economic terms. In such accounts, the people were largely invisible, except as they might contribute to the ease with which the region's resources might be exploited. In 1884 and 1888, Charles Dudley Warner, co-author with Mark Twain of *The Gilded Age,* made journeys into eastern Kentucky, where he found bad roads and illiterate and lawless people living in shanties on little farms set in the midst of magnificent mountains. But in Warner's view, these illiterate mountaineers could be lifted into civilization and made into productive citizens through industrial employment.

Beginning in the 1880s and reaching its climax from 1900 to 1910, a group of writers began to appear who were concerned with the growth of the cotton textile industry. Since many of those to be employed in this industry were Appalachians, and since wages in these new mills were low, Edgar G. Murphy, Walter Hines Page, Alexander J. McKelway, Samuel C. Mitchell, Thomas R. Dawley, and others were drawn into a debate on the nature of Appalachian culture. To these writers, Appalachians entirely "lacked culture," thus industry's coming could not help but have beneficial effects.

The view of Appalachians as a people to be valued during this turn-of-the-century Progressive Age drew largely from the writings of the missionaries, especially from William G. Frost and John C. Campbell. But some business writers, too, shared this optimistic view of Appalachian possibilities. Such writers were Philander P. Claxton, Samuel Tyndale Wilson, and Horace Kephart in *Our Southern Highlanders* (1913). Thus, from this rich complex of writings from 1865 to 1920, Appalachia was discovered by literate America. But the picture that emerged was often grossly inaccurate, based as it was on stereotype and self-serving characteristics.

Those living in the Appalachian backwoods, even in colonial times, had been characterized as people apart. The sense of backwoods is, in fact, older than the idea of the United States itself. Indeed, America was where disgruntled seventeenth- and eighteenth-century Englishmen went, and the backwoods was seen then as an even more remote place. The Virginia gentleman-scholar William Byrd II, for example, referred to backcountry people as "Lubbers" and complained that the men lazed about all day letting their women do all the work. So even before the United States emerged an Appalachian poetic was being developed, comprised of two contrasting images of the region—the one made up of William Byrd-style negativity (1728), the other of heroic images as seen in William Bartram (1773–1778) and James Filson (1782–1788).

Two fine studies about the discovery, indeed the "invention of Appalachia," have appeared in recent years, and they can provide excellent guides for our consideration of the emergence of the awareness of Appalachia. Henry D. Shapiro's *Appalachia on Our Mind* traces the emergence of the literature on Appalachia from the considerable popularity of Local Color writers from 1870 to 1920, especially of Mary Noalles Murfree and John Fox Jr. This Local Color literature, Shapiro says, firmly established the stereotypes of the violent, ignorant, malnourished, moonshining, and feuding mountaineer that has proven so durable for more than a century.

Shapiro also traces the influence of certain Protestant home missionary spokesmen who also emphasized the ignorance and violence of the mountaineers, whose inadequate religion had led them to accept superstition. Shapiro claims that William G. Frost, a college president seeking a mission for his school, "invented Appalachia" and developed what became the orthodox explanation of why Appalachia was as it was. Then, as American and British cooperation became particularly close during World War I, a kind of apotheosis of Appalachia developed as the locale where pure Anglo-Saxonism existed, as seen in the folk song collection of Cecil Sharp (1917) and the monumental study of Appalachia by John C. Campbell, *The Southern Highlander and His Homeland* (1921). Thus, Shapiro claims, emerged the orthodox Anglo-Saxon-oriented image of the Appalachian American as the individualistic, fundamentalist, and traditional mountaineer, who still spoke an Elizabethan dialect and sang the old ballads.

Building on historian Shapiro's ideas is anthropologist Allen W. Batteau, in his challenging book *The Invention of Appalachia*. Batteau traces the emergence of what he terms an "Appalachian poetic" from the Civil War into the 1980s. Using certain key writings he identifies as "Appalachian texts," Batteau traces how Appalachia was first invented by the Local Color writers and the missionaries in the late nineteenth century. In this invented Appalachia, Batteau says, the writers then created stereotypes that served their own purposes. In fact, as the writers' purposes have changed across time, so have the stereotypes themselves changed.

According to Batteau, some stereotypes can be seen as operating within a romantic universe, as with James Kirke Paulding, Frederick Law Olmsted, and John C. Campbell. On the other hand, there has also been a negative universe of stereotypes, dating all the way from William Byrd II to George Washington Harris and Mary N. Murfree. Yet all of these stereotypes were developed, Batteau claims, within contexts reflecting the purposes of the writers. William G. Frost, for example, created appropriate Appalachian characteristics and images in order to contrast with American developments in this time that needed to be reformed. And in the 1960s, there emerged apologists for the War on Poverty, particularly Harry M. Caudill and various writers for television, who Batteau claims made of the Appalachian environment a gothic horror of strip mining and crushing poverty, thus embellishing old stereotypes that filled their reforming intentions. Batteau therefore sees stereotypes as images created to serve the interest of some particular and self-conscious group. Consequently, in Batteau's view, traditional stereotypes are essentially undependable guides toward creating a realistic understanding of Appalachia.

So how much of our perception of the stereotypical Branchwater Mountaineers is myth, and how much is reality? James Branscome has written an angry article entitled "Annihilating the Hillbilly: the Appalachian's Struggle with American Institutions." In this article, Branscome contends that the abuse that the ordinary rural Appalachian suffers from deprecating stereotypes, as in "The Beverly Hillbillies," "Hee-Haw," "Lil Abner," and "Snuffy Smith," has in effect stripped the Appalachian soul. Others too have suggested a blatant media exploitation of Branchwater-style Appalachians for profit, seen as a part of a massive pattern of exploitation of Appalachia by the capitalistic system. What ought we make of this bitter attack on the American media as it seems continually to denigrate the Appalachian?

Billy F. Best, himself an Appalachian of rural background, has noticed that Appalachians have been long-suffering concerning abusive stereotypes. But unlike other ethnic groups in American society who have become hypersensitive about abusive stereotyping, Best claims that for the most part, Appalachians have not attacked those who have abused them. Best explains this by suggesting that Appalachians understand what the stereotypers are really doing. For example, Al Capp, the creator of "Lil Abner," was not really poking fun at Appalachians, Best suggests. Instead, Best says, Capp's purpose was to criticize modern America, and he used Dogpatch—a kind of Appalachian Never-Never-Land full of totally unlikely characters— as a metaphor from which to launch his criticism of materialism, industrialism, and business-dominated urban life. Whether or not Best's optimistic evaluation is valid may be debated, but it is certain that most Appalachians seem to enjoy programs that have used the most degrading stereotyping against them.

The effort of Appalachian scholarship to describe the region has been the slowest of all genres to develop. Though geographers, geologists, and botanists have been describing the region since William Bartram and Elisha Mitchell, serious studies of the life and culture of the region's people have been agonizingly slow in developing. Before 1925, the only serious scholarship underway was in Appalachian folklore and ethnography. Folk tale and folk song collectors clearly found the region a particularly rich field, though the early collectors usually merely collected the raw material and told us precious little about the cultural context that produced the music or the folklore.

Sociology and anthropology were fairly early scholarly disciplines that gave us significant insight into the way of life of traditional, rural-oriented Appalachian folk. Without claims of "discovery," still the insights of Robert Redfield in his 1947 study of "Folk Society" and the community studies pioneered by James Brown and others beginning in the 1940s, are important studies that offer real insight into traditional Appalachian life. It may be true that the "old-fashioned," rural Appalachian is harder for collectors to find today than in the days of Cecil Sharpe, but mountain folk can still be found speaking in the traditional way and even living the simple yeoman's life in the 1990s. Modernization has come to these mountains, but tradition has persisted as well.

As far back as the post–World War I era, several scholars wrote insightfully about the Appalachian American, principal among them the scholar-missionary, John C. Campbell. In his classic 1921 study, *The Southern Highlander and His Homeland*, Campbell suggested four major mountaineer traits: 1) individualism, 2) familism, 3) fundamentalism in religion, and 4) ruralism. Modern scholars comparing Campbell with other early twentieth-century students of Appalachian society modified this fourfold listing of regional characteristics to be: 1) individualism, 2) traditionalism, 3) fatalism, and 4) fundamentalism.

In a late 1950s survey, Sociologist Thomas R. Ford thought he saw a passing of provincialism in the region, since as he saw it, all of these regional characteristics were being eroded, and Appalachians were becoming more and more like other Americans. Others, however, especially ethnologist and religious scholar Loyal Jones, believe they see Appalachians as even more unique as compared with other Americans than in the past. Jones even lists ten particular Appalachian values that he believes set those in the region apart. In fact, Jones sees the Appalachian as perhaps the most traditionally Calvinist of any people. According to Jones, this Calvinism and the Appalachian's remarkable sense of humor has allowed him to survive hazardous occupations and being "gerrymandered, lied to and done unto," even "bilked of land, minerals and ballads," and still retain his sanity and sense of proportion.

Thus, we seem to be getting a fuller understanding of even the unusual, complex Branchwater Mountaineer—this unique and most isolated group within the Appalachian population that has been so much stereotyped and studied. A clear minority within the modern Appalachian experience, this group has been, nonetheless, influenced by the modern world and remains the modern inheritor of the yeomanesque tradition.

The Coming of the Machine Age

THE STORY OF THE Euro–American conquest of Appalachia since 1750 exactly parallels in time the emergence of the Industrial Revolution in England. At the very time of the Newcomen and Watt inventions in steam-engine technology, the first permanent European settlers were moving into the Shenandoah Valley. The earliest explorers in the region were, in fact, on the lookout as much for industrial fuel resources as they were for land for settlement and speculation. Thomas Walker's *Journal* in 1750, for example, notes the coal outcroppings present in the Cumberland Gap. And Jefferson's *Notes on Virginia*, written in the early 1780s, reflects the well-informed Virginian's knowledge of his state, and pretty well indicates where the timber and mineral resources are to be found.

Appalachian fossil fuels were explored and exploited from an early date. The Industrial Revolution has always been hungry for fuels, and by 1750 explorers were actively seeking new information, especially about the location of coal. Until 1840, however, most of the United States' small ironworks operated with charcoal as fuel. Iron deposits close to timber reserves from which the charcoal was made were found in Appalachian Pennsylvania, Maryland, and Virginia. Governor Spotswood owned furnaces on the upper Rappahannock that smelted six hundred tons of iron in 1760. However, Pennsylvania became America's leading manufacturer of iron products in the pre–Civil War period, and its major center became the Scranton area. After 1840, coal was increasingly used as the fuel for the growing American iron industry, and Pennsylvania anthracite and eastern Appalachian bituminous fields were exploited early on. As the American steel and iron industry grew beyond the simple forges of colonial times, it was still predominantly Appalachian fuels and ores that fired that industry.

Thus, the machine age came early into Appalachia. Although large isolated areas remained—especially in the more mountainous regions, as in the Blue Ridge or in the Cumberland Highlands of eastern Kentucky—from an early date the Shenandoah-Tennessee Valley areas provided important transportation corridors. The Ridge and Valley section was the natural way through the mountains. Although a few lines of transport were built over the numerous mountain ridges especially in Pennsylvania and Maryland, as the National Road and other roads that were built after 1790, the bulk of the railway and road building in the southern mountains prior to the 1880s was in the Ridge and Valley section. By the 1850s, the only rail route across what was to become the Confederate States passed through Appalachia by way of the Roanoke Gap, the upper Roanoke and New River Valleys, and the Tennessee River. Central to this prewar, trans-Appalachian railroad was the Virginia and Tennessee Railroad. From Virginia, this line made its way into the Tennessee Valley, and by the late 1850s had been driven to Memphis on the Mississippi River.

The Civil War destruction suffered by the Shenandoah Valley towns, such as Winchester and Staunton, hurt the budding commercial growth of these regional trade centers for a time. But other areas in Appalachia were actually given a boost by the war. Foremost among Southern Appalachian industrial towns aided by the war and the Union Army's repair of railways was Chattanooga, which grew from a village of thirty-five hundred soon after the war, to a town of twelve thousand by the early 1870s. Chattanooga was then a town in the heart of much mineral wealth served by five railways. Many of Chattanooga's new citizens were Union Army veterans who had campaigned among the mountains around and "noted its wonderful advantages as a railway center in one of the richest mineral regions in the world."

Knoxville, too, witnessed a considerable commercial revival after the war, although the city suffered greatly from divisions of opinion and destructive campaigning during the war itself. By the early 1870s, it had "more capital than Chattanooga," and enjoyed a large wholesale trade as a supply depot for the mountains.

In the post–Civil War years, one of the great industrial areas in the United States was developing to the south and southwest of Chattanooga. Atlanta and its Appalachian environs was becoming the industrial capital of the New South. And in northern Alabama a development occurred as noticed by historian Charles Beard when he posited that the real meaning of the Civil War was that American industrial society was freed from the shackles of sharing power with the plantation South. Northern Alabama's remarkable combination of iron ore, coal, and limestone had been known for over a generation. Once local politics recovered from the war and it was decided which group of competing railway entrepreneurs would build and operate the roads into the region, the economic success of Birmingham and its environs was assured.

By 1890, the Appalachian area with its great mineral wealth had been integrated into the nation's transportation system by a series of rail corridors. The Louisville and Nashville was built from the Ohio Valley southward into northern Alabama. Two coal-oriented railroads crossed West Virginia: the Norfolk and Western and the Chesapeake and Ohio. For a time, Southern capital controlled the Richmond-based Virginia and Tennessee Railroad as well as other shorter routes, but these were later integrated into the vast Southern Railway, which passed through Appalachia at several points. As railroads penetrated the region's more remote areas, the towns that developed along them became enclaves of mainstream American mercantile culture, complete with schools, churches, and stores usually little different from similar institutions in the small towns in the rest of the nation.

Major industrial development also emerged in Appalachia apart from the coming of the coal industry. However, the availability of coal often dictated where these industrial developments would take place. The major industrial developments tended to concentrate in either the southern or the northern extremities of the Appalachians. To the north, Pittsburgh became the center of a vast coal-based, industrial complex that allowed Pittsburgh and its industrial satellite cities—Johnstown and Altoona in Pennsylvania, and Morgantown, Fairmont, and Clarksburg in West Virginia—to become one of the world's major industrial centers. The development of the Carnegie Steel Corporation during the 1870s and 1880s was largely a Pittsburgh story, and with Carnegie's success, the area became the chief steel center in the United States. With steel came a dozen other industries—coking, machine tools, refractories, and general manufacture.

At the southern end of the Appalachians, a nearly equally dramatic industrial development occurred in the "A.B.C. Triangle of the New South," the area bounded by Atlanta, Birmingham, and Chattanooga. In this area, a steel industry emerged from the fortunate accident of the presence of all three of the raw materials necessary for steel production: iron ore, coal, and limestone. Nowhere else in the world can all three be found in such close proximity. In 1870, Birmingham was only a cotton field where two railroads crossed; a decade later it was a budding steel center. By 1901, its Tennessee Coal and Iron Company properties became a major part of the U.S. Steel Corporation, the nation's first billion-dollar corporation.

In many areas of the Great Valley from eastern Pennsylvania to the Tennessee Valley, significant industrial developments followed the railroad lines. Winchester, Staunton, Covington, and Roanoke became industrial towns based on the Shenandoah Valley's resources and railroad availability. After World War I, Kingsport, Tennessee, became a "model" industrial town, reflecting a 1920s, pro-business point of view. Kingsport became the center of an important petro-chemical industry as well as other industries. Textiles, too, came into the southern edge of the region from Dalton, Georgia (the nation's rug-making center), to parts of the cotton mill crescent of the upper Piedmont and intruded into Appalachia's fringes.

The Kanawha Valley of West Virginia, sometimes called "the American Ruhr," (calling to mind the rich industrial region in Germany) became part of the major petrochemical complex of the upper Ohio River, which had its beginnings just after World War I. Charleston, West Virginia, became one of its major centers.

The growth of the forest-based industries is also an important post–Civil War story in the region. The Great Appalachian Forest, with its luxurious growth of poplar, oak, chestnut, spruce, hemlock, and other woods, had provided the yeoman pioneer with ample building material and a major challenge from which to carve out his fields. With the appearance of sawmill technology after the Civil War, timbering became a seasonal and serious second occupation for thousands of regional farmers who were located close to streams and rivers. Timber in those immediate post–Civil War years was selectively cut and floated downriver in rafts of seventy to one hundred logs, and usually cut into lumber at such centers as Frankfort, Nashville, or Cincinnati. Until the 1880s, this locally controlled way of cutting and marketing dominated timbering in the Kentucky, Big Sandy, Guyandotte, Kanawha, Cumberland, and Tennessee River Valleys.

By 1890, after exploiting the great Lumber Lost of Michigan and Wisconsin and converting that area into a vast cutover district, the nation's timber barons began turning to the Southern Appalachian Forest. Such companies as the Kentucky Coal and Timber Development Company of New York; the Chicago Lumber Company; the American Associates Ltd. of London, England; Burt and Babb Lumber Company of Michigan; the Yellow Poplar Lumber Company of Ohio; and W.M. Ritter of Pennsylvania, began to develop Appalachian operations. Corporations with more local roots also joined the absentee corporations, such as Thomas J. Asher and Sons Lumber Company, originally of Clay County, Kentucky. In cooperation with various railway corporations, these corporate timbering operations drove farther and farther into the mountains. Vast cuttings exploited whole mountainsides as timber production soared between 1890 and 1920. By 1909, the year that Champion Fiber Company began its operations in western North Carolina, the boom days in Appalachian timber began to wane. The industry leveled off to become a consistent major producer of hardwoods and to supply the furniture and other wood-using industries that had emerged.

Tourism was another avenue of outside commercial and cultural influence that invaded traditional Appalachian society. From an early date, the mountains had provided a summertime retreat from the heat of the coastal cities. This was as true for the elite of Charleston, South Carolina, as for Boston, Massachusetts, for Savannah as for New York City. In fact, the southern mountains perhaps became a more compelling place for retreat than in the North, for even the beach offered little relief from the heat of the Southern Coastal Plain, an area of malarial threat throughout the nineteenth century.

As early as 1748 Berkeley Springs, (West) Virginia, was a well-known mountain retreat with its healing hot springs. Lord Fairfax and George Washington both enjoyed their health-giving relief. By the 1830s, the Virginia Springs area, including White Sulphur Springs and at least a dozen smaller places, had become a favorite vacation area for the Virginia elite. And early in the nineteenth century, Carolinians and Georgians founded the mountain village of Clarkesville in north Georgia. The Asheville area was an even older tourist mecca. As early as 1795, western North Carolina was known to be a good area for health seekers, and the Hot Springs in Madison County became particularly popular with Carolina planters. A Dr. Hardy began coming to Asheville in 1821, and he interested many in coming there who were bothered with various "lowland summer ills." Frederick Law Olmsted found Asheville in 1854 a "beautiful place among the hills, with a number of pretty country-seats about it, which I suppose are summer residences of South Carolina planters."

To the north was Virginia's Springs area. The area had been a place to go as early as 1818 and by 1837 was a well-capitalized development with substantial properties. Yet even the famed White Sulphur Springs then seemed to consist of a group "of unpromising-looking huts or cabins" around "an oblong square." At the "entrance into the establishment—which has the air of a permanent Methodist camp meeting—you have . . . a miserable looking barrack, badly constructed of wood, with a dilapidated portico."

A number of Charleston planters discovered the Asheville–Hot Springs area in western North Carolina in the 1840s, but it was after the Civil War that both the Virginia Springs and Asheville areas rose to real significance. The journalist Edward King, in the early 1870s, noted that post–Civil War Virginia society literally moved to the mountains in the summer time. At least ten well-developed springs resorts above Roanoke and Lexington were built, each with its central hotel—with dining room, reception parlor, and ballroom—surrounded with pleasantly spaced cottages for guests. All were thriving when King visited them, and he compared them favorably with the best that he had seen in Europe.

Even in the 1870s, the Greenbriar White Sulphur Springs was the grandest of all the Virginia Springs hotels. The central hotel was "a remarkable structure, resembling the Krushal at the German baths rather than the vast palaces . . . of Saratoga." It was "amply provided with verandas, with a huge ballroom and a colossal reception parlor." Between the two was a "dining room three hundred feet long, in which twelve hundred guests may at once be seated." The cottages were arranged along paths marked "Alabama, Louisiana, Paradise, Baltimore, Virginia, Georgia, Wolf, and Bachelor." During "the early morning the parlor was filled with ladies who make their engagements for the day, and with the customary rows of invalids who chat cheerily." But not one-tenth of those at such spas were there for the health-giving baths. Creative use of leisure time was spent making contacts and matches, which was the business of most. After the dinner hour, "the crowd separates into small parties, who linger on the verandas, or under the oaks, or along the shaded paths . . . where hundreds of hearts have been broken."

The Virginia Springs season was from July until September. Farther south the season was longer—from May until October. But the hotels and springs resorts in the Asheville region in the 1870s were not as grand and popular as were those in the Virginia Springs. In these years, the great figures of the defeated Confederate States of America were in frequent attendance at the Virginia Springs spas.

Robert E. Lee lived in nearby Lexington, and even Jefferson Davis made occasional visits.

The railway had not yet come to Asheville when Edward King visited there in 1873, although at the great White Eagle Hotel you could catch a stagecoach that traveled the roads west of the Blue Ridge. A few Asheville hotels and the Warm Springs Hotel in Madison County, forty miles northwest, were the only resorts that King noted. After many difficulties, the railroad was finally driven to Asheville in October of 1880. By then the city bristled with hotels and boarding houses and boasted two spas built in the "Virginia tradition." Frances Fisher Tiernan's novel, *The Land of the Sky*, had featured Asheville's great promise in 1875, and the boom was on. The splendid Battery Park Hotel was opened in 1886 by Colonel Frank Cox, a multimillionaire who had first visited Asheville only a few years before and had been unable to find accommodations. The Battery Park dominated a prominent hill site of twenty-five acres above the downtown section. It was four stories high, 473 feet long, turreted and "modern and strictly high class in every way." From its porches there was "a magnificent panorama of mountain views in every direction."

It remained for the grandson of one of America's most successful captains of industry to build the ultimate in Appalachian accommodation. George Washington Vanderbilt, grandson of Commodore Cornelius Vanderbilt, began in the mid-1880s looking for a place to build the finest country home in North America. In December of 1887 he visited Asheville, and as he sat on the veranda of the Battery Park looking south, he "saw a giant pine rising above the other trees in the forest." There on the spot of that tree, he told his friends, he intended to build his estate. In the year following, he bought 125 thousand acres of mountain forests. Securing the services of America's most famous architect, Richard Morris Hunt, and the nation's foremost landscape planner, Frederick Law Olmsted—who forty years before had traveled through the region—George W. Vanderbilt erected a 250–room palace in the French Provincial style that rivals the grandest palaces of Europe. His home was a virtual museum loaded with European art treasures, one of the grand showplaces of America, and placed in the magnificent setting of Carolina's Great Smoky Mountains.

Asheville had begun as an imitation of the Virginia Springs, with the advantage of a season two months longer. And across the Appalachian Mountains were many other imitations of the Greenbriar and the Battery Park. At Mary Noalles Murfree's Beersheba Springs in Grundy County, Tennessee, or Crab Orchard and Estill Springs in Kentucky, or Demorest in north Georgia, these smaller spas had a down-country, Southern clientele who came loyally into the mountains each summer.

The conservation movement in America owes much to developments in the Appalachian South and is part of the development of the National Forests of Appalachia and the emergence of "The Park"—The Great Smoky Mountain National Park—which did not reach success until the 1930s. Much earlier at George Washington Vanderbilt's Biltmore Estate outside Asheville, America's first modern school of forestry was founded. Here modern conservation methods were the first tried in North America. Another early champion of conservation was Horace Kephart, then living in Bryson City, North Carolina, who at the turn of the century was perhaps the nation's best-known outdoorsman and writer on woodsmanship. He wrote regularly for *Outdoor Magazine,* and in 1913 he wrote the widely read *Our Southern Highlanders.* Kephart was one of the major champions of conservation in the Appalachian South, one of the fathers of The Great Smoky Mountains Park and the Appalachian Trail. And there was Gifford Pinchot, who learned modern forestry while employed as the Biltmore's forester with Carl A. Schenck, the pioneer forester who ran the forestry school at the Biltmore Estate from 1895 to 1914. So significant was the Biltmore School of Forestry and other western North Carolina-centered conservation champions of forestry practices, that within American forestry at that time, the whole was referred to as the "Appalachian Movement."

These pioneers of conservation were important in the development of the idea of "The Park," the Appalachian Trail, and the Blue Ridge Parkway. The view that the proper use of the beautiful Appalachian area was to set it aside as national forests and parks was largely an "outside," middle-class hope, and an essentially urban movement. A number of bitter legal condemnation proceedings had to be made in order to remove the natives from their traditional lands. This removal has continued as urban Americans have supported government land-buying schemes for forests, parks, and reservoirs. And urban Americans have also bought second homes in Appalachia's favored sections at prices so inflated that native owners could not afford to hold their land and pay the rising taxes. One author concerned about this problem has pointed out that through its national forests and national parks, the United States government has become

Appalachia's largest "absentee landowner." The national forests in Appalachia exceed 5.388 million acres today, an area larger than Connecticut, Rhode Island, and Delaware combined.

The major industrial invasion of Appalachia, however, has involved the exploitation of the region's fossil fuels—mainly coal. The world's first commercial oil well was drilled in Appalachian Pennsylvania, the 1859 well drilled by Edwin Drake near Titusville. Gas also has been and remains a major Appalachian fuel product. In fact, Appalachia was the world's major producer of oil and gas before 1902. But among the fossil fuels, coal has had the major twentieth-century impact upon the region.

Since the American Revolution, the region has been the major supplier of coal to the nation. The first fields exploited were those nearest the population centers on the east coast—the anthracite fields of northeastern Pennsylvania and the bituminous fields of Virginia and Maryland. As the appetite of American industry for fuel increased, mineral-hunters were sent out to explore—Thomas Walker in 1750, Professor David T. Anstead in the 1850s, General John Daniel Imboden in the 1860s, Jedidiah Hotchkiss in the 1870s, and Richard M. Broaz in the 1880s. The 1880s and 1890s were climactic decades for explorers and industrial promoters in the region. Charles Dudley Warner, William Mahone, Henry Watterson, and John H. Debar as well as Edward King, traveled through this "Switzerland of America," representing such journals of opinion as *Harper's, Atlantic, Lippincott's, Cosmopolitan,* and *Century.* Explorers and promoters together combined to make the region's mineral resources quite precisely known by 1900.

First came the explorers and "scholars" like Broaz, Anstead, and Hotchkiss, who discovered and precisely located the coalfields. Then came the buyers who secured title to the minerals when they were not able to deal directly with absentee owners of vast tracts of mountain land. When small owners were involved, buyers gained control of mineral rights by outright purchase of the mountain lands or by purchase of the mineral rights only, leaving the surface to the original owners. After a careful search for title in the state capital or county seat, and into the legal chaos that has troubled Appalachia's lands since the American Revolution, the mineral buyers came to the Appalachian farmer with gold, charm, legal maneuver, and sometimes fraud. They came into western Maryland, western Pennsylvania, northern West Virginia, and northern Alabama during the 1860s. During the 1870s, the buyers went into central Tennessee, then into

REGIONAL NATURAL RESOURCES

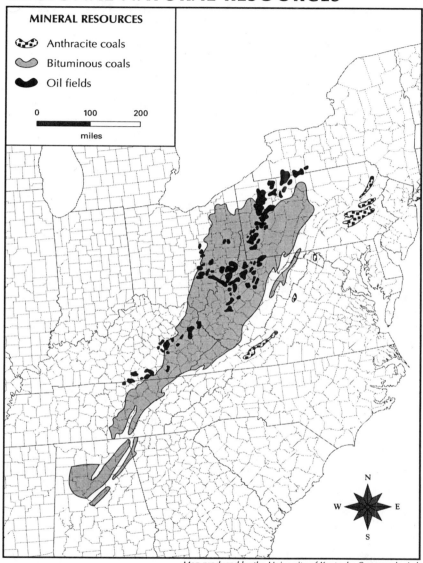

MINERAL RESOURCES

- Anthracite coals
- Bituminous coals
- Oil fields

0   100   200
miles

N
W   E
S

Map produced by the University of Kentucky Cartography Lab

southern West Virginia in the 1880s, and finally into eastern Kentucky in the 1890s.

Prior to 1870, most of the large coal mining operations had been confined to Pennsylvania, Virginia, and Maryland. Although as early as 1840 investors in New York, Philadelphia, Cincinnati, London, and Paris knew that one of the world's greatest sources of fossil fuel energy was locked under the Appalachian Mountains, it took more than a recognition of these resources to bring persons to actually invest in such speculation. Titles to these minerals had to be consolidated into large blocks. Only after title to large blocks of coal rights was procured could railways or other lines of access be built. Then the coal camps and mines could be established and the coal actually brought out.

In the 1870s, when the active coalfields spread into the new state of West Virginia, Edward King traveled down the New River and found its canyon cut through fourteen "coal strata for nearly its whole length." Other rivers, he said, cut "through most of the coal-bearing strata on their courses, leaving the coal entirely above water-level." King added that "there is no region in the world where less physical labor will prepare a mine for the delivery of coal at its drift mouth." The Chesapeake and Ohio Railroad was built into the area in 1870, so King was seeing the region on the eve of massive mine growth. David Thomas Anstead, Professor of Geology at Kings College at the University of London, had explored the New River reserves in the 1850s and had given as his opinion that "there is no coalfield more important." Nor were there others, in his opinion "more accessible or of better quality." Furthermore, he thought the supply "might be looked on as inexhaustible."

Twenty years after Anstead had proven the mineral reserves of the New River field, railways were built. The boom in this field is reflected in the growth of Charleston, which had been a tiny trade center for Kanawha Valley farm produce. Then in 1885 it was designated as the capital of West Virginia. By 1900, its population was 11,099; by 1929, it was nearly 60,000.

By 1900, all the coalfields in West Virginia—the south, central, and northern—were in full production. Furthermore, the exploitation of the Newcastle, Montevalle, Warrior, and Cahabe fields in Alabama had been begun in the 1870s and 1880s—fields associated with the late-century rise of the iron mining and steel production in Birmingham, Bessemer, Fort Payne, Anniston, Gadsden, and Talladega. Annual mineral production in Alabama had expanded from $779,242

RAILROADS, 1860 & 1880

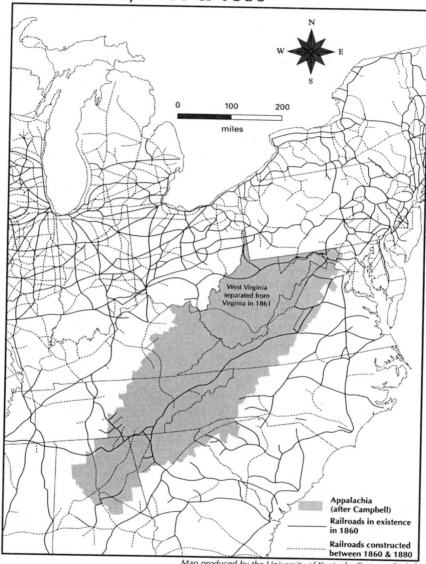

West Virginia
separated from
Virginia in 1861

0   100   200
miles

N
W   E
S

Appalachia
(after Campbell)

Railroads in existence
in 1860

Railroads constructed
between 1860 & 1880

Map produced by the University of Kentucky Cartography Lab

in 1880 to $13,701,525 in 1900. The Birmingham boom continued un-abated through the early 1890s, but the Panic of 1893 threw the more ill-conceived iron mills and mines into receivership. The larger Tennessee Coal and Iron Company, however, continued to thrive.

Historian Ronald Lewis has noted the different racial labor patterns that developed in the various parts of the Appalachian coalfields. In the southernmost fields of northern Alabama, Georgia, and Tennessee, predominantly black labor was used during the nineteenth and early twentieth centuries. In the mining fields Lewis calls "northern," which included the fields of northern West Virginia closest to Pittsburgh, blacks were almost totally excluded from the mines. However, in Central Appalachia, which included southern West Virginia, eastern Kentucky, and southwestern Virginia, the most remote and the last-developed fields, owners sought what was deemed a "judicious mixture" of blacks, native whites, and foreign-born whites. These three groups were brought to the new coal camps and coal towns in a balance that the owners thought would keep labor most easily controlled and docile.

At the Cumberland Gap, where Virginia, Kentucky, and Tennessee meet, an aggressive foreign-owned enterprise developed in the 1880s. Alexander A. Arthur, a Canadian lumberman, visited the Gap in 1885 and became enamored by the coal possibilities that he saw. He formed a syndicate to buy up lands, mineral rights, and rights-of-way, which he successfully sold on the London market to form a British firm, The American Associates, Ltd. Feverish activity during 1888 to 1890 built a railway tunnel near the Cumberland Gap, laid some one hundred miles of track connecting Knoxville to the south with Pineville to the north, and began development of several mineral properties in the area. A well-laid-out city, Middlesboro, was built in the Yellow Creek Valley and an elite suburb built at Harrogate, Tennessee. The massive Four Seasons Hotel was built there at a cost of $1 million. Proper Englishmen mingled at the hotel with mountaineers, and barroom brawls shared the attention of Middlesboro with one of the first golf clubs established in America. But the 1890 failure of a major London bank brought the scheme to a temporary halt. Instead of a new Birmingham, the new city had to be content with being only a rather large mountain mining town. The American Associates, however, was able to maintain control over their vast properties despite the disaster of 1893 and the failure of the original company.

The golf course at Middlesboro was an ironic "new event." Built in 1889 for the enjoyment of the English elite and their friends, it was laid out amid spectacular hills above the town of Middlesboro. Thus, one of the first golf courses built in North America was in the heart of Appalachia, and it is still used today by that small city.

The seekers for the mineral wealth of the area usually overlooked or disdained the people and the society that had grown up in the area. Alexander Arthur at Middlesboro, for example, believed that he had civilized a barren wilderness and brought rails, mines, and enlightenment to a backward people. Edward King spoke of eastern Kentucky in a similar way in the 1870s, when he noted that eastern Kentucky may be said to be "one immense bed of coal and iron." In fairness to King, however, it should be said that when he traveled through the isolated region between Maryville, Tennessee, and Asheville, North Carolina, he came to appreciate the mountaineers there, whom he described with some sympathy.

Appalachian yeomanry was directly and dramatically challenged, even as in the pre–Civil War period when plantation capitalism had challenged this beleaguered mentality. Intruding industrial culture threatened this war-wounded way of life, and it was no wonder that many mountaineers were attracted to a different kind of life. Historian Crandall Shifflett has recently made the point that the yeomanesque way of life had been in serious economic trouble for many years as population pressure kept driving down the standard of living in rural areas in Appalachia. When left alone on sufficient acres, yeomanry was able to provide a "good life." But as its acres per farmer gradually decreased—thanks to very large families—that way of life, never an affluent one, became more and more difficult. Some modern writers have insisted that yeomanry never provided a comfortable life. One historian has even characterized the yeoman's approach in Appalachia as "self-defeating," while another has characterized rural Appalachia as dominated by "family fecundity." Mountain yeomen, this historian says, "struggled to preserve their way of life," yet they lost out because of "high birthrates, population growth, and land scarcity."

In contract to the yeomanesque farm, the coal town and other parts of the nation's expanding market-oriented economy in the mountains seemed to provide many goods and services and a higher standard of living. Though yeomanry had been able to pretty well resist the blandishment of plantation capitalism, it proved much less able to resist the post–Civil War appeals of industrial capitalism.

That "outside" entrepreneurs such as Edward King and

Alexander Arthur might have negative sentiments concerning the traditional yeomen of Appalachia is hardly surprising. But many "insiders" also came to believe that the region's destiny lay in wholehearted cooperation with the progressive spirit of American business, and they participated actively in bringing the benefits of industry and mineral development to Appalachia. Perhaps the regional native who did most to bring the machine age to the region's remote corners was John C. Calhoun Mayo.

John C.C. Mayo was a native of Pike County, Kentucky, raised in Floyd County, and schooled at Kentucky Wesleyan, then in Winchester. After college he returned to teach in another eastern Kentucky county, Johnson. In time, teaching took less and less of his time, and he began organizing companies that bought up land and mineral rights in the 1880s and 1890s.

Mayo went among his people on horseback and by buckboard wagon with his pockets full of gold dollars, buying thousands of acres of mineral rights. He had his farmer-customers sign a "Broadform Deed," which gave the owner of the mineral the privilege of using the surface, which the mountaineer retained, in any way necessary to get at the minerals beneath the surface. Of course, with his yeoman values, the mountaineer could see value only in the surface. Obviously the mountaineer had in mind only the deep mining methods used at that time, the kind of mining he had seen at Millers Fork on the Big Sandy or the few holes that were hacked into the coal seams then operative in the Kentucky River or the Big Sandy Valleys.

Mayo bought thousands of parcels of mineral rights, and then consolidated these titles into blocks of mineral rights, which he sold or leased to companies that might actually do the mining. These dealings made him a rich man and a respected "benefactor to his region." His mansion in Paintsville, Kentucky, a huge Victorian structure, is still a showplace in the region. His funeral in 1914 was the largest ever held in eastern Kentucky.

The expenditure of funds, human blood, and energy that had built the railways into the hitherto remote mountain areas of Appalachia is legendary. Whether in West Virginia, where John Henry died in competition with the machine, or in North Carolina, or Kentucky, the per-mile cost of building these railroads in dollars and human lives was staggering. And so great was the financial risk in opening a new coalfield in a remote mountain area that the resources of great rail companies, such as the Louisville and Nashville and the Chesapeake and Ohio, had to be combined with those of great energy corporations, such as the Consolidation Coal Company of Maryland.

Perhaps it could not have been otherwise. Few towns outside small county seat villages existed in all of eastern Kentucky in 1900. Mary Beth Pudup's study of Prestonsburg, Harlan, and Hazard, shows that these eastern Kentucky towns shared only modestly in the South's antebellum and postbellum farmer-commercial developments. By 1880, Prestonsburg's population was 275, and Harlan's was only 76 persons. So to accommodate the thousands of miners then necessary to extract the coal from Appalachia's new coalfields, the companies had to provide housing, public services, and frequently whole towns, complete with schools, stores, churches and hospitals. Such new towns, of course, were a wonder to the surrounding yeoman population. Most of those recruited into the eastern Kentucky mines were from the surrounding counties, and were brought from a lifestyle then largely devoid of industrial discipline. The plutocratic developers who brought industrialism into the mountains thus set in motion forces that created a society very different from the yeoman society that dominated the traditional life in remote Appalachia. In a few decades, a special kind of Appalachian proletarianism emerged in the region's coal camps and coal towns that was to have a lasting impact. Historian Ronald Lewis has noted that the late-developing Central Coalfield of northeastern Tennessee, eastern Kentucky, southwestern Virginia, and southern West Virginia, transformed a vast farming and virgin forest area in 1880 into an area covered with coal towns and small cities dedicated to coal. Population boomed as coal production "tripled by 1900 and multiplied fivefold by 1930."

In the coal towns, immigrants from Wales, Italy, Poland, Hungary, and other European countries joined the locally recruited miners; blacks, too, were particularly prevalent in the Kentucky and West Virginia mining camps of Central Appalachia. Black miners were recruited from northern Alabama and the Deep South, and blacks reached a particularly high percentage of the miners in southern West Virginia. Of course, Jim Crow patterns of segregation existed in Southern Appalachia at the time, and blacks found themselves living in separate sections of town or in separate towns that became wholly black.

By the time the Eastern Kentucky Fields were opened in 1910, the coal town had largely replaced the earlier and cruder coal camps. Clearly a coal town culture developed. In eastern Kentucky, native white miners were recruited from the farms in nearby areas, and they moved into the new towns with their families. The sudden boom in mining population in such counties as Harlan County, Kentucky, where a 1920 population of 10,566 mushroomed to 75,274 in 1940, meant a virtual revolution in institutions and values for those who moved to the coal towns.

Even prior to the great mine strike in 1902, the United States had most unfortunate experiences with industrial paternalism. In Pullman, Illinois, George M. Pullman had attempted to build a model town, only to have the intolerance inherent in such paternalism exaggerate his differences with labor that exploded into the terrible strike of railroad workers in 1894. Hershey, Pennsylvania, offered a similar spectacle. In almost every case of industrial paternalism—some called it "corporate feudalism"—it worked badly. In the Appalachian coalfields, the company towns—necessarily built by a company needing the workers in areas remote from regular urban services—often became centers of oppression. Appalachia, in fact, had a much higher concentration of company towns than any other area of the nation. Some towns quickly became fiefdoms run by the resident manager or mine manager, using the leverage of the company store, the company-financed church, and the school, or control of company housing, to strengthen the company's control.

Until World War II, the technology for mining coal was such that armies of miners were needed. Thus, sizeable cities sprang up as the fields were opened—Cumberland, Maryland; Clarksburg, West Virginia; Welch, West Virginia; Lynch, Kentucky; and scores of others. The last real coal town built in Appalachia was Wheelwright, Kentucky, largely developed during World War II. These and scores of other coal towns, many constructed as shacks row on row, spread across the Cumberland-Allegheny portion of Appalachia. They became at best small cities of romance for those wishing to escape the confinement of the mountains and the poverty of mountain farming. For others they were a grim lure into a neo-feudal vassalage to some mining corporation.

In many of these towns, one company literally owned the whole. The coal company paid the preacher, owned the company store, the houses, the hotels, and the school. A wage check-off paid for the doctor, the teacher and other services. The very smallest towns—jerry-built villages erected by get-rich-quick developers—provided only the barest housing and no services. In the large company-built towns, important amenities were provided, and a sense of permanence and community existed. Usually only company men could bring their families to live in the company houses. The company often paid its wages in scrip convertible only at the company store, where prices were often higher than in competing stores in the county. Miners frequently came to think of themselves as virtual vassals, working for the company in unsafe mines for low wages, renting a company-owned house, and paid in scrip. In some communities, a reputation for being a "model town" was widely recognized by elite and worker alike, although in times of industrial trouble such "model" towns often suffered from particularly bitter divisions.

The coal mines were among the first of the work places in America to organize. Thrust below ground in a wilderness of mysterious tunnels, management could not possibly control labor's contacts on the job as well as they could in a more confined factory setting. Furthermore, mining has always been inherently dangerous—miners have been killed by the thousands in every decade in American history until recently. Working conditions were miserable at worst and tolerable at best. Thus, grievances were present everywhere. And the profit-conscious owner tried to keep wages as low as he could. Whenever mine unions developed, they were fought tenaciously.

Coal mine unionism probably began in Appalachia in 1842 at Shenandoah, Pennsylvania. The early Molly McGuire strikes in the Anthracite Fields of northeastern Pennsylvania came during the 1860s and 1870s. The bitterest battle was fought between the Miners National Association (MNA)—a union that combined class interests with wartime and ethnic differences and that was run by and for the mostly Irish miners themselves—and a company union, the Miners and Mine Laborer's Benevolent Association. In the midst of this jurisdictional difficulty, owners cut wages, and the miners who were members of the Miners National Association walked out. Open warfare soon broke out, with MNA loyalty reinforced by the secret mysteries of the Molly McGuires, a pro-Catholic and Irish secret society. A hired Pinkerton detective, James McParlin, risked his life to infiltrate the "Mollies"; he learned their secrets and discovered who their leaders were. The trial, in the fall of 1875, completely destroyed the Miners National Association, and ten of the Molly McGuires were hanged for murder. Fourteen were sentenced to prison terms.

The modern era of mine unionism began with the organization of the United Mine Workers of America in 1890. The UMW operated with success in the anthracite region around Scranton, Pennsylvania—the area of the old Molly McGuire difficulties. Under the lead-

The Cherokee dominated southern Appalachia for centuries, living in some fifty towns along the major rivers of East Tennessee, western North Carolina, and North Georgia before Desoto entered the region in 1540. (Above) The Hiwassee Island site near Cleveland, Tennessee.

(Right) House construction (Reproduced by permission of the University of Tennessee Press. From Thomas M.N. Lewis and Madeline Knebergos, *Tribes That Slumber: Indians of the Tennessee Region*, 1958).

Homes reflected one's wealth in the region, and logs were the main building material for many years. (Above) The Pigg house in Madison County, Kentucky, was a double-pen cabin with a "dog trot" and full attic (Photo by A.E. Todd, Berea Archives). (Below) Some log homes were quite dressed up (Berea College Photo Archives). *Unless otherwise noted, all photos courtesy of Berea College Photo Archives.*

(Above) Even a modest log cabin provided a warm environment. (Below) Until the 1890's much of a woman's time was taken up with the textile arts—carding, spinning, dying and weaving. Looms were often massive, and of varying complexity—one to four harnesses were used.

(Above) When the Appalachian area was settled by Euro-Americans, it was transformed from a forested environment into farms, even on steep hillsides. (Below) The whole family was involved in producing the crops—corn, oats, hay, wheat, cotton, flax, barley as well as animals—and always a big garden.

(Left) It took many years for adequate transportation to be built into a forbidding mountain environment. (Above) Yet visiting was nicely done on horseback.

(Above) Railroads were built into many counties.

The major coal production era for Appalachia was from 1861 until 1990, when the region was the nation's major source of fossil fuels. (Above) At first coal was very easy to bring out but later mining became complex. (Below) Seco, a fairly comfortable coal town, was built by South East Coal Company in eastern Kentucky to accommodate the thousands of miners needed to work the mines before 1950.

Important timbering was done in the whole Appalachian region from the 1870s until its peak year, 1909, and has continued at a more modest rate. Sawmills sprang up throughout the Appalachian forest.

Wherever possible, rivers carried the logs to market, but railroads and trucks carried them in more recent times.

(Above) Some grist mills were rather advanced. (Below) Stores grew up at strategic spots along country roads (Courtesy of Warren H. Brunner, Brunner Studio, Berea).

Appalachia maintained a traditional rural flavor through World War II, and towns and schools represented the modern "outside" life that was intruding into the lives of the rural mountaineers. (Above) Hazard, Kentucky, ca. 1925. (Below) A rural one–room school with teacher and children at play (Courtesy of Warren H. Brunner, Brunner Studio, Berea).

Most churches in the region are independent, believing the King James Bible literally and depending upon a spiritually-called ministry, and they identify with independent Baptist and Pentecostal denominations (Courtesy of Warren H. Brunner, Brunner Studio, Berea).

Not all churches in Appalachia fit the Independent Baptist/Holiness pattern. This Log Cathedral at Buckhorn, Kentucky, was once Presbyterianism's largest rural church.

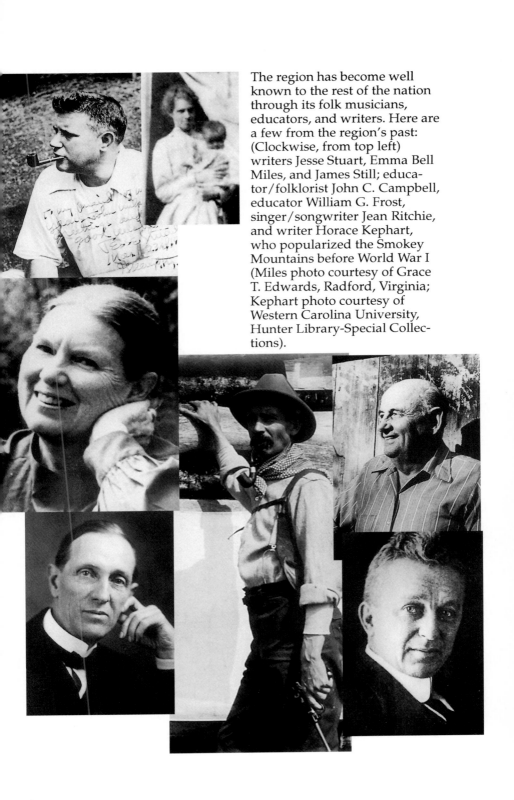

The region has become well known to the rest of the nation through its folk musicians, educators, and writers. Here are a few from the region's past: (Clockwise, from top left) writers Jesse Stuart, Emma Bell Miles, and James Still; educator/folklorist John C. Campbell, educator William G. Frost, singer/songwriter Jean Ritchie, and writer Horace Kephart, who popularized the Smokey Mountains before World War I (Miles photo courtesy of Grace T. Edwards, Radford, Virginia; Kephart photo courtesy of Western Carolina University, Hunter Library-Special Collections).

Since 1950, modern mining machinery has invaded Appalachia's mines, cutting drastically the numbers of miners needed. (Above) The bulldozer prepares the land (Courtesy of Warren H. Brunner, Brunner Studio, Berea). (Below) This dragline in western Kentucky is similar to machines now used in eastern Kentucky and West Virginia. Note the figures in the foreground. (Courtesy of Earl Dotter, Silver Spring, Maryland.)

(Above) The result of surface mining is a badly disrupted landscape (Courtesy of Kentuckians for the Commonwealth). (Below) Pilot Knob in the morning mist (Courtesy of Shean Perry, Berea).

The spectacular beauty of the Appalachian Mountains has always played a role in the life of its people and of people fortunate enough to visit its valleys and peaks. (Above) North Carolina mountain homes. (Below) Tourism has become a major attraction, which has actually threatened some of the region's wilderness. The dimensions of Appalachian adventure are many, including lake and river sports (marina photo by author; kayaking photo courtesy of Phoenix Poke Boats, Inc.).

Since 1970, a majority of the Appalachian people have lived in the region's cities, or close enough to these cities to have their lives revolve around modern urban life. Roanoke's market area (photo by author).

A stylized building in downtown Knoxville, Tennessee (photo by author).

Appalachia's complexity assures that examples can be found to reinforce stereotypes, no matter how misguided they might be.

A captured moonshine still.

The prevalence of rifles reinforced the view that mountain society was violent.

A frequently overlooked group has been the region's Blacks, who have usually made up about 10 percent of the region's population (Courtesy Warren H. Brunner, Brunner Studio, Berea).

ership of the charismatic John Mitchell, who headed the United Mine Workers of America from 1898 to 1908, the UMW won some very significant strikes, especially the great West Virginia strike of 1902. Careful always to avoid the violence that had destroyed the Molly McGuires, Mitchell even gained the support of President Theodore Roosevelt, the first American president to give his support to a union in a strike.

Mine strikes everywhere in America, and certainly in Appalachia, have had more than their share of violence. Perhaps violence is inevitable in such an industry, for coal miners live with death daily, and explosives are commonplace at every mine. Whether at Cripple Creek, Blair Mountain, or in bloody Harlan, coal operators, too, have felt themselves justified in using all the force they could summon— mine guards and sheriff's armies, the National Guard, and even the United States Air Corps—in order to protect their properties.

In the eyes of the operators, the American way of life depended upon the small businessman running his own business, risking his own capital to mine the coal that the nation needed. To him it was persons from the outside with alien ideas, like the union, who were threatening free enterprise and regional well-being. To the miner, on the other hand, the justice of his cause was clothed in terms of the freedom to join a union and the fairness of a living wage. On both sides it was easy enough to surround one's cause with righteousness and to condemn the opposition as tools of exploitation and corruption.

Until the 1960s, the coal industry was immensely competitive— even overly competitive. The natural resource of coal was readily available, and until safety regulations proliferated and expensive equipment requiring well-paid labor became the rule, anyone who could borrow as little as $10,000 could become a coal operator. As a result, thousands of individual mine operating units emerged. In good times, small operators flooded into the industry, raising the supply of coal so quickly that no one could make much of a profit. In bad years, the marginal producers were driven out of business by the thousands, and even the larger, more efficient corporations were in for hard times. During some of the industry's more desperate years, prices for coal were so low that the larger companies could show a profit only by raising the prices at their company stores and the rent on the houses in their company towns. These tactics, of course, placed the main burden of economic maladjustment squarely upon the backs of the laboring miners.

After World War I, West Virginia became a center for some of the worst mine violence in U.S. history. During World War I, the UMW had agreed not to strike and to hold the line on wages as a patriotic gesture. But prices continued to rise during the war, and with the return of peace, the union made strong wage demands. When these demands were not met, a general strike was called in 1919. In Logan County, West Virginia, the coal owners made a concerted effort to destroy the union, and Sheriff Don Chaflin led an army of deputies and mine guards against the strikers.

Rigid antiunionism was centered in Logan County, but operators in neighboring Mingo County shared strong antiunion sentiment as well. Yet in Mingo the law enforcement institutions were sufficiently divided that open warfare broke out between armed miners and the operator's forces, here made up of private detectives supplied by the Baldwin-Felts Detective Agency of Bluefield, West Virginia. A shoot-out at the railroad depot in Matewan killed six detectives and two miners in May of 1920. The terrorism in the minefields was heightened as nearly half of the six thousand mine union members in Mingo County who had been fired from their jobs were evicted from their company homes and forced to live in tent colonies. In August of 1920, terrorism erupted into a three-hour gun battle in which six more miners were killed.

Crisis conditions continued into 1921. In August, the pro-union sheriff of Mingo County, Sid Hatfield, was assassinated. The much loved organizer, Mother Jones, returned to West Virginia on August 23 a little over three weeks after Hatfield's murder. Soon, three thousand union miners from the central fields of West Virginia in the Cabin Creek and Kanawha County area began their dramatic one-hundred-mile march across the mountains toward Logan and Mingo Counties to support their embattled brethren. Many U.S. Army veterans who had fought in Europe during World War I were in this miners' army of three thousand and gave leadership and discipline to the march. They were well armed and determined to "hang [Sheriff] Don Chaflin to a sour apple tree."

West Virginia's governor, Ephraim F. Morgan, called out the state police and the state militia and appealed to President Harding for help. On the last day of August 1921, the two armies met at Blair Mountain at the crest of the watershed between the Central Mine Fields and the fields of Mingo and Logan. Twelve hundred state police, militia, and sheriff's deputies and mine guards met the three thousand UMW marchers in a pitched battle that probably had more sophisticated logistics across a twenty-five-mile front than was involved in the Battle of New Orleans in 1815. Both sides were supported by scouts, physicians, nurses, and even chaplains.

On the side of the State of West Virginia and the operators, airplanes dropped bombs on the miners' army during the battle. The operators defending their domain suffered three deaths and about forty wounded. The "invading" miners' casualties were not known. Neither side gained any particular advantage until a detachment from the U.S. Army arrived on September 4 to support the operators' army. With the appearance of the U.S. Army contingent, the miners withdrew and the battle ceased.

The leaders of the miners' army, Frank Keeney, William Blizzard, and others, were tried for treason by the State of West Virginia. Their trial was conducted in the same mountain-valley courthouse where John Brown had been tried some seventy years before in Charles Town. A total of twenty-two miners were tried. The defense contended that the miners' action was taken only against autocratic operators and their arbitrary actions and that they had no quarrel with the State of West Virginia. Though acquitted on the treason charges, subsequent trials at Berkeley Springs, Fayetteville, and Lewisburg on charges of murder did result in the conviction of three union leaders.

The coal operators in the Southern Appalachian fields were quite suspicious of their northern competitors and the UMW when, after a serious strike in Illinois, the "Jacksonville Agreement" was signed in February of 1924 between the union and the northern operators. John L. Lewis, the new president of the UMW, desired a more stable industry and the elimination of high cost, fly-by-night mines. A more efficient and stable operator was what Lewis wanted to encourage, and a $7.50 daily wage was agreed to. In return for this "high wage" and a check-off of wages for union dues, the UMW agreed to move into the Southern coalfields in a large organizational campaign.

The Southern coalfields in West Virginia, Kentucky, and Tennessee were not then unionized and paid wages that were no higher than six dollars per day. Yet more and more of the nation's coal was coming from these Southern fields. From the first, the Jacksonville Agreement was met with deep suspicion by the Southern Appalachian operators. Such operators were quick to see a conspiracy between their northern competitors and the hated union, "a damnyankee plot aimed at Southern free enterprise." Though the Jacksonville Agreement was to operate for only three years, from 1924 to 1927, it was avoided from the first. When first Consolidation Coal then Pittsburgh Coal reneged in the summer of 1925, the Jacksonville Agreement collapsed entirely.

The 1920s, though hard years for the coal industry generally, were also years in which the control of the region seemed wholly within the hands of the region's coal operators. Not only had the union been beaten back and the rising consciousness of labor frustrated, but the handles of power seemed to rest rather totally in the hands of the region's coal and railroad barons. Perhaps the major manifestation of this kind of plutocratic power concentration was in the rise of the so-called "Fairmont Ring" during the early decades of the twentieth century. This was a small group of West Virginia politicians and coal-owners, including Peter H. Watson, Johnson N. Camden, Clarence Wayland Watson, and Aretas B. Fleming. These gentlemen sat atop a network that included such great corporations as the Standard Oil Company of Ohio, the Baltimore and Ohio Railway, the Fairmont Coal Company, Consolidation Coal Company, and the Monongah Coal and Coke Company. This combine openly bought U.S. senatorships for Johnson Cameron in Kentucky and for Clarence Watson in West Virginia.

Clearly by 1930 the yeoman's way of life was in decay in Appalachia. Despite hard times, the most successful of the yeomen continued to move into petty agricultural capitalism. Yet within Appalachia, something fairly close to true yeomanry still persisted among many traditional rural folk. In the 1920s, the intrusion of industry, especially in coal mining, attracted many farmer–yeomen into a basically proletarian life with a value system substantially different from his traditional one. The Appalachian yeoman farmer as early as 1900 was conscious that his position was deteriorating. The attractions of coal town life and his own relative poverty combined with the progressive climate preached by the schools and the local chambers of commerce to place the rural way of life on the defensive.

From Plutocracy to Welfare State and Back

WILLIAM G. FROST'S *Atlantic Monthly* article on Appalachia in 1899 referred to the southern mountain area as the "Republican backyards" of nine solidly Democratic states. This political evaluation is essentially accurate if we accept the characterization of the South from 1880 to 1928 as "solidly Democratic." There were exceptions, of course. West Virginia, an entirely Appalachian state, enjoyed a classic two-party system. Furthermore, there was such a large Republican population in East Tennessee that it could not be ignored by Tennessee's normally dominant Democratic Party. North Carolina also developed practices that kept the mountain section of that state, which voted predominantly Republican, with strong representation in that state's politics after the 1870s. But in the other Southern states with "mountain backyards,"—Kentucky, Alabama, Georgia, Virginia, and Maryland—mountaineer Republican constituencies were consistently ignored by the Southern Democratic state governments until the 1930s.

The reason for the hostility of some Southern Democratic state governments toward southern mountaineers is not difficult to discover. In pre–Civil War days, the Cohees in the mountain South represented a clear counterforce to planter domination. When the Civil War came, the mountain areas were frequently strongly Unionist, and thus became a "sword of treason thrust into the heart of the Confederacy," an indiscretion Southern Democrats did not forgive easily. Even worse, during the Reconstruction period when Radical Republican governments were forced upon the South, many mountaineers showed their continued identification with the Union by voting for "Constitutional Unionist," and then Republican candidates. Most of the scalawag votes that helped keep Republicans in control during the years of the Reconstruction era were southern mountain votes.

Gordon McKinney, the principal historian of politics in late nineteenth-century Appalachia, has noted a dual pattern in the rise of the Republican Party in Southern Appalachia. In the mountain sections of Kentucky, Tennessee, West Virginia, Georgia, and Alabama, he says, mountaineers were strongly Unionist during the Civil War and became the base of the Republican Party in these states. But another pattern developed in southwestern Virginia and western North Carolina, which were predominantly Confederate for much of the Civil War. Southwestern Virginia and western North Carolina came to their strong Republican orientation much later because of events between 1876 and 1896. Though many Virginia and North Carolina mountaineers ultimately supported the Unionist side late in the war, most of their sons had to desert the Confederate service in order to join Union armies, a fact that later impaired their chances of benefits for their Union service. Furthermore, in southwest Virginia, the remarkable political success of William T. Mahone had the effect of converting many mountaineers in the state to the Republican Party. Also the modest growth of urbanism and industrialism in that area turned many "progressives" toward the Republican Party.

After the Democratic Party, with its call for white supremacy, "redeemed" the South in the 1870s, the continued loyalty of the mountaineers to the Republican Party became a convenient means by which mountain voters were effectively disfranchised, simply because Southern state governments after 1880 were dominated by the Democratic Party. Blacks were also deprived of the right to vote in these years by their continued loyalty to the Republican Party, reinforced after 1890 by the poll tax, literacy tests, and white primary laws. Both Appalachian whites and Southern blacks, thus, were shut out of significant participation in Southern state government by their loyalty to the Republican Party. In addition, after 1877 the national Republican Party ceased to raise serious objections when local Southern political arrangements allowed the disfranchisement of these two loyal Republican constituencies.

After 1900, the Republican leaders in the states of the old Confederacy accepted their continuing minority status, making little effort to contest statewide races. Southern Republicans seemed content to play at presidential politics during the quadrennial Republican nominating convention. Then because of their small number, they would have only a few people to share in the federal largesse that Washington distributed.

The Civil War's devastating effects, which many mountaineers blamed on the planter elements and the Democrats, was the initial reason for the mountaineer loyalty to the Republican Party in West Virginia, Kentucky, Tennessee, Georgia, and Alabama. However, the individual labors of Republican leaders such as William G. Brownlow and Leonidas Houk in Tennessee; Arthur Boreman, Archibald Campbell, and John Jacob in West Virginia; Robert Hughes in southwest Virginia; and Tod Caldwell in western North Carolina, were very significant. Though Appalachian and Negro loyalty provided the major sources of late nineteenth-century Republican strength in the South, neither constituency had a particular love for the other.

As the nineteenth century moved toward its end, the Republican Party in the South became increasingly oriented toward the traditions of the prewar Southern Whigs, those sons of Henry Clay and of the New South interested in business development and tariff protection. Southern leaders of this New South were raising their voices, calling for a new, business-oriented South, and the Republication Party in Appalachia also took a most aggressive pro-business stance.

Moreover, the groups in the South to which the national Republican Party paid closest attention were the emerging champions of this New South. Protective tariffs, conservative monetary policies, internal improvements at national expense, anti-open range laws, and even subsidies for "essential" business developments were all policies that attracted most businessmen, North and South, to the Republican Party. Government in those years was fiercely anti-labor union and considered any workingman's organization as a potential restraint on trade. Thus any strike became a disruption of law and order requiring the intervention of the police power of the state. "Progress" meant the promotion of business ventures designed to bring economic growth.

A group of Appalachian business leaders—coal operators, railroad entrepreneurs, and steel mill owners—came increasingly to control the Republican Party in the region. Gordon McKinney traces the changes in Republican Party leadership in the Appalachian South through three different periods between 1865 and 1900. The earliest group of Republican leaders in the region was composed of those whom McKinney calls "issue-oriented leaders," such men as

Archibald Campbell in West Virginia and William G. Brownlow in Tennessee. These men were determined to lead their states back into the Union and were prepared to accept quite radical social measures, in terms of Negro civil rights, in order to accomplish this reconciliation. These leaders were particularly close to the Republican Radicals in Congress. Campbell in fact had been an abolitionist before the Civil War.

The second generation of Republican leaders in Appalachia, McKinney says, were essentially local bosses who organized a "party army" in their respective areas through the strength of their own personalities and the exploitation of purely local issues. Such "party army" leaders were Leonidas Houk in Tennessee, Nathan Goff in West Virginia, and J.J. Mott in North Carolina. These leaders succeeded in making the Republican Party broadly acceptable and overcame the party's earlier identification with Radical Reconstruction.

In the late 1880s and 1890s, McKinney contends, a still different type of leader began to move into Republican Party leadership positions in Appalachia. These were the successful businessmen and industrialists, the "plutocrats," the region's new aristocrats of wealth. Thanks to their driving ambitions and superior organizational skills that had led to success in business, these leaders turned their skills toward politics, and they moved quickly into the positions of leadership in the Republican Party. Such leaders as Stephen B. Elkins in West Virginia, Henry Clay Evans in Tennessee, William O. Bradley in Kentucky, and John B. Eaves in North Carolina were typical of this kind of plutocratic leader. By the 1890s, the Republican Party in the mountains was under the control of these captains of coal and commanders of railroads.

Stephen Elkins was probably the best known of these plutocratic leaders. Ohio-born, Elkins was raised in Virginia and Missouri, graduated from the University of Missouri in 1860, and served in the Union Army during the war. Following the Civil War, he was admitted to the bar—first in Missouri, then in New Mexico where he held various political offices. In 1875, he married the daughter of Senator H.G. Davis of West Virginia and transferred his interests to that state until his death nearly forty years later. First he focused his attention upon business success in coal and railroad building, then upon politics. Even though his father-in-law was a Democrat, Elkins joined the Republican Party and ultimately served as U.S. senator from West Virginia from 1895 until his death in 1911. For twenty years, Elkins was probably the most powerful man in West Virginia and always saw the interest of coal and railroads as primary. He kept a regular office in New York City. His name became nationally known because of his connection with much of the so-called "Progressive legislation" passed during the Presidency of Theodore Roosevelt. The Elkins Act of 1903, for example, prevented the then-widespread practice of railroad rebates—special returns in money from a competitor's rates to a large user. By 1903, railroads had become uncomfortable with this practice, and the legislation was apparently written by railroad lawyers.

The major challenge to Elkins's continued domination of West Virginia politics came not from labor or from yeoman and rural interests, but from other businessmen. According to historian John Alexander Williams, four factions of capitalists contended for the state in the Elkins years. One was the Davis–Cameron–Elkins faction, with its Rockefeller and Washington, D.C. connections. The second was John B. Floyd and his associates, who represented various absentee capitalists, principally the Mellon and Morgan interests. The third group was those businessmen associated with the Democratic Party in West Virginia and who supported the popular governor, Henry D. Hatfield. Fourthly, a group of lawyers in Charleston, the state capital, known as the "Kanawha Ring," was perhaps the most reform-minded, but even they saw the state's interests as closely tied to continued business success. All were coal-oriented, and all four factions were convinced that West Virginia's interests should be identified with the continued good fortune of business within the state and the nation.

Many Appalachian states were equally identified with the fortunes of coal and its owners. Perhaps the supreme example of the power of coal in the early twentieth century was coal's purchase of a U.S. Senate seat for Johnson N. Cameron in Kentucky, even though he was a coal operator living in West Virginia. And at the time, Clarence Watson was the U.S. senator from West Virginia, though he was a coal operator living in Maryland. In these years when U.S. senators were chosen by state legislatures, coal money openly purchased both of these seats for millions of dollars.

Harry M. Caudill has studied the interlocking tentacles of coal's power during these years. The central group he calls "the Fairmont Ring," a small group of West Virginia politicians and coal barons, which included Peter H. Watson of the Baltimore and Ohio Railroad and friend of John D. Rockefeller; Senator Johnson N. Camden of the Standard Oil Company and the Monongah Coal and Coke Company;

and Senator Clarence Wayland Watson of the Fairmont Coal Company. Aretas B. Fleming, attorney for the B & O Railroad and Standard Oil, was the key figure in relating them all into a Maryland corporation, the Consolidation Coal Company. Consolidation Coal carried the "Fairmont Ring's" interest westward into Kentucky, where the group was prominent in the opening of the Elkhorn Field and attracted allies in Kentucky among that state's coal people, including John C.C. Mayo.

Another example of regional "inter-state" corporate cooperation, which developed as early as the 1880s in West Virginia, was the decision of John D. Rockefeller's new Standard Oil Company of Ohio, working through its chief ally in West Virginia, Johnson N. Camden, to close all West Virginia oil refineries except for a single plant in Parkersburg. A similar interstate agreement between West Virginia and Maryland, with Maryland's interest represented by Consolidation Coal and the Baltimore and Ohio Railroad, allowed Consolidation Coal to absorb Fairmont Coal, a West Virginia corporation run by Clarence Watson. Watson then moved to Baltimore to head Consolidation Coal Company, a convenient residence for him when he became senator from West Virginia.

Since conservative Democratic "Bourbons" had gained control of most Southern state governments after the Reconstruction period, and the Republican Party in the Appalachian South came under an aggressive, coal-oriented business leadership, rural Appalachian voters became a target for appeals from various reformers and radicals who challenged the influence of businessmen upon the party. From time to time during this period, issues and personalities arose to challenge those in control of the political processes within the region.

The "Fusionist Movement" in Virginia, for example, emerged in the 1870s and 1880s under the leadership of William T. Mahone, an ex-Confederate general and originally a Democrat. Mahone was a "Readjuster," a group that called for an increase in governmental services such as schools and roads, though such programs might lead to higher taxes. Mahone allied himself with Virginia Republicans and won control of the legislature in 1879 with a "Fusion Ticket" that combined former Democrats like Mahone himself with Republicans in a program that readjusted the state debt, taxes, and services. In 1881, Mahone won a U.S. Senate seat for himself with this coalition. But the "Fusionist" constituencies—mountaineers, blacks, Readjusters and disgruntled Democrats—were too diverse to hold together for long. McKinney regards Mahone as the most creative politician in the South during this era.

Tennessee, too, had a Fusionist movement in the 1880s, which brought Democratic desertions sufficient to allow a Republican victory in the gubernatorial election of 1880. As Bourbon Democratic conservatives took control of Southern state governments after Reconstruction, Appalachian voters were prime candidates for the appeals of various reformers who attempted to build coalitions strong enough to oust the Bourbon Democrats. In the end, however, the conservatives defeated the Readjuster and Fusionist challenges in both Tennessee and Virginia. But soon a much larger revolt faced the Bourbon masters of the South.

The Populist Movement was a broad farmers' revolt that emerged in the 1890s, centered mainly in the American West and the South. It attempted to unite all farmers—"the true producers" of America—against the "plutocrats" (their term), whom they saw as malefactors of wealth. Populism was a protest against the kind of industrial and urban nation that the United States was becoming. The Populists objected to an America that was increasingly controlled by the elite captains of industry. They saw American politics in terms of a struggle between the "plutocrats" and the people. One historian has called the Populist Movement the largest mass movement in American history. The Populists spread across the rural areas of the United States in the depression-ridden 1890s, sweeping congressmen, governors, and legislators from office and replacing them with colorful rural types, such as "Sockless" Jerry Simpson of Kansas; "Pitchfork" Ben Tillman of South Carolina, who promised to "stick his pitchfork in Grover Cleveland's fat old ribs"; and Thomas D. Watson of Georgia, "the orneriest man in the South."

Appalachian Mountain Republicans, many of them yeoman farmers, often responded favorably to the appeals of Southern Populist candidates. In North Carolina, the Populist leader Marion Butler gained considerable support from both blacks and mountaineers in a strange coalition that also included the tobacco tycoon, Benjamin N. Duke. Populist leaders Tom Watson in Georgia and Reuben Kolb in Alabama also received strong mountain support.

In Tennessee, East Tennessee mountaineer Robert Love Taylor used an essentially Populist rhetoric in campaigns, though his program was decidedly "moderate" and was associated with the Democratic Party. Bob Taylor dominated Tennessee politics from the late 1880s until the end of the century as one of the region's most colorful

politicians. A particularly memorable campaign was the gubernatorial campaign of 1888 between Bob, as the Democratic nominee, and
his brother Alfred, who was the Republican candidate. Bob won this
campaign, known locally as "the War of the Roses." But in the
governor's office Bob Taylor did not bring in policies significantly
different from those of his predecessors, despite the Populist flavor
of his campaign rhetoric.

In the end, the Populist challenge to Southern Bourbonism failed,
even as the Readjuster challenge had been defeated. In fact, as the
1890s gave way to the new century, the Republican Party, usually
with strong mountaineer support, consistently took a pro-business
stand. By the 1890s, Appalachian business groups, drawn primarily
from coal and railroad men, had moved into effective control of the
region's Republican Party. And Appalachian farmer voters for the
most part remained loyal to the Party, although Republican policies
on the state and national level seemed frequently at odds with the
best interests of these rural people.

The persistence of the traditional Appalachian rural loyalty to
the Republican Party, even in the face of the appeal of the Populists,
seems most puzzling. It appears to demonstrate an almost unbreak-
able Appalachian yeoman's tie to the Republican Party, despite its
business-orientation. Surely the Populists, a farmer's party specifically protesting the increasing business control of the two major parties, *should* have had a major appeal to Appalachian yeomen. Despite
the success of the Populists in many areas of the South, in Appalachia this appears not to have been the case. How are we to understand this?

In Kentucky, the failure of the Populist Movement was partly
due to active Appalachian opposition. Forces in Kentucky conspired
to place mountain Republicans on the side of the corporate interests
of the state and against the Populist forces. And the industrialist–
Appalachian combination prevented the state's major Populist leader,
the anti-railroad Democrat William Goebel, from ever effectively occupying the governor's chair. In an atmosphere made critical in part
because the L & N Railroad gave free passes to hundreds of mountain Republicans, this mountaineer presence in the state capital at
Frankfort in January 1900 was crucial in preventing Goebel from gaining the governorship until sworn in on his deathbed.

Nevertheless, Populism during the 1890s did represent a major
challenge to the continuing identification of Appalachian mountaineers with the Republican Party. On its face, the Populist protest

seemed ideally suited to represent the needs of a predominantly rural, still heavily yeomanesque population threatened by the growth
of American industry. Yet the Populists proved to be unpopular in
most of the Appalachian South. No doubt, this was partly due to the
Populist's "capture of the Democratic Party" during the election of
1896, with the nomination of the "silver-tongued" William Jennings
Bryan of Nebraska. In the West, the Republican Party more clearly
represented a conservative, pro-business sentiment. In the South in
these years, the conservative party was the Democratic Party. Thus
Bryan's nomination in 1896 threw the Southern conservative Democrats into confusion. And Southern anti-industrial Republicans were
equally confused.

In the end, mountain Republicanism persisted and the Populists
failed. The reasons are complex, but part of the reason may be the
lack of any religious connection with Populism in the Appalachian
South. In the West, a kind of "pietistic fervor" accompanied Populism. Appalachian farmers were certainly religious, but their religion
then did not translate into political protest. And there are scholars of
Populism who make much of the role of racial prejudice in the South
to explain why essentially class-oriented issues failed.

There was also substantial ideological confusion. Populism's
answer to the business and industrial domination of government was
to place the farmer at the handles of power of an activist government. But this view of government as an instrument of reform violated the yeoman's Jeffersonian philosophy of government that "the
least government is the best government." The self-sufficient yeoman indeed has often been a kind of anarchist who has believed in
minimalist government. The Populists conceived of government as
an instrument that could bring new monetary rules to the market-
place with a bi-metal (thus inflationary) monetary standard, and the
Populists moved actively against the perceived enemies of the farmer,
the railroads, and the modern corporations, using government to
regulate these powerful institutions.

What's more, the traditional clientage system in the region had
been thoroughly integrated into the Republican party-army tradition by 1890. The plutocratic party bosses were well connected in the
nation's capital and the various state capitals, and these personal ties
held despite the threat of the Populists.

Perhaps even more important were the blunders of the regional
leaders themselves. In most states, the Bourbon, ex-Confederate
Democrat's disdain for the "mountain scalawags" produced an abid-

ing Appalachian suspicion of all Democrats. When Populism merged into the national Democratic Party in 1896, Southern mountain yeomen could never follow the western farmers and become Democrats.

In Kentucky, moreover, the Populist leader, Democrat William Goebel, was responsible for an election reform law that seemed particularly aimed at Republican Party practices in the eastern part of the state. Mountaineers strongly resented this and were angered by Goebel's abrasive personality. His gubernatorial candidacy was particularly odious to mountaineers, and the presence of thousands of mountaineers in Frankfort following the extremely close election of 1899 was part of an attempt to guarantee the apparent victory of the Republican, Alfred A. Taylor. Goebel's dramatic assassination probably by a mountaineer entirely changed the dynamic of Kentucky politics for decades, and despite his plurality, Taylor was denied the governorship.

In vain we search for a consistent, effective reform-minded leader prior to 1920 from the region who developed a program aimed at bringing the resources of government to bear upon the region's very real problems. In Tennessee Bob Taylor's populism was more stylistic than substantial; and Ben Hooper, an East Tennessean who was the only Republican to be elected governor between 1883 and 1921, was a leader who at best could be called "progressive" because of his support of prohibition, fair election laws, and the right of labor to organize. But Hooper was always essentially pro-business and a believer in the wonders of free market competition. Other progressive leaders from the region worked hard for educational reform but in no way hampered the continued control of the handles of power by plutocrats in or out of the region.

Probably the only important Appalachian Populist was Milford W. Howard, a lawyer, congressman, educator, and resident of Fort Payne, Alabama. Howard served two terms in Congress from 1895 to 1899. He wrote two widely read books: one a novel, *If Christ Came to Congress* (1894), and *The American Plutocracy* (1895). Howard saw the nation divided between the people and the plutocrats, who were engaged in a desperate struggle for mastery of the nation. In that struggle, he warned, "constitutional methods" may not "avail . . . [and] . . . this continent will be shaken by a mighty revolution."

The great invasion of the machine age into the Appalachian South after the Civil War meant the enlargement of plutocratic influence. By 1920, the success of the plutocrats seemed complete. In the labor difficulties of West Virginia, which reached their tragic climax at the

Battle of Blair Mountain in 1921, the new mountain proletariat, led by the United Mine Workers, was totally frustrated by the power of the region's businessmen. The power of coal and of railroad politics was most dramatically shown in the 1920s influence of the "Fairmont Ring," which operated especially effectively in Kentucky, Maryland, and West Virginia. Throughout the region, the plutocrats' control seemed to be complete. And the mountain yeomanry seemed content with this arrangement.

Thus the 1920s represented a high point of business control and influence in both regional and national politics. The Republican Party was in control of the nation's destinies. Business interests led the nation in pursuit of what President Harding called "normalcy." President Coolidge put it best when he proclaimed, "the business of government is business."

Within the Appalachian region, the political success of the business-oriented Republican Party also reached a high point in the 1920s. Kentucky, normally a Democratic state, had a Republican governor for eight of the twelve years between 1919 and 1931. And in West Virginia, the Elkins Era (1895–1911) was continued as the Republican Party dominated the state until 1933.

In the coal-producing areas of Appalachia, coal company owners and operators largely dominated local politics, which usually involved the struggle for control of the sheriff's office, the county judge-executive, the tax assessor, and control of the highway department. Southern state governments, however, were then usually dominated by the Confederate-style Bourbon Democrats. Yet as Virginius Dabney, editor of the Raleigh *Observer*, noted at the time, "many Southerners who currently profess allegiance to the Democratic Party . . . would be far more congenially suited as Republicans if they could but forget Thad Stevens and Ben Wade." Money talked loudest in the 1920s whether one was a Bourbon Democrat or a Republican, and any suggestion that significant change was needed in politics was greeted with charges of socialism.

During the 1920s, the aristocracy of wealth was in charge, and challenges to that control were sporadic and confused. Kentucky's Republican governor, Flem Sampson, for example, was closely associated with Kentucky Utilities, then part of the national electrical empire owned by Samuel Insull. And the local governments of Kingsport, Tennessee, and Asheville, North Carolina, along with most of the other towns in the region, could not readily be separated from the local chambers of commerce.

But signs of economic trouble were everywhere. These signs began to accumulate during the decade of the 1920s, with bank and land-speculative failures, bad crop years, international disruption of trade and credits, and miners' strikes. A deeply troubled coal industry, overvalued real estate, economic maladjustment left over from the World War, a bitter tariff war, and unstable farm prices, all played their role to bring on a worldwide financial crisis. The signal for disaster was the collapse of the New York stock market in late October 1929. By 1932, the Dow–Jones industrial average was only 20 percent of what it had been three years earlier. Radicals openly anticipated a rebellion, and signs of a possible revolution appeared. Farmers revolted in the Corn Belt, and armed and angry Bonus Marchers were camped on the Washington Mall in the nation's capital.

Across the nation, over five thousand banks collapsed between 1930 and 1932. Within the Appalachian region, probably the most widely known Depression bank failures were the collapse of the banks associated with the Tennessee-based empire of Rogers Caldwell and the failure of the Central Bank and Trust Company of Asheville, North Carolina.

Rogers Caldwell, known as the "J.P. Morgan of the South," was a Nashville broker and banker who specialized in Southern bond issues. Closely associated with Colonel Luke Lea, boss of the Republican Party in Tennessee, and Governor Henry Horton, also a Republican, Caldwell's whole empire collapsed in November of 1932. The failure of one of his flagship banks, the Union Bank of Knoxville, was the signal for the collapse of nearly two score smaller banks. And worse, a scandal developed because of the loss of over $6.6 million in state funds that went down with the Caldwell banks. Both Colonel Lea and Governor Horton went to trial along with Caldwell, but only Colonel Lea spent any time in prison.

In Asheville, North Carolina, the land boom of the 1920s was derailed by the collapse of the city's major bank and the deep involvement of the city and county government in the ill luck of the city's land speculators. This incident sent one bank president to the state penitentiary and prompted the suicide of Asheville's mayor, who had lost public funds in his effort to prop up the Central Bank and Trust.

The whole region was caught in the grip of the deepening crisis. Whether miner, businessman, or professional, wages and prices plummeted, and the whole market system seemed in collapse. In eastern Kentucky, one mountaineer reported that in the early 1930s where he worked, "there'd be anywhere from seven to fifteen men every morning begging for work." Conditions in the mines grew desperate, and the struggle between labor and management sharpened.

The possibility of making a living on the old family farm, however, was the ex-yeoman's option for many Appalachians who had gone to the mine or factory in earlier and better times. One Kentucky mountaineer remembered, "We raised a garden. Mom managed some way or other to sell eggs; we even dug May Apple roots and scoured the hills for ginseng; gathered walnuts and hickory nuts and sold them; and she usually managed to have a hog." One woman in Hot Springs, North Carolina, even remembered the Depression as "the happiest time in my life. People came back. A few were poor, but there was no despair," and the churches were full. In fact, the collapse of the market system appeared to breathe new life into the yeoman system of self-sufficient agriculture. It came as no surprise that as the crisis of the Depression shattered factory employment and mercantile trade, yeomanry in Appalachia made a comeback.

Because the Republican Party was in power in the national government and in so many states when the Great Depression of 1929 struck, it was blamed for the disaster. In the election of 1932, the Democratic Party under Franklin D. Roosevelt was swept into office. Yet despite the heavy vote nationally for the Democrats in 1932, the Appalachian region as a whole still voted heavily Republican.

The program that Roosevelt and his supporters rushed through the Congress during the "100 Days" in the spring of 1933 was built on the assumption that action was necessary and changes were needed. But the "New Deal" philosophy held that there was nothing fundamentally wrong with the economic system. What was needed was "pump priming"—governmental aid to get the economic machinery moving again. Although some reforms were needed to prevent the "economic royalists" from keeping too much power, reform could correct the system to prevent the extreme boom-and-bust cycles in the market economy. But in place of the businessman's blind trust in the market, the Democrats promised a "New Deal for the American people."

The New Deal programs have frequently been summarized as promoting the "three R's: 1) "relief," to care for the immediate needs of people; 2) "recovery," to get the economy back on its feet again; and 3) "reform," to change certain things that were wrong with the economic system that had let us into the Great Depression.

As relief measures, the New Deal established a number of agencies designed to put money into the pockets of those who had real need. The WPA (Works Progress Administration) gave jobs to people who needed income. The PWA (Public Works Administration) provided employment by building sewer systems, post offices, sidewalks, and city halls—permanent public monuments that still dot Appalachian towns. The CCC (Civilian Conservation Corps) placed young men under army discipline, gave them a private's pay, and set them to work in the national forests planting trees, building forest roads, and fighting forest fires. The CCC had a wide impact upon Appalachia, for many of the newly established national forests were in the region. Another New Deal program that had a wide impact—nationally as well as regionally— was the NYA (National Youth Administration). This program attempted to keep the nation's youth in school and off of the labor market, which was then suffering from a 25 percent unemployment rate.

The recovery aspect of the New Deal program was aimed primarily at agriculture and industry. In agriculture, several Agricultural Adjustment Acts (AAAs) were passed that established the principle of price supports accompanied by government controls on the quantity of crops produced. The "parity price" program established a "fair price" for farmers that the government would guarantee. But the government also knew it had to have some control of the quantity of crops or animals produced, thus it initiated acreage allotments or limiting the number of animals farmers were allowed to bring to maturity. These AAAs inaugurated a new era in American agriculture and had an immense impact upon Appalachia, particularly in tobacco growing areas.

The New Deal's industrial recovery program proved to be less permanent. The basic legislation, the National Industrial Recovery Act (NIRA), established fair codes of business practice in order to get production started again. The NRA (National Recovery Administration) was set up to administer the program. No one was forced to participate in the new fair practices, though taxes were levied to pay for this voluntary program of market cooperation. It was this taxing element that was declared unconstitutional by the U.S. Supreme Court after only a year of operation.

One aspect of the NIRA that was to have an important long-run effect in the Appalachian region was that component of the act (Section 7–A) that encouraged the formation of labor unions. In establishing the fair codes of business practice, representatives of management, labor, and consumers were instructed to meet. The only agency that was in a position to represent labor was the union. And where no union existed, one was supposed to be formed. As a result, the effect of this act was to greatly enhance the growth of unions. When the act was struck down as unconstitutional, labor was in no mood to lose the benefits of governmental guarantees of unionization. So in 1935, Congress passed and President Roosevelt signed the Wagner Act. This act guaranteed labor its "essentials": 1) the right to organize and bargain collectively, and 2) the right to strike in defense of legitimate demands. A National Labor Relations Board (NLRB) was established to oversee fair labor practices on the part of both labor and management. Probably the union in the nation most able to take advantage of the new legislation was the United Mine Workers of America.

The Tennessee Valley Authority (TVA) was one of the first measures passed by the new administration. It represented a new idea for the United States. The notion of an "Authority" was an invention of the time, a publicly owned corporation set up to serve a particular region, three-fourths of it within the Appalachian area. This Authority was semi-governmental and had the "right of eminent domain," but it was to operate essentially as a private corporation. It had no stockholders, but was owned by all the citizens of the United States, with its three directors appointed by the president of the United States to govern it.

The area chosen for the TVA to serve was largely within the Appalachian area. During World War I, Wilson Dam had been built across the Muscle Shoals of the Tennessee River in northern Alabama with the purpose of generating electricity to facilitate making nitrates for explosives. A better German process for obtaining the nitrates became known after the World War, which left the technology at Wilson Dam outmoded. Consequently, the government was left with an enormous white elephant on its hands. During the 1920s, the government nearly sold the works at Wilson Dam for a fraction of its value. But a senator from Nebraska, the independent-minded Republican George Norris, prevented its sale. With time, the dream of the TVA was matured by Senator Norris, and twice in the late 1920s he guided legislation through the Congress establishing the TVA as an agency for regional development. The idea involved building a series of dams to control the flooding and navigation of the Tennessee River, and the project would establish a governmentally owned utility of electricity production. Twice, two different Republican presidents vetoed the Tennessee Valley Act. With the new administration in Washington in 1933, Norris again prepared the act, Congress passed it, and President Roosevelt signed it.

Norris Dam was first constructed, followed by the others on the main rivers: Watts Bar, Cherokee, Chickamauga, Guntersville, and Douglas. The Tennessee River—one of the nation's most notorious flooders—was tamed. Its full length to Knoxville was made available to navigation. In developing the Valley, the dams were the key—they provided cheap electricity, they maintained the flow of the rivers, and they provided the power for making fertilizer. With better fertilizer, modern farming practices were encouraged. In the process, the government obtained a major electrical utility, thus enabling it to have an accurate yardstick by which to gauge proper electrical rates for the regulated private utilities in the rest of the nation.

When World War II came, the TVA went into the business of making and selling vast quantities of electricity that the nation needed. The heart of the infant nuclear industry was established in the Valley at Oak Ridge, Tennessee. The vast K–25 Plant, which made radioactive fuel for the atom bombs and other uses, was a consumer of immense quantities of electricity: one-half of the TVA's total electrical production by 1945 went to keep this single plant in operation.

In addition to the government's atomic program, another major electricity-using industry, aluminum, also came into the Valley. Thus the TVA was pressed into providing great amounts of electricity. The Authority's largest dam was built during World War II: Fontana on the Little Tennessee in North Carolina. But even with this new dam, TVA was pressed to provide the dependable power demanded. Therefore, large steam-generating plants were built to provide a less seasonal supply of electricity than the dams provided. As a utility, the TVA succeeded far beyond its original dreams. But in its effort to serve the electrical needs of the Tennessee Valley area, the TVA has sometimes acted in ways that have been detrimental to other parts of Appalachia. This has been particularly true of its coal-buying practices. In seeking the lowest possible price for its coal, the TVA in its pricing policies led the coal industry during the 1950s and 1960s into terribly destructive strip-mining practices. Strip-mined coal in those largely unregulated days could provide coal at much lower prices than coal mined by underground methods. Since 1950, the TVA has been the nation's largest buyer of strip-mined coal, thus contributing heavily to the ravishing of massive areas in the Appalachian Mountains.

The nation's welfare system, too, grew out of reform measures instituted during the New Deal. The idea of welfare is a simple one: that a rich and powerful national should not allow its citizens to live in grinding poverty. The idea was fifty years old before the United States adopted the practice in the 1930s. Welfare was actually the invention of European conservatives in order to undercut the appeal of Europe's socialist parties.

The welfare state is concerned with the well-being of all its citizens. "To promote the general welfare," indeed, is a stated purpose of government identified in the preamble of the United States Constitution. In the days of Populism,·the formula was suggested that the "welfare of the people" ought to be promoted rather than the welfare of plutocrats. In the United States, welfare state practices have developed from the pragmatism of the New Deal. A number of new programs were instituted during the 1930s designed to promote the general welfare. Among these was Social Security, a government insurance program that "taxed" (taking premiums from its citizens during their working years), then provided participating citizens with income if they became unemployed or when they reached the age of retirement.

What is generally designated as "welfare," however, are those programs that attempt to give some income to the nation's poorest citizens. Such programs were first enacted on a national level during the New Deal. Before the 1930s, local governments had supported poor farms and orphanages. But the New Deal initiated massive national programs for poor relief—WPA, CCC, NYA, etc.

Because of the great economic maladjustments in Appalachia's major industries, particularly coal mining and agriculture, large numbers of people were able to qualify for welfare benefits. Circumstances have drawn many Appalachian people into the welfare system. So large has this system become in Appalachia that in certain communities in the region, welfare has effectively become a major "employer." There are some who are convinced that the welfare system has corrupted the Appalachian soul. Some people claim it has undermined the mountaineer's traditional independence, and others claim that it has corrupted mountain politics. Certainly the system has become pervasive.

Appalachia was deeply influenced by the New Deal, notably through the TVA, the welfare system, the AAA, and the CCC. Also as a result of this latest labor legislation, a new day dawned for the American labor movement. With the Wagner Act of 1935, the American labor movement was provided with basic legal protection under which to grow. With guarantees of the right to organize and the right to strike, labor union membership boomed. In the six years from 1933 to 1939, national labor union membership grew from three million to eight million. A totally new federation of labor unions, the Congress of Industrial Organizations, was born. And in Appalachia, the United Mine Workers of America moved into its most significant era, with its membership growing 300 percent in just five years. And the United Mine Workers, as then probably the nation's best organized union, provided some of the most significant leadership for the organization of the new industrial unions, particularly the steel workers and the automobile workers. No longer could anti-union operators legally refuse to recognize the union. Yet in eastern Kentucky, the coal operators of Harlan, Bell, Letcher, and neighboring counties held out amidst the bitter strikes of 1931 to 1939. A final settlement in eastern Kentucky did not come with mere passage of the Wagner Act. Settlement there had to await a Kentucky law forbidding privately paid sheriff's deputy armies.

Perhaps the most important impact of the New Deal upon basic makeup of the Appalachian region had to do with how the agricultural policies of the 1930s influenced the region's yeoman farmers. A case can be made that the original impact of the Depression had been to strengthen yeomanry. The market system had collapsed, and many families returned to their rural homesteads in order to survive. Early on, New Deal agricultural policies moved in many directions. But though the several Agricultural Adjustment Acts themselves improvised in various directions in their attempts to increase the farmer's buying power, New Deal agricultural policies ultimately did not improve a rural person's condition unless he owned a fair amount of land. Sharecroppers and tenants and even the small owner lost out in the political maneuverings under the new farm policies, as the intentions of the Farm Bloc, the National Farm Bureau Federation, and the various state agricultural colleges tended to be decisive. At the heart of the New Deal agricultural policies was the market-oriented, domestic allotment plan of parity prices—a very unyeomanesque solution to the problems of American agriculture, which still left rural America dependent on outside forces and government policies.

One political effect of the New Deal was to substantially strengthen the Democratic Party in the region and to pose something of a threat to the Republican Party in some areas of Appalachia. The region's traditional political affiliation had been with the Republican

Party since the Civil War, yet during the 1930s many mountaineers shifted their loyalty to the Democratic Party. Most members of the UMW, for example, became Democrats, thus the coal-mining areas developed as centers of Democratic strength. Often this shift in allegiance was sufficient to change the affiliation of whole Congressional districts from Republican to Democratic. Such was the case of the old seventh district of Kentucky, the third district of Tennessee, and the fourth district of West Virginia. Yet even with these large defections to the Democrats, the region as a whole remained predominantly Republican.

The Democrats' support in the Tennessee Valley Authority had an important, if brief, influence upon Tennessee politics. After World War II, a strong liberal wing of the Democratic Party emerged in Tennessee under the leadership of Governor Gordon Browning and Senator Estes Kefauver. Albert Gore, also a liberal Democrat, was elected to the U.S. Senate to sit alongside Kefauver, and another liberal, Frank Clement, succeeded Browning as governor. The strength of this liberal bastion in Tennessee during the 1950s was probably due in part to the TVA's popularity and provided what some regard as the South's first significant reform voices since the days of Andrew Jackson.

One result of welfare politics in the 1930s was to enlarge the patronage available in the patron–client system. To simple gifts (bribes?), road contracts, and jobs were now added federal moneys for properly qualified poor people. The signal for the arrival of this kind of welfare politics was the 1938 Democratic senatorial primary campaign in Kentucky. Kentucky's aggressive young governor, Albert B. "Happy" Chandler, challenged the New Deal's Senate Majority Leader, Alben Barkley. "Dear Alben," as FDR referred to him, was such an integral part of the New Deal team that President Roosevelt came to Kentucky to campaign for Barkley. Chandler's challenge brought in the Kentucky "statehouse machinery," which mobilized the state's highway department and other departments to "deliver for Happy." The infant welfare bureaucracy of the WPA and other New Deal agencies in each of Kentucky's counties were frightened into using their special relationship with their clients and urged the recipients of their largesse to "vote right." A journalist for the Scripps-Howard newspaper chain, Thomas L. Stokes, discovered this abuse and won a Pulitzer Prize in 1939 for his special series focusing on Kentucky politics, most of it dealing with eastern Kentucky.

Barkley was the victor, and although a special investigation agreed that Stokes's charges were valid, the state-controlled system supporting Chandler had been equally corrupt. Barkley claimed no knowledge of the corruption, and nothing came of the charges. But the long-run effect of this campaign was to bring the new welfare money into the traditional client–patron system that had traditionally dominated mountain politics. In fact, powerful new county machines were built throughout the region, basing much of their power upon control of welfare.

In the late 1950s and early 1960s, several developments conspired to identify Appalachia as a problem area within the nation. Across nearly two generations, various social science and missionary studies had been published that identified the region's educational and economic deficiencies. In 1957, a conference of church leaders from those denominations with the major home missionary concerns for the region concluded that more up-to-date information was needed in order to get an accurate profile of the region. The Ford Foundation was approached and $250,000 was acquired to produce this regional profile, to be researched by the best scholars from the area's universities and colleges. This study was published in 1962.

The beginning of the War on Poverty did not come from any strong demands within the region itself. True, the research project financed by the Ford Foundation came in large part from individuals living within the region. That project was largely the inspiration of Willis D. Weatherford Sr., of Black Mountain, North Carolina, who approached the Ford Foundation and was the person who had presided at the meeting of 1957. After identifying the scholars to provide the up-to-date profile, Dr. Weatherford visited each Appalachian governor and enlisted each of them in a united approach to the region's problems. Weatherford was particularly successful with Governors Bert T. Combs of Kentucky, Millard Tawes of Maryland, and Terry Sanford of North Carolina. Even before the presidential campaign of 1960 began, several Appalachian governors met to talk about regional problems, meeting in May in Baltimore at the invitation of Governor Tawes and later in Lexington, Kentucky at the invitation of Governor Combs.

Also, a Junior Chamber of Commerce initiative in eastern Kentucky enlarged into an organization of coal executives, a university president, and regional professionals and called for a federal and an Appalachian state "Regional Development Agency." Spearheading this group was John D. Whisman, who obtained the confidence of Kentucky's governor, Bert T. Combs, in an initiative that called for better roads, schools, and health facilities for eastern Kentucky.

Meanwhile, the 1960 presidential campaign was beginning. John F. Kennedy became the Democratic nominee that year and ran against Richard M. Nixon, who received the Republican nomination. Even before Kennedy won the nomination, he became involved with Appalachian problems. His most crucial primary campaign was in West Virginia, the first state in which Kennedy ran that was overwhelmingly Protestant, and a key state for America's first Catholic aspirant to the Presidency since Al Smith's defeat in 1928. Kennedy's experience in West Virginia had an immense impact on him. As Theodore H. White told it:

> Kennedy's shock at the suffering he saw in West Virginia was so fresh that it communicated itself with the emotion of an original discovery. Kennedy, from boyhood to manhood, had never known hunger. Now, arriving in West Virginia from a brief rest in the sun in the luxury of Montego Bay (Florida), he could scarcely bring himself to believe that human beings were forced to eat and live on those cans of dry relief rations, which he fingered like artifacts of another civilization. "Imagine," he said to one of his assistants one night, "Just imagine kids who never drink milk." Of all the emotional experiences of his pre-Convention campaign, Kennedy's exposure to the misery of the mining fields probably changed him most as a man.

In winning that crucial primary, Kennedy promised "to do something for West Virginia." During the campaign that followed, the Republican nominee, Richard Nixon, made much of the fact that Kennedy seemed to be critical of American well-being. Forced to defend the previous administration, Nixon emphasized America's continuing prosperity. Speaking in Michigan, Kennedy reminded Americans that there were still Americans in poverty. He promised that if elected he would inaugurate a War on Poverty.

Americans at the time appeared to be ready to make a real effort to alleviate poverty in the nation. In the late 1950s, the Harvard economist John Kenneth Galbraith wrote a widely popular book, *The Affluent Society*, which analyzed the consumer-oriented society that had developed by that time. But in 1960, Michael Harrington reminded Americans that there was an *Other America*—the America of the poor and powerless found in the rural South, the urban ghetto, the Hispanic Southwest, and among our elderly. One of these "Other Americas" described by Harrington was Appalachia, where the region's natural beauty made its poverty all the more ironic.

In 1963, an eloquent native Appalachian voice was added to the cry for regional justice: Harry M. Caudill's *Night Comes to the Cumberlands*. Caudill, a lawyer and politician, angrily chronicled the rape of eastern Kentucky by the coal industry and dramatically outlined the region's plight.

During Kennedy's thousand days in the presidency, he did relatively little to fulfill his pledge to "do something for West Virginia." He did establish the Area Redevelopment Administration (ARA), but this agency merely identified poverty-impacted counties where, if industry would locate there, the federal government would give special assistance in loans and tax breaks. A heavy concentration of those counties was in Appalachia, but few industries actually located in the region. The other major Kennedy initiative relating to the region was the establishment of a research agency, the President's Appalachian Research Commission (PARC), with Franklin D. Roosevelt Jr. as its director. PARC's economic development-oriented team identified the region's problems. But PARC's researchers had progressed only to the point of issuing a publication before Kennedy's assassination in late November 1963.

The new president, Lyndon B. Johnson, dedicated a major part of his administration to the continuation of Kennedy's War on Poverty. During the December following Kennedy's assassination, Johnson called most of Kennedy's old advisors to his LBJ Ranch in Texas, and there they outlined their strategy for the War on Poverty and the major agenda of the new administration's domestic policy. The full weight of the Johnson Administration was then turned toward getting the program across to the American people and through Congress.

The War on Poverty as it related to Appalachia had two major dimensions. The earliest enacted was the Economic Opportunity Act of 1964, which established the OEO (Office of Economic Opportunity) and was first administered by the "martyred President's" brother-in-law, Sargent Shriver. The OEO established numerous "human" programs such as job training; Headstart (which gave kindergarten experience to children from poor homes to enhance their chances of succeeding in the early grades); a domestic peace corps called VISTA (Volunteers in Service to America); the Job Corps (a War on Poverty resurrection of the New Deal's CCC); and Upward Bound, a summer program for potential high school dropouts; etc.

These OEO programs were mostly educational and aimed mainly at the Appalachian young in order to lift them out of the cycle of poverty.

An unexpectedly significant part of the OEO was the establishment of the Community Action Programs, the CAPs. In this element of the War on Poverty, community organizers went among the poor to discern what they wanted. In the enabling legislation, a phrase was inserted that programs were to be developed "with the maximum feasible participation of the poor." Sociologist Kenneth Clark has identified this part of the legislation as the only truly revolutionary aspect of the War on Poverty. It was certainly central to much of the conflict that emerged in Appalachia.

The other major strategy of the War on Poverty program in Appalachia, economic development, had to await the results of the election of 1964 before it could be enacted. The report on Appalachia prepared by the President's Appalachian Research Commission during the Kennedy years had recommended the establishment of a joint federal and state agency to guide the region's development. Legislation was passed in 1965 that established the Appalachian Regional Commission (ARC), with a "new federal-state cooperative structure" to be controlled as much by the governors of the thirteen Appalachian states designated in the act as by the federal government. Many in Washington were as interested in this "creative federalism" as in the developmental strategies attempted.

The ARC provided various "hardware programs" in contrast with the human or "software programs" of the OEO. The Appalachian Regional Commission built things, mostly highways, in the belief that infrastructures—transportation, health, and educational facilities—were necessary before significant development could occur.

The ARC soon realized that its broadly defined Appalachian region, portions of thirteen states, was far too complex an area to be treated with a single strategy. As a result, the ARC defined four, later three, different Appalachian sub-regions. Its "Northern Appalachia" was basically industrial Pennsylvania; its "Southern Appalachia" was north Georgia and surrounding areas sharing in the growth of greater Atlanta, Birmingham, and Chattanooga; and the "Highlands" were those portions of the Smoky Mountains and eastern West Virginia that are spectacularly beautiful, thus most appealing for tourist development. The last sub-region, "Central Appalachia," was that part of the region with the most difficult problems, resulting primarily from its experience with the coal industry.

APPALACHIAN REGIONAL COMMISSION SUBREGIONS

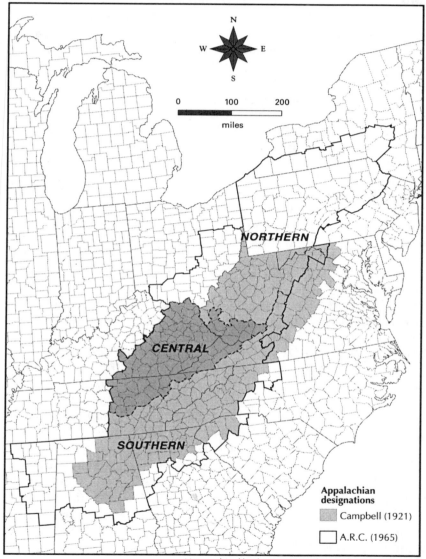

N
W E
S

0   100   200
miles

NORTHERN

CENTRAL

SOUTHERN

Appalachian
designations

Campbell (1921)

A.R.C. (1965)

Map produced by the University of Kentucky Cartography Lab

The ARC also identified "growth centers" within the region and spent much of its money in aiding their development. Most of these growth centers were in the developing industrial centers in the sub-regions designated as Northern and Southern Appalachia. The most truly problem-prone area of Central Appalachia was pretty much left to its own devices, except for some particularly spectacular projects, such as the mountain-moving project at the designated growth center of Pikeville, Kentucky.

Since its inception, the ARC has been administered from the nation's capital and by developmental economists and managers largely from outside the region, though they responded to many local initiatives from Area Development Districts that were built into the ARC strategy. But by its very nature, the OEO had to deal with the people of Appalachia directly and often. A number of community developers were recruited from the region. These persons were then sent to develop programs in cooperation with the region's people themselves. In this potentially reformist aspect of an otherwise fairly traditional program, many community developers took seriously the directive to operate with the "maximum feasible participation of the poor." This led to programs that were often in serious collision with the projects of those in power within the region.

The so-called "poverty warriors" were these community developers, together with many VISTA volunteers, who were recruited from various colleges and universities to serve in this "domestic peace corps." A privately funded and initiated program, the Appalachian Volunteers (AVs) focused on recruiting graduate students and para-professionals who could give the poor such aid as legal services, architectural planning, health services, and agricultural guidance. From 1965 through 1968, a virtual flood of young people from throughout the nation came into Appalachia to serve the people.

In the process, the poverty warriors ran squarely into the vested interests of the region's political/economic establishment. The leading political leaders of the region had initially welcomed the new programs and funds. But when the young AVs and VISTAs began taking seriously the provision concerning the "maximum feasible participation of the poor," and connecting this directive with the potentially revolutionary notion of "participatory democracy," the establishment politicians responded negatively. The collision came in 1967, and it proved to be no contest. The traditional leaders had strong ties with Washington, while the young community developers were wholly dependent upon Washington's continued funding.

Power was clearly and effectively shifted away from the poverty warriors when the so-called "Green Amendment" was placed on the OEO Appropriations Act of 1967. This amendment required that all programs funded through the OEO have the approval of the local elected county officials. Then, with the election of Richard Nixon in 1968, the War on Poverty as a significant change agent in the region was effectively ended.

What were the real effects of the substantial federal largesse expended upon Appalachia during the War on Poverty? By 1971, the ARC had built 550 miles of roads in the region and 181 health centers, and nearly $250 million had been spent for health, educational, and reclamation projects. The Office of Economic Opportunity had spent an additional $21.5 million on training and educational projects. But had the region changed substantially? Had the persisting problems of the region been significantly addressed?

The assessment of the War on Poverty continues, and the answers to its effects and impact are not totally clear. Serious studies have come to diametrically opposite conclusions. But one thing is quite apparent—the political impact of the War on Poverty within the Appalachian region was minor. Although certain "reformist enclaves" may have been left here and there, and remnants of some of the "Land and the People" organizations may persist, for the most part political patterns of the area were not significantly changed.

Political scientist Stephen L. Fisher is convinced that radical reform groups have made a real impact upon the region, beginning with the community action groups during the War on Poverty and continuing through to the later anti–strip mine efforts. Particular victories he sees for these "change agents" were the remarkable strike "won" in southwest Virginia against the Pittston Coal Company and the occupation of the Moss 3 Plant in 1989, and the success of the 1988 anti–strip mine "Homestead Amendment" in Kentucky.

However, evidence of the rather negligible political influence of the War on Poverty within the region is not difficult to find. The election of 1968 is evidence in itself. In that election, Hubert Humphrey, as the Democratic candidate, might have been expected to inherit whatever appreciation Appalachian people had for the expenditures given to the region. Humphrey was then running against Richard Nixon, Kennedy's opponent in 1960, as well as a third-party candidate, Alabama's Governor George Wallace. In a survey of regional political sentiment made by *Mountain Life and Work* in October 1968, just one month before the election, Nixon was running first in Appalachia, as he had in 1960, and as a Republican he might be expected to be in the lead. But Wallace was then running second, with Humphrey a poor third. It was indicated then that of all the Appalachian states, Humphrey would carry only West Virginia. By election day, Wallace's support had eroded to the extent that Humphrey outpolled Wallace within the region. But this appears to have been due to various state laws making it difficult in later elections for the party coming in third to appear on the ballot without a massive petition campaign. Thus loyal Democrats organized so as to come in second and thus avoid the inconvenience of later petitions. Clearly, War on Poverty Democrats were not very popular in the region.

A further indication of continued anti–War on Poverty strength supporting traditional Republican sentiment in the region was the response to the "coming-out party" for Richard Nixon in Leslie County, Kentucky, in August of 1979. This was former President Nixon's first public appearance after the scandal of Watergate and his resignation. Nixon had stayed in virtual seclusion since Watergate, and a secure Republican area was needed for him in any "coming out." Mountainous Leslie County was deemed such a place. Accordingly, neither the expenditures of the War on Poverty nor the scandal of Watergate dimmed the region's loyalty to the party of Lincoln and the Union.

The War on Poverty represented a high point in the realization of the welfare state in the United States. But the results of the War on Poverty placed enough onus on the welfare state idea itself, that a reaction against "welfare statism" set in following the election of 1968. In place of the larger welfare state concern for all citizens, there was a return to the Hamilton/Clay/Coolidge view of national prosperity, which viewed well-being in terms of individual initiative within a benevolent market system.

Nineteen seventy-two represents one highwater mark of Republican success in the South, as Richard Nixon overwhelmed the Democratic candidate, George McGovern. Nixon ran extremely well in all of Southern Appalachia as the Republican Party began to reap the benefits of its "Southern strategy." In 1972, of the eleven states in the old Confederacy, three states elected Republican governors—James Holhauser in North Carolina, Winfield Dunn in Tennessee, and Lynwood Holton in Virginia. But Republican congressional gains in 1972 were still rather minimal, electing only six of twenty-two Southern senators, and thirty-four of ninety-five congressmen in districts in the Southern Appalachians.

The success enjoyed by Jimmy Carter in his campaign for the presidency in 1976 seemed a possible break in the developing conservatism of the region and nation. The Carters had many Appalachian Georgia connections, including the banker from Calhoun, Bert Lance. His Secretary of Commerce was eastern Kentucky-born Juanita M. Kreps. Both Minority and Majority Leaders in the Senate at this time were sons of Appalachia—Howard Baker of Tennessee and Robert Byrd of West Virginia. And several significant congressional chairmen represented Appalachian areas—Jennings Randolph of West Virginia was Chairman of the patronage-rich Senate Public Works Committee; Carl Perkins of Kentucky chaired the House Education and Labor Committee; Joe L. Evins of Tennessee was Chairman of the House Small Business Committee; and Robert Jones of north Alabama served as Chairman of the House Public Works and Transportation Committee. Never had chances seemed better for the emergence of an effective Appalachian coalition in the nation's capital than in early 1977.

On the state level, too, Appalachian coalitions seemed at last to be emerging. In Kentucky, a coalition of eastern Kentucky legislators organized in 1975. In West Virginia, an organized people's movement emerged in conjunction with the United Mine Workers in the state. It successfully pressured for the passage of new "Black Lung legislation," making it possible for miners to claim benefits from this occupational hazard.

Yet the 1976 election also provided signs that the old power of the plutocracy was increasing. Although there were liberal victories—such as young Albert Gore's victory over Congressman Joe Evins in Tennessee's Fourth District, and James Sasser's victory over William Brock for Tennessee's U.S. Senate seat—Ken Hechler, Appalachia's most anti-establishment voice in Washington, D.C., for eighteen years, lost his seat. Meanwhile the young Jay Rockefeller, scion of America's foremost business family, who had come to Appalachia as a poverty warrior, lost his first bid to be West Virginia's governor, largely because he wanted to control strip mining.

President Jimmy Carter himself became caught between several dilemmas that probably stretched his administration across too many issues. His major concerns were the substantial economic and environmental problems of the nation—an unemployment rate of nearly eight percent, double-digit inflation, an energy crisis, and rising defense costs. The Carter presidency became increasingly frustrated despite important regional legislation, such as the Surface Mine Control Bill of 1977. In the end, Carter began lecturing his opponents, Democrats and Republicans alike, and finally even the American people.

By 1980, the Appalachian region strongly supported the nation as a whole as it returned to Republican conservatism by voting for Ronald Reagan for president. Perhaps the best-known Appalachian politician in these years was Senator Howard Baker of Tennessee, who came into enormous power after 1980 as the Majority Leader in the newly Republican-dominated Senate. Baker was the son of a conservative Tennessee congressman, a lawyer and mineral owner. The region's congressmen and senators generally supported Reagan's program of lower taxes and increased benefits for the wealthy, in the belief that they were the persons most likely to invest in American growth. In 1980, three conservative, Reagan-style Republicans were swept into the Senate from Appalachian states: Jeremiah Denton of Alabama, Mack Mattingly of Georgia, and John East of North Carolina. All three represented states with strong Appalachian constituencies.

During the Reagan years, the region's political complexion seemed to demonstrate an increasingly conservative temper. Some observers, however, claimed to see a persisting radicalism among mountain politicians, if one can call "radical" those that believe that the coal industry—now being swallowed by great outside, multinational energy conglomerates—needs significant new and closer controls. Still the nation as a whole seemed determined to continue to enjoy the benefits of Appalachia's mineral wealth, yet to continue to impose on the people of the region most of the costs of this exploitation in terms of strip-mined mountains and smoking gob piles. Regional political spokesmen who have attempted to defend the mountain people and who have spoken out against the continued abuse of the Appalachian environment by largely outside multinational energy conglomerates—such politicians as Congressman Ken Hechler and Paul Kaufman in West Virginia or Harry Caudill in Kentucky—have been labeled "radical" and denied significant governmental responsibilities. Those "liberals" who have been able to gain election have tended to be persons such as Senator Jay Rockefeller in West Virginia or Senator Wendell Ford in Kentucky, both of whom, though they may have seen the need for serious corporate regulation, have found that they must accommodate their programs to the demands of the region's key corporate forces.

The political climate of the Appalachian region from 1968 to 1998 was one of retreat from welfare state concerns. The mountaineer's loyalty to the Republican Party, once mildly threatened during the New Deal era, demonstrated its persistence through the War on Poverty and the supply-side tax cuts and welfare reductions of the 1980s and 1990s. Regardless of the hopes of several New Left scholars, the evidence seems to indicate that, despite its poverty, Appalachia will probably remain one of the nation's bastions of conservative politics.

On the other hand, in 1988 Kentuckians did agree to amend their Constitution to forbid the stripping of coal by the mineral owner without the consent of the surface owner. On numerous occasions since 1956, the Kentucky Court of Appeals, alone of the state supreme courts in the nation, has defended the right of the mineral owner— thanks to the broadform deeds signed in the 1890s—to acquire his mineral by surface methods even without the approval of the surface owner. The coal industry interpreted this move against their property rights and "contract rights to not have to buy the right to their mineral again" as a move by radicals. But by a margin of more than four to one, Kentuckians in every section of the state approved this amendment. However, the successful rhetoric of this campaign for what was called the "Homestead Amendment" was couched in purely yeomanesque terms, emphasizing the right of the individual farmer to his own acres. Even yet in Appalachia, it may be that the only reform that can succeed must be seen through the lens of yeomanry.

In the 1990s, the election and re-election of Democrat Bill Clinton as president of the United States suggests the possibility of some modification of the suspicion toward the welfare state. Though a "new world order" seems to be emerging, still a conservative-induced welfare reform succeeded, new legislation that has had immense effects in the region. Yet in the Clinton's presidential races, Southern Appalachian constituencies remained mostly loyal to the Republican Party. Four Southern states with important Appalachian areas— Alabama, North Carolina, South Carolina, and Virginia—have become strongly Republican, and North Carolina failed in 1992 to return the veteran liberal and longtime regional friend, Terry Sanford, to the U.S. Senate. Appalachian voters still seem to give most of their votes to Republican candidates, no matter how plutocratic their philosophies.

Regional Society and Social Change

IT HAS BEEN MENTIONED previously that Cratis Williams, for years recognized as the "Dean of Appalachian Studies" and himself a native of the region, observed that there are three quite distinctive groups among Appalachian mountaineers. The first he termed the town-oriented elite and city folk, who are little different, he said, from the rest of middle-class Americans. Members of this group that are the region's elite and the professional and commercial people. The second group, he says, are the substantial farmers in the region's more fertile valleys. This is a quite prosperous group, and at the time Williams made this observation in the late 1950s, it was a group almost as numerous as the town and city folk. The last group, whom Williams called "Branchwater Mountaineers," was actually the least numerous of the three, but it was also by far the most unusual and the group about whom so much had been written and upon whom the well-known regional stereotypes have been based. The Branchwater Mountaineers, Williams said, were those who lived in the region's more remote areas, at the end of the hollows (hollers), along the ridges and the worst roads, and were the farmers who have tried to farm the region's most marginal lands.

Recently, Professor Charles Smith of Cumberland College, and a candidate for Congress in Kentucky's old Fifth District, designated a similar three-category description of Appalachian social structure. Professor Smith spoke of three groups of persons he would expect to find in any Appalachian county. The first group he called the "town folk." These are the lawyers, doctors, teachers, and businessmen and their families of the county-seat towns who "run things." The contrasting group to this controlling elite in each county he termed the "hollow folk," or those who live in the county's most remote sections—"up at the head of the holler." They are the ones who present the major problems to the town folk of the county seat. Their children are the school dropouts and the problems for the truancy officers. Overall, they are not very dependable employees. Furthermore, they are often the ones whose petty crimes cause them to fill the county's small jail. The third group, Professor Smith says, are the "Big Road Folk." These are the people that live in the small houses that line the county's main roads where transportation is relatively easy. Essentially, he says, they are "hollow folk on their way to town." These Big Road Folk usually live with some economic precariousness, but they work hard. Their children attend school with some regularity, and they thus represent a middle group between the culture of the town folk and the culture of the hollow folk.

Other observers have seen a two-part structure for Appalachian society. Harry Caudill, for one, claimed that there were only the *few*, who held the wealth and the power, and the *many*, who were poor and powerless. David Hsiung's recent study of East Tennessee claims that "two worlds" have existed in mountain society since well before the Civil War.

Most sociologists and anthropologists who have looked into small Appalachian rural communities have found that the local community, apparently fairly democratic, is actually divided by family reputation, income differentials, and the degree of urban sophistication. Other useful analyses trace the distance from urban ways, placing the person closest to the city as "superior," with the rural "back forty" places next, and the remote "holler" as the poorest and least powerful.

Sociologist John Stephenson found that the traditional folk of his community, Shiloh, had their highest regard for "good church folk" with steady jobs. Then Shiloh's class structure descended in four steps down to the "no-good families" who had no steady employment. Recent immigration has brought many retired folk and mainline families into Appalachia's rural communities. In the 1960s, "back to the landers" came in considerable numbers to set up their own groupings, and the 1980s brought a steady flow of refugees from the American mainstream who were attracted to the region's lack of serious crime and other urban problems.

Many scholars and observers have focused on the region's problems, such as lack of income and low educational level—in fact, seeing the region itself as identified by the appearance of several negative indicators in a county's statistics. Such scholars also make much of the convergence of such indicators as the proportion of persons accepting a premillennial approach to religion or a general hostility to the agencies of government, which all seem to appear from the same county statistics. Ironic as it may seem, those fleeing urban violence have found in many truly remote counties in Appalachia a caring neighborhood that clearly looks out for their welfare and respects their property.

Yet every county has a county-seat elite who seem to control the county's major institutions—its banks, principal stores, the courthouse, and the schools. Usually they attend essentially mainstream churches—the dominant Baptist Church, but also Methodist, Presbyterian, Christian, and even occasionally an Episcopal church. In the earliest-settled areas in Appalachia, especially in the Shenandoah Valley, churches of the German religious tradition are frequent—the Brethren and Lutheran Churches. These county-seat town churches are quite different from most of the rural churches in the region, for most rural churches share a very conservative Baptist or Pentecostal faith. This denominational differentiation sets up a religious difference that further increases the distance between hollow folk and town folk. Occasionally there is a Catholic church, and in coal-mining areas, an occasional Orthodox church or Jewish synagogue.

The town elites are market-oriented, commercial folk who have broad family and social connections as far afield as New York, Philadelphia, Chicago, Atlanta, and even Los Angeles. Essentially, Appalachian town elites have emerged to a rising degree of dominance as modernization has proceeded. The main difference of opinion that has emerged between the scholars of the region's elite has to do with how early these elites emerged. Historical geographer Mary Beth Pudup, for one, claims that these elites had developed strongly as far back as the years just following the Civil War. Historian Wilma Dunaway, however, sees them emerging much earlier than that. Others have seen this process as in some measure related to the coming of coal.

The place of blacks in Appalachia is an often-overlooked part of regional life. While it is true that in some mountain counties, blacks were almost totally absent, and that during the Jim Crow era, some mountain counties drove blacks from the county entirely, in other areas of the Appalachian Mountains, blacks were a significant minority. One scholar has suggested that in 1860, blacks made up 15 percent of the region's population, and one county at least—Madison County in northern Alabama—had a majority of blacks. By 1980, it is clear that the proportion of blacks was about 9 percent. Until 1900, about 40 percent of the region's blacks were concentrated in northern Alabama. As West Virginia and Kentucky developed their coalfields in the early twentieth century, many Alabama black miners were recruited, and the black population in Appalachia became much more widely dispersed.

During the era of Jim Crow segregation, blacks were thrust into neighborhoods and schools of their own. Yet the black population in West Virginia's coal communities offers a particularly interesting group to study, because even in those segregated days, the state of West Virginia provided an essentially equal system of schools for blacks. And even in Kentucky, where equal educational opportunities were not provided, and in the non-mining areas where significant black communities developed, such as in the Shenandoah Valley, stability of those black communities provided a quite positive background for young blacks, who later were able to take advantage of the increasing opportunities available after 1954. In fact, a remarkably large number of important leaders in today's national black community come from Appalachian childhoods.

Despite what might be seen as fairly good race relations in the region, many examples of clear racism and stubborn prejudice must also be recognized. During the Jim Crow era, some 125 blacks were lynched in the region, and the many examples of the "racial cleansing" of rural counties in the region demonstrate a situation that not only sent blacks from their traditional homes but also left a legacy of racial and fear hatred that was not soon forgotten.

Since 1910, blacks have moved from rural to urban areas in a migration that saw the black population move from the rural South and concentrate more and more heavily in the North. In each Appalachian city, significant black communities have developed. This is especially true in Birmingham, Chattanooga, and Knoxville. Although these urban black communities did not enjoy the quality of black leadership experienced by the black communities of Atlanta and Nashville, few communities have ever been able to enjoy the kind of leadership that was developed by the major black colleges of Nashville and Atlanta.

An important aspect of any society is the fact of change. Even a reasonably stable society is not totally static, and Appalachia, particularly since World War II, has been a society that has experienced rapid social change. Gender relations, for example, as in the rest of the nation, have undergone dramatic changes in the region. The traditional Appalachian family had been clearly paternalistic, with the father's authority sanctioned by religion, law, and tradition. Yet even in traditional times, there were women whose force of personality led them to be dominant in the churches and even in their families and communities. Nevertheless, tradition allowed various disciplining actions to be used against "uppity" women—community pressures, even actual legal mechanisms and scripturally sanctioned actions. So long as a woman's tasks involved such time- and energy-consuming jobs as spinning, weaving, cleaning, cooking, bearing children every other year, and child care, it was less disturbing for such a woman to be content with her leadership role in her church, her quilting circle, in health care, or gardening, or in the textile arts.

As schools penetrated the region, at first it was more likely that girls were allowed to attend than their brothers, for boys were needed in the fields. Therefore, as modernization proceeded, often it was the women who were the most employable in the new industries, for they were better educated. In fact, many of the region's young men were destroyed emotionally, since with modernization they were not able to provide for their families, while their wives easily found work. Farming was usually not very profitable, and after 1950, increasingly men were not even needed in the mines. Despite their traditional authority, the men were not able to deliver as the major family provider, and many sank into despondency.

In traditional times, the more isolated the family, the more completely the family itself dominated the life of its members. But this also meant that other institutions such as the church, the country store, and the agencies of local government, played little if any role in the life of the especially isolated family. As isolation broke down, these other institutions played increasingly important roles—the school in education and socialization, the store in trade, and the agencies of local government in law enforcement and order. Just as the yeoman farm broke down before better transportation and increased economic contact, the coming of schools brought a broadening of opportunities and a wider awareness of the world. And in government's tasks of justice and order, particularly interesting political patterns developed, all of which had a very close relationship to the families of the region.

The family structure that was operative for the earliest, isolated families was built upon a mix of inherited European patterns and the demands of the Appalachian frontier environment. The frontier's complete wilderness, along with the resources of soil, stone, rainfall, the presence of wildlife, the challenges of the Indian threat, and the remoteness of government, gave the family its earliest patterns. Europe's paternalistic family norm was the beginning, and other things being equal, the father was the authority, with tasks related to his strength, abilities, and preferences—the planting and the tending of the fields and animals and trading whatever surpluses were grown. The wife was responsible for the home, its care and cleaning, the cooking, the care of small children, and frequent childbearing, as well as the never-ending demands of the textile arts. The gender task-division line was just outside the walls of the house, usually including the garden and chicken yard within the women's domain, and all beyond, including the fields and ranging hogs and cattle, considered as man's work.

As time went on, the pattern of gender–work relations changed. The man was drawn into social relations at the store, saloon, and courthouse, and these frequently developed even broader contacts. In the church, women as well as men, were given an opportunity to broaden themselves. And when the Sears Roebuck catalog came into the mountain home late in the nineteenth century, the flight from women's textile tasks became precipitous.

As the twentieth century's modernization proceeded, the influence of roads, schools, the coming of coal in parts of the region, radio, and television all broke down the family's isolation and changed most aspects of the lives of the family's members. It often seemed as if everything was changing. The children were attracted to other neighborhoods, interests, and vocations. The wife was attracted to other tasks more in keeping with her special interests, often under the influence and guidance of mission schools. And the men, kept from schooling in the early days because they were needed on the farm, were often less well-prepared for the modern world. The disparity caused by the man's poorer educational preparation, while remembering their traditional authority and responsibilities, drove many men to alcohol and despair. Modernization clearly brought dramatic change, with remarkable successes mixed with tragic failures.

Sociologist Richard Couto, though recognizing that the region might have been influenced by notions drawn from nostalgia, contends that the unusual and persisting poverty in the region really does set Appalachia apart from the rest of the nation. The region is, he says, less a place and more a "set of economic relations." Yet Appalachia has long played an important role in the economic history of the United States. Appalachia has had both successful areas and areas of economic privation. There are wealthy areas in the Southern Appalachians, especially concentrated largely around Atlanta, Birmingham, and other urban centers. But it is true as well that the region still has many poor counties, mostly in West Virginia and eastern Kentucky. In recent years, however, the poverty rates, population growth, and average age of the population have basically followed the rates of the rest of the nation. Clearly, regional population growth is lower and poverty rates have remained higher than in the nation, particularly in the area designated as "Central Appalachia"—i.e., the rural and coal-producing areas of eastern Kentucky, West Virginia, southwestern Virginia, and East Tennessee.

Actually, Appalachian society is more complex ethnically than the story of black and white. There are several other important ethnic minorities within the mountain region of the South. The continuing life of the some six thousand Cherokee within the Qualla Boundary in western North Carolina parallels the life of Indians elsewhere in the twentieth century. And a remarkable and puzzling minority called "Melungeons," never precisely enumerated in East Tennessee and neighboring states, has been a mysterious dark-skinned group subject to much prejudice for many years. The Melungeons are just now beginning to put together their own story in a fairly convincing way.

Clearly, the region's society is far more diverse than the traditional picture painted as a stable enclave of Anglo-Saxons, Scotch–Irish, and Germans. As coal mining developed in the region after 1880, numerous immigrants from eastern Europe came with their Catholic, Orthodox, and Jewish congregations. And in the twentieth century, Hispanics and Asians have moved into the region's urban centers, principally those urban centers with large universities.

The whole aspect of the Appalachian region has changed dramatically since World War II. Hard-surface roads were extended deep into every county, and radio and television spread the doctrine of consumerism into every mountain cabin. In fact, this formerly rural region became perhaps as much as 50 percent urbanized by 1977. The great and small metropolitan areas on the edge of Appalachia— Atlanta (2.9 million), Pittsburgh (2.25 million), Charlotte (1.2 million), Greenville–Spartanburg (640,000) and Lexington (450,000)—all extend far into the region. At the same time, at least 40 percent of the region's 11 million population today lives within the region's Standard Metropolitan Statistical Areas (SMSAs): Birmingham (.9 million) and the smaller SMSAs in northern Alabama (.5 million); the three SMSAs of East Tennessee (Knoxville, Chattanooga, and the Tri-Cities, 1.4 million); plus the Ashland–Huntington–Charleston corridor in West Virginia and Kentucky; Roanoke, Virginia; Asheville, North Carolina; and the northern West Virginia area of Morgantown–Fairmont–Clarksburg–Wheeling. All of these combine for an urban population of some 4 million wholly inside the Appalachian region itself.

Since the late 1950s, it has been the contention of some sociologists that the mountains were being flattened by the influence of radio, roads, and television so that the distinctive traits of Appalachian Americans were being blurred. At the same time, some mountain values and attitudes appear to have gone out into the rest of the nation, along with the movement of some four million sons and daughters of Appalachia who have left the region in the "Great Migration." This migration began during World War II and went mainly to the great Midwest cities—Cincinnati, Dayton, Cleveland, Gary, Detroit, and Chicago. This movement can be coupled with the dramatic growth of Pentecostal Protestantism, which is in part an Appalachian-born phenomenon, as well as the spreading popularity of bluegrass and country music and the spread of other esthetic parts of the mountain soul. Thus there is a larger and larger acceptance of mountain values and styles by the rest of the nation. This dynamic has flowed both ways and is very complex. But even though many forces move toward integrating Appalachia's more remote people into mainline America, still important and discernable differences persist.

The health revolution in Appalachia during the twentieth century has paralleled in many ways the growth of the health industry in the United States, though in the region's more remote sections, there has been a remarkable leap from a health system depending upon folk remedies and "grannywomen" to the more male-oriented medical system of doctors, nurses, and hospitals. Still, in some areas the folk system persists, and the emergence of a modern medical system in the more remote areas lags considerably behind the rest of the nation. Early in this century, the emergence of the modern medical system is associated with a number of medical "heroes," nurses as well as doctors.

Modern medicine came to Appalachia's more remote areas in the early decades of the twentieth century. The story began with a few pioneer doctors such as Dr. Joseph A. Stucky, a Louisville physician who became famous for research in diseases of the eye, trachoma

METROPOLITAN STATISTICAL AREAS

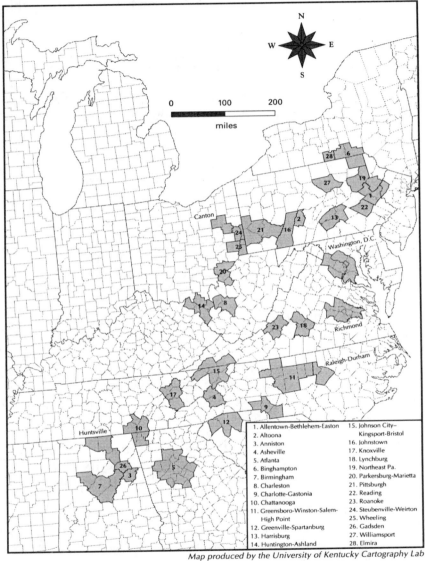

1. Allentown-Bethlehem-Easton
2. Altoona
3. Anniston
4. Asheville
5. Atlanta
6. Binghampton
7. Birmingham
8. Charleston
9. Charlotte-Gastonia
10. Chattanooga
11. Greensboro-Winston-Salem-
    High Point
12. Greenville-Spartanburg
13. Harrisburg
14. Huntington-Ashland

15. Johnson City–
    Kingsport-Bristol
16. Johnstown
17. Knoxville
18. Lynchburg
19. Northeast Pa.
20. Parkersburg-Marietta
21. Pittsburgh
22. Reading
23. Roanoke
24. Steubenville-Weirton
25. Wheeling
26. Gadsden
27. Williamsport
28. Elmira

Map produced by the University of Kentucky Cartography Lab

mainly, and from his work on trips into eastern Kentucky at Hindman Settlement School. Dr. May Cravath Wharton became a remarkable medical missionary who set up her practice in connection with a mission at Pleasant Hill, Tennessee. Other important medical missionaries who brought remarkably fine health care to thousands were Dr. Robert F. Thomas at the Pittman Community Center in Sevierville, Tennessee (who delivered Dolly Parton); Dr. Mary Sloop at Crossmore, Tennessee; and Dr. Everett W. Schaeffer and others at the Red Bird Mission in Kentucky. Furthermore, an outstanding group of missionary nurses also became agents of exceptional health service to thousands, as provided by Mary Wright at Buckhorn, Kentucky, and Nola VanDermeer at Morris Fork near Buckhorn.

Most famous, perhaps, was the multicounty mission begun by Mary Breckinridge known as the Frontier Nursing Service, which specialized in modern childbearing service, centered near Hyden, Kentucky. Noteworthy also was the medical service rendered by Dr. Louise Caudill at the small university town of Morehead, Kentucky, and of Dr. Louise Hutchins to the Mountain Maternal Health League, which operates through much of eastern Kentucky.

In eastern Kentucky today, fine medical services are provided in a variety of ways by dedicated doctors following several philosophies of service. Dr. Bennie Lee Bailey and Dr. Grady Stumbo, for example, made a pledge while still in medical school to go back to the mountains and serve the region. They have done this ably through their for-profit practices and active political careers. Dr. Paul Maddox of Campton has been called the busiest doctor in Kentucky, where he runs a practice that literally never closes. The cause of the rights of miners suffering from Black Lung disease raised an otherwise average local physician, Dr. Isador E. Buff, to prominence in West Virginia reform politics as this industrial disease became recognized and protected by health insurance and governmental policy. Not-for-profit medicine has also had an important place in the region's health story, as Dr. Philip Curd and his associates have demonstrated as they serve populations in several eastern Kentucky counties through their White House Clinic.

In 1946, the United Mine Workers began its Welfare and Retirement Fund in an attempt to bring health services to miners under union control and away from the whim of the mining companies. In a major effort financed by a fee levied on every ton of coal mined, the Fund developed a remarkable medical reform program that, among other things, built eleven fine hospitals in the coal-mining areas of eastern Kentucky, West Virginia and southwestern Virginia. However, thanks to mismanagement and dramatic economic change in the industry, this effort failed in the late 1970s. As a result, other agencies have had to take over the hospitals. But the hospitals and clinics begun by the Fund were built and their long-run effect established.

Since the 1950s and 1960s, thanks mostly to local efforts and federal grants through the Hill–Burton Act and various War on Poverty initiatives, especially the Appalachian Regional Commission, many hospitals and clinics were established and/or enlarged throughout the region. The National Health Service Corps scholarships have been offered to new medical school graduates as an opportunity for service in the region, as well as to pay off their costs of medical school. Moreover, a number of foreign doctors have set up practice in the region. Thus the region's physician gap has at least been partly filled. The present movement in health services—in the nation as well as the region—has been to form various hospital alliances and to build a growing networking of health services tied to major medical centers. In the region, Appalachian people have been particularly aware of the aggressive networking generated by the medical centers of the University of Kentucky, the University of Tennessee, the University of Virginia, Vanderbilt University, and the University of North Carolina.

Dramatic change had clearly come even to the more remote areas in the southern mountains during the early and mid-years of the twentieth century, and often that change came rather quickly. By the 1970s, the region's yeomanry was on the verge of disappearing as the region's people became more and more urbanized.

"The New Appalachia," 1930–2000

THE 1930S BROUGHT important changes to the Appalachian economy. But while the American market economy floundered, yeomanry made something of a comeback in Appalachia's rural areas as thousands retreated from the nation's cities and returned home. The Great Depression placed immense strains on the nation's commercial institutions, and at times the market system seemed on the verge of collapse. Some even suggested that the basic principles of market capitalism should be abandoned. In Appalachian Virginia, for example, the number of farmers rose by some 16 percent between 1930 and 1935; and according to one scholar, though agricultural conditions had been deteriorating for twenty years, farming in that state survived the Depression because it was "little changed from nineteenth-century self-sufficiency."

Another scholar of Appalachian agricultural conditions notes that "even before the Great Depression, Appalachia had contained 166,000 'self-sufficient' farms—one third of the U.S. total concentrated in about 3 percent of the country's land area." Much of Appalachian agriculture, then, had retreated to its yeomanesque roots and appears to have provided a living for several hundreds of thousands of people in the region.

Also during the dark days of the Great Depression, chronic troubles appeared in the Appalachian mine fields of Harlan, Bell, Letcher, and neighboring counties. Eastern Kentucky mine operators in these areas were belligerently antiunion. Their brief experience with unionism during World War I had convinced these operators that they could have a significant price advantage over their northern competitors only if they could operate on a non-union basis. The union outsiders—in their view, "carpetbaggers" with principles they considered un-American—had been effectively ousted from the Southern fields in the early 1920s, and the iron hand of the operators was laid on their men through control of the company-owned stores, schools, and churches, as well as the company's paid deputies. These deputies operated under the control of the county sheriff's office, and the cost of these substantial armies was borne by the local coal companies. Their justification was the preservation of law and order and the protection of mine property.

In March of 1931, the miners in Harlan and neighboring counties in eastern Kentucky went on strike—a "purely spontaneous affair" apparently brought forth out of misery and hunger. The National Miners Union, a Communist-dominated union, came to the aid of the miners when the United Mine Workers, fearful of the mine owner's power, refused to support the strike and wildcatted it. Even the American Red Cross would not give any relief to the wildcatted miners.

Violence in Harlan reached its height in the Battle of Evarts in May of 1932, when a well-armed, roving party of sheriff's deputies was waylaid. At least four persons were killed. National attention was focused on the plight of the miners by several committees, one a group of prominent writers headed by the novelist Theodore Dreiser. Soon thereafter, many Harlan miners were paraded before audiences in Madison Square Garden in New York City by their northern, left-wing benefactors. Much zeal, rhetoric, and indignation was expended without significantly changing conditions in Harlan or its neighboring counties. However, changes in labor's situation in eastern Kentucky, as elsewhere, had to await developments later in the 1930s.

The crisis of the Depression and the New Deal programs that followed did bring changes. In agriculture, conditions had developed by the first third of the twentieth century to the point that the ten million farm units in the United States were producing so much food and fiber that under laissez-faire market conditions the quantities produced were driving prices down to disastrous levels. It was only in unusual years, when conditions in Europe and elsewhere took overseas farm areas out of production, that the massive amounts of American food and fiber could command strong prices. American farmers in general, and small farmers in particular, were producing "at a loss." By the 1920s, it was clear that the old government policies favoring American agriculture, particularly through protective tariffs, would not work.

During the 1920s, farm state legislators increasingly suggested that the government should intervene in the pricing mechanism of the market for the benefit of farmers in order to guarantee a base price. But President Coolidge vetoed the bill supporting this tactic, the McNary–Haugen Bill of 1927. As a consequence, its passage and implementation had to await the several Agricultural Adjustment Acts of the New Deal. During the New Deal, the government began guaranteeing a parity price for agricultural products—cotton, wheat, tobacco, hogs, etc. But along with this guaranteed price, the government protected itself from agriculture's tendency to overproduce by entering into various schemes to limit production.

Therefore, in American agriculture since the 1930s, farmers generally accepted a role for government to determine what the parity price was to be—a price arrived at by a complex formula relating to good years for farmers. The various methods used to limit production involved the government with each farmer, measuring his acreage allotment and even buying his crop if the market price did not match the percentage of parity agreed upon. Tobacco particularly—a major money crop for tens of thousands of Appalachian farmers—has had a history of dependence upon government guarantees and controls. A small number of corporate buyers placed the many tobacco growers in a particularly vulnerable market position. So government since the 1930s has intervened within the market structure as a "friend of the grower," thus guaranteeing better prices for the farmer. Ironically, many small farmers sharing a "yeomanesque mentality" have continued to operate reasonably successfully thanks to government price supports.

Despite the intrusion of government into the agricultural pricing mechanisms—especially in tobacco—as late as 1960, the average rural Appalachian was a small, yeomanesque-style farmer depending largely on family labor. Though not strictly a self-sufficient operation, it was the yeoman's dream mixed with the guaranteed price for tobacco that kept many Appalachian farmers in operation.

For example, as late as 1960, though only 25 percent of the region's people were full-time farmers, the average Appalachian farm then contained eighty-one acres. One authority described this eighty-one-acre farm as having fifteen of these acres in croplands, with these crops grown largely for home consumption, thirty-six acres were in pasture, and the remaining acres were in woodlands or allowed to lie fallow. This average Appalachian farmer, according to this authority, owned seven cows, three pigs, and forty-three chickens. He had an average annual income of $1,267, which allowed this average rural Appalachian family in the mid-twentieth century to have electricity (92 percent did) but did not allow most to have a telephone (only 22 percent), a truck (36.4 percent), or a tractor (22.2 percent). Although the traditional small Appalachian farmer in the mid-twentieth century owned his own acres (only 14 percent were tenants, according to this authority), the Appalachian farmer in 1960 still farmed with animals (80 percent did). And although the traditional Appalachian farmer still farmed acres he himself owned, the standard of living that most rural Appalachian families enjoyed was vastly poorer than the standard of living of most Americans.

New Deal policies in agriculture generally had a favorable impact upon rural Americans if the farmer owned his own land. Parity prices, farm loan opportunities, rural electricity, and marketing aids all had a beneficial impact for farmers who held land. Sharecroppers and tenants by the hundreds of thousands, however, were shut off from "their" acres and found it necessary to migrate northward to the Midwest cities. The Appalachian rural population actually enlarged through the 1930s, and New Deal policies seemed for a time to enhance Appalachian rural life in many areas. But because New Deal policies focused on commodity prices and allotments, small farmers had particular difficulty in qualifying for the new programs and remaining on them once accepted. It all seemed like so much red tape.

Organized labor's remarkable success during the late 1930s was largely the result of the New Deal policies. When the Wagner Act was passed in 1935, it gave labor what it considered its "Bill of Rights." These rights were the twin guarantees—the right to bargain collectively, and the right to strike in redress of grievances. With the majesty of the law of the nation now on the side of the unions, the United Mine Workers finally won the desperate strikes in eastern Kentucky, which continued from 1931 to 1937. Management at last recognized labor's rights. Thus strengthened, the UMW launched unionizing drives, which increased its membership by some 300 percent from 1935 to 1939. The UMW, then one of the nation's strongest unions, was able to lend organizers and leaders to the unions of the new Congress of Industrial Organizations—the autoworkers, steelworkers, and others—which mushroomed quickly following the passage of the Wagner Act.

World War II brought a quickening of the nation's economy, and in Appalachia a "boom" was enjoyed in the coal-producing areas. Coal was still the nation's primary fossil fuel then, and as employment rose, new operators entered the fields in large numbers. Towns throughout the coal areas enjoyed increasing bank deposits and rising mercantile sales. Especially in the region's Ridge and Valley cities, from Winchester to Chattanooga, a rising economy brought significant growth and increased prosperity.

More dramatic than the internal wartime growth in the Appalachian area, however, was the movement of people from the Appalachian region into the fast-growing industrial cities of the upper Midwest, into such cities as Cincinnati, Dayton, Akron, Cleveland, Willow Run, Detroit, Gary, and Chicago. It was in such cities that major national expansion occurred in the war industries. This "Great Migration" from Appalachia, which began during World War II, created whole Appalachian sections and suburbs in the North. By 1950, some two million sons and daughters of Appalachia had joined this Great Migration, which continued into the 1970s and the 1980s.

A major regional industrial development has been the emergence of the chemical industry centered in the Kanawha and Ohio River Valleys in West Virginia. As salt production declined in the Charleston area in the late nineteenth century, the manufacture of alkalies and other chemicals rose to take its place. The major growth of the chemical industry accompanied developments during the two world wars when supplies were cut off from Europe. As a wartime measure, the federal government encouraged this industry, as with the high explosives plant built at Nitro, West Virginia. Major corporations such as DuPont and Union Carbide led the way toward the establishment of an industry that employed over twenty-five thousand people in West Virginia by 1976. A major Southern dimension of the chemical industry also spread into East Tennessee at Kingsport, where the massive Tennessee Eastman plant was built.

Industrial growth within the region also followed the fortunes of cotton textiles. During the late nineteenth and early twentieth centuries, this industry fled New England for the low wages of the New South, which centered largely in the "great crescent" from Danville, Virginia, through the North Carolina Piedmont and the area around Greenville–Spartanburg, South Carolina, then on to Atlanta. Though this industry provided employment for thousands in the region, textiles has proven a most mobile industry, and it has continued to be attracted by low-wage areas. This means that during the late twentieth century, American textile plants have closed and gone to Mexico or locations overseas.

Industries that have proven to be less "low-wage driven" that have impacted the region are the wood-products and furniture industry, as well as the tobacco industry. Tobacco remained quite concentrated in the North Carolina Piedmont. The furniture and wood-products industry has more often penetrated the Appalachian Mountains themselves, as a fairly strong concentration of furniture factories has arisen from High Point, North Carolina, into East Tennessee.

A most remarkable industry in Appalachia continues to be tourism, claimed by some to be the "world's largest industry." This industry has long held a prominent and growing place in Appalachian life. An industry that is remarkably interrelated with various other mostly service industries—restaurants, travel, accommodations, commercial sales generally, recreation, etc.—this aspect of modern life in Appalachia is expanding rapidly, perhaps at twice the rate of the Gross National Product. However, it seems that the region may not be expanding its efforts in this industry as rapidly as it might. Despite the remarkable scenic advantages that the region enjoys, the nation's most popular national park in its heart, and vast areas designated as National Forest, the income enjoyed from this industry lags substantially behind that of most of the United States.

Furthermore, tourism seems to enjoy an insatiable market, for technology and new tastes are creating new dimensions for tourism through new uses of leisure time. The recent development of whitewater canoeing, for example, has found the Ocoee, the New, the Nantahala, the Youghiogheny, the Chatooga, and other regional rivers to be some of the best in the world. This has developed a demand for river guides as well as services and manufactures totally unappreciated before the rise of this recreational outlet. The same could be said of hunting and fishing in its various dimensions, hiking, mountain climbing, and even the regionally invented stock car racing.

The area's sports heroes—from Junior Johnson, Johnny Mize, and Hal Greer to Jerry West, Earl Combs, George Brett and Mary Lou Retton—as well as its musical stars—from Loretta Lynn to Bill Monroe and the Carter family—attest to the opportunities taken by some of the region's sons and daughters to move into national prominence because of their particular excellence. The region is and has always been an integral part of the nation's experience, even its sports and entertainment experience.

A World War II development within Appalachia was the birth and early growth of Oak Ridge, Tennessee. The Oak Ridge story changed a rural area of remote valleys and hills near Knoxville, Tennessee, into a mysterious city of seventy-five thousand scientists and workers laboring on the top secret, wartime project that made the fuel for the nation's first atom bombs. At its vast Centrifuge Plant, Oak Ridge made the fuel that went into the bombs dropped on Japan and the first reactors that brought the world into the nuclear age.

Nevertheless, alongside the developing areas within Appalachia, a still-active folk economy existed. But although the Great Depression appears to have strengthened the family unit, self-sufficient yeomanesque way of life inside the region, as times got better, the world seemed to demand the services of Appalachia's sons and daughters. So again there was movement toward the cities and the towns—this time usually to destinations outside the region.

The lure of the wartime industries at Willow Run, Detroit, and other places proved irresistible. The military draft took many thousands more, because the United States Armed Forces proved a popular way for sons in the region to get ahead. Appalachian men had always made excellent soldiers, for few Americans were as deadly with the rifle or as willing to face the dangers of combat. In fact, a remarkably high percentage of Congressional Medal of Honor winners in each of our wars have been natives of Appalachia.

And once a mountaineer had tasted the thrill of travel and the marvels of Paris, London, or Sydney, it was hard to keep him in his Appalachian hollow. The whole of the 1940s were dynamic years in Appalachia, and even the region's slowly increasing prosperity was not enough to keep most of its young people at home.

Internally the 1930s had seen the growth of the National Park and the National Forest systems. From these developments, and the development of the TVA to build dams to create lakes, many rural acres were subjected to condemnation proceedings. With over one million acres in the region moving from private to government ownership during this decade, there was further impetus for migration. Many of these acreages acquired by the government were small farms, thus more and more mountain yeomen were separated from their traditional lands.

Within each Appalachian county, at least one town developed as the county seat. The county government and various business and professional services emerged around the town's courthouse square. For the most part, these people shared the values of the nation's middle class. But within each of these counties, too, were numbers of traditional Appalachian farmers living on their acres in the far coves and hollows of the country who still represented a different way of life. Usually these other people in the county were the ones that the town professionals and businessmen complained to the outside about—those troublesome "hillbillies," whose children didn't stay in school and who made difficulties for the town's police.

The persistence of what may be termed the "yeomanesque" into the present may seem strange to many. But the appeal of this way of life in English and American history, from Oliver Goldsmith to Thomas Jefferson, Henry David Thoreau and Wendell Berry, demonstrates its strength. In Appalachia—the locale in America where this attitude seems most persistent—its isolation within the mountains has appeared to reinforce the appeal of this lifestyle. As noted above, even as late as 1960, the reality of Appalachian farm life coincided with most of the yeomanesque way of thinking.

Even as the yeomanesque way of life was being threatened by modern life, organized labor in the region also began to fall from the heights of power it had enjoyed in the late 1930s and early 1940s. An early sign of the decline of labor's status was the passage of the Taft–Hartley Act of 1947. This act set up prescribed rules of proper conduct for unions; strengthened the hand of workers not choosing to join unions; and established machinery for suspending strikes if the nation's safety required it. Although this last Taft–Hartley provision has been seldom invoked, its presence as law has substantially decreased the power of the unions.

During the 1950s, the frustrations of the coal miners mounted. Mines were hardly less dangerous. For example, in 1940 a Barley, West Virginia, mine disaster killed ninety-one people; in 1957 a Bishop, Virginia, mine explosion killed thirty-seven; twenty-two more were killed there in a 1958 explosion. And in 1969 a Pittston, Pennsylvania, mine disaster killed twelve people.

Even more devastating in its long-run effects upon the condition of miners was the Love–Lewis Agreement, signed in 1950, between the president of the Bituminous Coal Operators Association, George Love, and the president of the United Mine Workers of America, John L. Lewis. This agreement established the principal of high wages (then twenty-five dollars per hour and more), as well as certain health benefits for the miners' welfare fund. In return, the union agreed not to oppose the introduction of any level of technology that management desired to bring into the mines. In fact, according to this agreement, the union would actively interpret the "need for technology" to its membership. John L. Lewis apparently believed that mining was such a dangerous occupation that as few men as possible ought to go underground. But those who did go underground should be very well paid. Unfortunately, this agreement set the stage for the human tragedies in the coalfields during the 1950s and 1960s brought on by massive technological unemployment. The coal industry, in fact, was the first industry in America to have to deal with this phenomenon.

In its history, the United Mine Workers of America has taken a middle-of-the-road position as a labor organization. More radical unions, such as the Molly McGuires, the International Workingmen of the World, and the National Miners' Union, preached class solidarity and a deep suspicion of all businessmen. Most radical unions accepted the Marxian analysis of history as class struggle and rejected capitalism as a system. At the other extreme have been the company unions, such as the Southern Miners' Union, which have been particularly concerned about the health of the mining companies that employ the miners, assuming that only as business prospers will labor prosper. The UMW has followed neither philosophy, and since its founding in 1890, it has taken a "safe and sane," or labor-oriented but businesslike, approach to labor's problems. It has been in the business of selling labor, and it has tried to get as high a price for its product from its consumers, management, as it could. Under Lewis, the UMW apparently assumed that only the larger and more dependable operators could pay the price labor demanded. John L. Lewis, the UMW president from the 1920s to the mid-1960s, got his price, but its effect was to limit the need for miners. With fewer and fewer miners employed by the industry, the union was inevitably weakened.

The result of 1950's Love–Lewis Agreement was the first massive invasion of technology into an American industry. From the mineowner's point of view, if high wages were to be paid, the workers needed to be made more efficient; thus the latest machines should be placed in their hands. Old pick, shovel, and blast methods were abandoned, and in their place was substituted continuous miners, or the more efficient auger and stripping methods; and in more recent years, the massive Long Wall method. The result has been an amazing efficiency. But fewer and fewer miners have been employed. Whereas over 500 thousand men went under the Appalachian Mountains to mine coal during World War II, by 1960 less than 150 thousand were needed. And employment in the mines has continued to shrink through the 1970s, 1980s, and 1990s.

The coal industry itself underwent another revolutionary change after World War II as well. Government energy policy and tax breaks for oil corporations have allowed Middle East oil and domestic petroleum production to dominate the nation's energy markets at a growing pace. This has helped bring on a substantial shift away from coal to oil. The retreat from coal has been very broad—on the railways (dieselization), home heating, and even for electrical generation prior to 1973. The result has been a shrinking market for coal and an increasing national dependence on foreign sources for oil. As a result, coal has faced a generally depressed market during most of the years since World War II. The numerous "truck mine" operations with the older technology were driven from the market, and increasingly conditions changed so that the wildly competitive coal industry of the period before 1940 has become controlled by fewer and fewer giant corporations and with ownership of these large corporations usually concentrated outside the region. The escalating use of expensive technology, the growing state and federal regulation of the mines, as well as general market conditions, have all conspired to drive the small operator from the coal industry, except as it suited the purposes of the larger corporations to maintain the appearance of general competitiveness.

When in the late 1960s and early 1970s it became clear that the nation was as dependent as it ever had been upon Appalachian fossil fuels, the corporations that had the economic strength to dominate the region's coal production turned out to be the large oil companies that had been built during the growing petroleum era from 1920 to 1960. In the early 1960s, Occidental Oil purchased Island Creek Coal, Appalachia's second largest coal producer, and Continental Oil bought Consolidation Coal, the industry's largest producer within Appalachia. Increasingly, the coal industry has become controlled by giant energy conglomerates, so that by 1972, even before the so-called "Energy Crisis" consolidated outside control more solidly, the ownership of coal's top ten producers together accounted for 52 percent of the nation's coal extraction. In more recent times, low-grade coals from the American West have penetrated the industry in an important way, and this further makes Appalachian coal apprehensive about its future.

In fact, the storm of difficulties never seems to lift from the coal industry. In the old, overly competitive days, clashes were the most bitter in the mines of small operators who managed operations on the barest of profit margins. Often wage cuts were the small operator's only way of survival in bad times. The bitter battles of the 1920s and

1930s generally had been between the mine unions and small local owners. As the industry changed with the introduction of new technology and larger corporate control, the struggle in the coalfields has centered principally on two areas: 1) organizational strikes against specific giant corporations, and 2) the clash over what is called "strip-mining."

The major mine strikes of the 1960s and 1970s have reflected the UMW's two basic internal problems of a declining membership and a crisis of leadership. A number of major coal companies have dropped their UMW contracts and have become either completely non-union, through the free elections of their workers, or company unions have emerged. The UMW has apparently been helpless to prevent this, but it has fought back by focusing on strategic organizational battles with particular large corporations, such as the Duke Power Company in the strike at Brookside, Kentucky. Such conflicts have been fought on a broad front, from the corporate boardrooms of Wall Street to general nationwide boycotts, to the hollows of the mines themselves. Yet despite the drama and media attention, these battles have not been exceptionally successful.

Perhaps the most successful mine strike in recent years has been the remarkably imaginative strike of the UMW against the Pittston Coal Company in southwestern Virginia in 1989. The sudden and dramatic peaceful occupation of the massive Moss 3 Processing Plant, and the popularity of the union's "Solidarity City," which accepted and fed all who came, brought public support for the union and ultimately a fairly good settlement.

More bitter has been the battle over strip-mining and, more recently, mountaintop removal. This method of mining coal became possible only when World War II developed the technology for moving massive amounts of soil with bulldozers and giant shovels. Here the soil on top of the coal—the "overburden"—is simply moved away and the coal extracted by surface methods. As time has gone on, larger and larger machinery has been used, and more and deeper seams of coal have been extracted, with even whole mountains leveled.

In mountainous terrain, problems emerge that are not present when strip-mining is attempted on flatter lands. The "contour methods" used in rough land may follow a particular seam around a mountain, but the "overburden," when it is pushed down the mountain, creates an unstable "spoil bank" that may not stabilize for years. In areas of heavy rainfall, which is characteristic of all of Appalachia, streams become clogged, and mountains of mud destroy downstream farm acres. The small yeoman farmer, whose grandfather probably sold his mineral rights to some nineteenth-century mineral buyer for fifty cents an acre, now finds his home and farm inundated—often with little or no legal recourse.

In Kentucky especially, the courts have time and again defended the legality of the Broadform Deed, which gave the right to the mineral owner to use any means necessary in the use of the surface to get at the mineral beneath it. Despite the fact that a technology such as we have today could scarcely have been imagined by the nineteenth-century ancestor of the mountaineer who signed his mark to a complex Broadform Deed, the Kentucky courts continued to accept these signed documents as valid, following the principle of the sanctity of contracts. In an election in 1988, the people of Kentucky by a margin of four to one accepted a constitutional amendment prohibiting strip-mining by the mineral owner without the permission of the surface owner. And by 1993, the Kentucky Court of Appeals finally accepted the constitutionality of this Homestead Amendment.

Over the past forty years, a rather desperate situation has developed in some of Appalachia. Groups of small landowners banded together to fight for what they considered their way of life and against strip-mining. Dramatic folk heroes emerged who have, for a time, stopped the march of the bulldozers upon their valleys, as did Uncle Dan Gibson, the Widow Combs, and Jink Ray in eastern Kentucky. The groups that have gathered around them—the "Abolitionist Movement" in West Virginia, Save Our Kentucky (S.O.K.), Save Our Cumberland Mountains (SOCUM), or the Appalachian Group to Save the Land and the People—have had bitter and frustrating experiences. The industry, its employees, and their friends have fought back against the antistripper with the weapons available to them, thus bitterly dividing mountain society. Many have been killed. Rhetoric frequently outruns logic. In fact, a kind of "holy war" has developed, and people in some parts of the region are no longer talking with one another, so deep are the mutual suspicions.

Furthermore, the crisis of the UMW leadership since the late 1950s produced a tragic result for the union for many years. Even before John L. Lewis retired in 1963, his leadership was unsure. And his succession was filled with problems. Thomas Kennedy was briefly president, and in 1965, Lewis's longtime assistant Tony Boyle became president. Mismanagement of the Miner's Health and Welfare Fund, financed by a forty cent per ton "contribution" levied on all union-mined coal, was merely informal and careless at first, but later became fraudulent. Though Kennedy and Boyle had been Lewis's trusted lieutenants, that trust was betrayed.

In 1968 Jock Yablonski, a former union official who had broken with Boyle over actions that he charged involved fraud, ran against Boyle for the presidency of the union. Yablonski lost badly, so the widespread vote fraud on Boyle's behalf in the election was probably unnecessary. Then, just after New Year's Day 1969, Yablonski, his wife, and daughter were murdered. It was later established that certain Ohio men with eastern Kentucky and Tennessee UMW connections were the "hit men" who killed the Yablonski family under Boyle's orders. The National Labor Relations Board had to supervise the honesty of the UMW election of 1971 when Arnold Miller, a candidate for the reformist Miners for Democracy, won the presidency.

Miller, a soft-spoken ex-miner suffering from black lung, proved to be no match for the complex problems and forces swirling about the UMW, and he was defeated for the presidency by Sam Church in 1979. Church in turn was defeated in 1982 by Richard Trumka, a young lawyer close to the Yablonski brothers, sons of the murdered Jock Yablonski. Meanwhile, the union's beleaguered position continued, despite increasing stability under Trumka's leadership.

Looking at the economic history in Appalachia after World War II, at least five different periods stand out: 1) a "postwar boom" from 1945 to about 1950; 2) the frustrating 1950s; 3) the rise and fall of the War on Poverty from 1960 to 1968; 4) the hopeful decade from 1968 to 1978; and 5) a troublesome period since 1978.

The so-called "postwar boom" has been much overemphasized. In Appalachia, although times were relatively good, there was not much of a boom. Many veterans from World War II returned to their region, some to work in the coal industry or to set up their own businesses. In those days, one could still go into the coal business with a relatively small capital investment, and many of Appalachia's sons did just that. Others took advantage of the G.I. Bill of Rights and went back to school, returning to the region as teachers, lawyers, doctors, or politicians. The group of young leaders was a remarkable one and included Harry LaViers Jr. in coal, lawyer–author Harry Caudill, businessman William B. Sturgill, and Congressman Carl D. Perkins, all from eastern Kentucky.

The 1950s were a frustrating decade in the region. The coal boom faded as technology began ruthlessly invading the mine fields. And John L. Lewis's UMW made little or no effort to minimize the effects of the assault of technology upon the jobs of its members. These were heady days for the Mine Workers' Health and Welfare Fund, and the union built a string of hospitals across the coal areas, which dramatically demonstrated the union's power. But increasingly these hospitals became the privileged possession of those miners fortunate enough to keep their jobs, as more and more miners were laid off because of mechanization. Well over 50 percent of the miners of 1950 had lost their jobs by mid-decade, and the newly unemployed miners even found themselves cut off from their hospitals and the Welfare Fund. There was no one in those years to help those caught in this human tragedy—not the union, nor the owners, not even government. It was the miner and his family who had to bear the burden.

Many Appalachians solved their economic problem by migrating. Hundreds of thousands did. The Appalachian "Great Migration" to the cities of the upper Midwest was already in process by 1950. The flow northward continued, and until the "Depression of 1957," at which time the Detroit area suffered a significant economic setback, there was always a job if a mountaineer simply left his hills and struck out across the Ohio River. After 1957, the least-educated and older migrants often could not find work. Yet through the 1960s the flood continued. In all, over three million Appalachians left the region in the period from 1940 to 1970.

Despite the presence of many centers of dramatic economic development within the region—such centers as the Redstone Arsenal complex at Huntsville, Alabama; Oak Ridge, Tennessee, and its atomic research facilities; and the very real excitement surrounding Knoxville during its World's Fair of 1982—large portions of Appalachia remained depressed and by any statistical standard were poor areas. During the years since government statistics have been kept, large sections within the region continued to be characterized by negative indicators—low income per capita, low housing standards, high unemployment, and high illiteracy.

Some War on Poverty programs during the 1960s proved at least partly successful. But the two basic developmental strategies of the War on Poverty—the culture of poverty model and the economic development model—were tried for such a brief period and were subject to such large political stresses, that their long-run effect is hard to gauge. However, most social scientists concerned with the region agree that the characteristic of blaming the victim, a quality inherent especially in the culture of poverty model, which led the efforts of the Office of Economic Opportunity, was a most serious difficulty in that theory.

THE GREAT MIGRATION

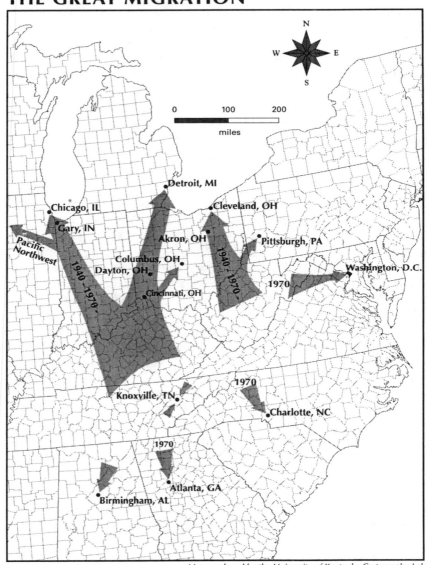

Map produced by the University of Kentucky Cartography Lab

The culture of poverty model had inspired many programs during the War on Poverty, but these programs did not leave an obvious institutional impact upon the region. Although some of these programs were continued (for example, Head Start and various vocational training programs), they were continued by other governmental agencies when the Office of Economic Opportunity was dismantled. However, many individuals had benefited from these programs. Thousands of the region's people were given schooling and training that enabled them as individuals to escape poverty and move into more comfortable lives.

The other major strategy for regional uplift tried aggressively during the War on Poverty years was that suggested by the regional economic developers. Based on theories emphasizing capital investment in infrastructures that would prepare an area for economic "take off," the Appalachian Regional Commission was established on such principles in 1965. The ARC was designed to give help to the region by providing the necessary prerequisites for development—roads, health facilities, vocational training buildings; "infrastructures." Capital investment, it was believed, would follow proper educational, transportation, and health facilities once they were in place. Three hundred ninety-seven counties in thirteen states, North and South, were designated as "Appalachia," within which federal monies on an eighty to twenty basis would match state supporting funds to provide infrastructures, mostly roads. The Appalachian Regional Commission, however, was wise enough to recognize the diversity within the region and set up first four, then three sub-regions as different "Appalachias." Furthermore, specific "growth centers" were identified to be the places where development would be particularly encouraged, and provision was made for Area Development Districts (ADDs) to be established, ensuring local initiatives in establishing programs. Development did occur within these growth centers, but usually these were already the most favored areas where development might have occurred anyhow. Despite the statistics that the ARC developed to show the effects of its programs, the overall success of this developmental model remains unclear.

A major flaw in the economic development strategy followed by the Appalachian Regional Commission was the specific exclusion in the ARC Act itself of any consideration of rearranging any parts of regional energy policy and the way the coal industry operated within the region. Harry Caudill, Gordon Ebersole, and others suggested in the early 1960s the development of Public Utility Districts (PUDs) built on the TVA model, which would buy up mineral properties with public monies and generate electricity for sale, with the benefits going for regional development. But this strategy was deemed "socialistic" and was never tried, despite the precedent in the TVA and Public Utility Districts in the Pacific Northwest. Apparently, the deal struck with the coal industry to get the Appalachian Regional Commission established in 1965 involved leaving coal out of any possible governmental strategy for Appalachian development.

During the decade following the effective end of the War on Poverty, from 1968 to 1978, the region's general economic mood remained hopeful. It was a time of some optimism in the region. The Appalachian Regional Commission, which survived the end of the War on Poverty, had developed its strategy for regional growth by the 1970s. Various growth centers were identified and real growth took place in many areas throughout the decade. The ARC-induced developments during the 1970s that appeared especially hopeful were various highway-corridor developments, such as the corridor across western Maryland and westward across West Virginia to Ohio, connecting Hancock, Cumberland, Morgantown, and Huntington. Another impressive project was the massive cut through Peach Orchard Mountain, which moved thirteen million yards of earth and changed the course of the Big Sandy River in order to give the city of Pikeville, Kentucky, 150 flat acres of developmental lands where the old riverbed had been located. Various developmental projects focused on growing areas such as Spartanburg and Greenville in South Carolina, Cookeville and Putnam County, Tennessee, and Beckley and Fairmont in West Virginia. By the late 1970s, the ARC claimed that the economic health of the region had turned around and that a "New Appalachia" had arrived. Though it was admitted that the development in the region was not as rapid as most other places in the United States, the ARC claimed by 1979 to have reduced poverty to 14 percent of the population and to have helped create 1.35 million jobs in the region.

A 1974 ARC study further claimed that a closer look at migration patterns from the region showed a more complex picture than the south-to-north migration across the Ohio River that had been characteristic of the 1950s and 1960s. The overall out-migration from the 13–state, 397–county area designated as "Appalachia" by the ARC showed that the major cities to which rural Appalachians were then migrating were Atlanta and Washington, D.C. Furthermore, several cities within the region were then attracting migrants from rural areas in Appalachia in substantial numbers—such cities as Birmingham and Huntsville in Alabama; Knoxville and Chattanooga in Tennessee; Charleston, West Virginia; and Pittsburgh.

The oil crisis of 1973 seemed to throw the nation into a renewed dependence upon coal. President Nixon's hope for energy independence looked to the region's coal, using new methods of utilizing this coal in gasified and liquefied form. The region's large reserves of oil shale were also explored enthusiastically. Besides increasing demand for the region's coal itself, which raised the demand for some labor by opening new mines, the hope for coal-based synthetic fuels further raised the outlook for coal.

But the boom of the early 1970s was as mild as the boom of 1945–1948 had been. Better times changed little fundamentally. In fact, perhaps the major impact of these years was the emergence of the multinational energy conglomerates already mentioned. What Occidental Petroleum, Ashland Oil, Diamond Shamrock, Continental Oil, and Standard Oil of Ohio were seeking was a larger array of options for fossil fuels to place alongside their massive and unstable dependence upon Middle Eastern oil. By the 1980s, the oil crisis had turned into what industry spokesmen claimed was an oil glut, and the schemes for gasification and liquefaction of coal were forgotten.

By 1978, it was apparent that the region was again a most troubled area economically. With the energy crisis cooled and the nation turning away from coal and coal-based research to the more economical sources of power (i.e., oil from the volatile Middle East), coal production dropped and employment plummeted. Many Appalachian counties came to suffer from over 50 percent unemployment. When the "environmental crusade" cooled, the low-sulphur coals of Appalachia increasingly lost out in the battle for utility market to the cheaper, western lignite coals with high sulphur content. In the Reagan years of market-determined policies, the region's coal future looked increasingly bleak.

Ronald Reagan's old-fashioned faith in the effectiveness of laissez-faire economics, despite the region's tragic experience with market economics, would seem to have made his notions unpopular in such a poor area as Appalachia. Furthermore, Reagan's tax policies lowered taxes for high-income Americans while lowering government services for the poor of the region. And his pro-oil and pro-western coal policies placed Appalachia's fossil fuels at a considerable disadvantage. Besides, Reagan's farm policies, especially in tobacco, placed the region's farmers in a very difficult position. Yet for all this, Reagan as president remained one of the most popular political figures ever in Appalachia.

The regional picture in Appalachia since the 1980s has been generally gloomy. The unemployment rate in the region stands consistently at 10 to 12 percent, substantially above the national rate of 2 percent to 7 percent; and some areas within the region have an unemployment rate of over 20 percent, with the real unemployment rate substantially higher than that. The industrial outlook for the coal industry is bleak. Agriculture, especially tobacco, is in poor condition. The regional outlook for merchandising and services is somewhat better, but in Appalachia, times have consistently been hard.

The time is ripe for some fresh thinking on how the region might develop most meaningfully. The various missionary approaches to development, whether from the point of view of religious or business sectarians, have proven not very useful. From such a perspective, Appalachia is seen as an area to be "saved." The area is viewed to be in need of some sort of uplift, overcoming its problems by introducing something that the missionary deems the region needs.

The developmental approach favored by most economists seems to betray this missionary paternalism. To most developers, Appalachia is seen as an area that needs to be changed and brought into the industrialized world. Such developers seek to move Appalachia from its underdevelopment, with inadequate infrastructures and attitudes, into a new situation that will allow the region to take off into an affluent future.

A promising modification to the traditional developmental theories of the economists is suggested by President Clinton's appointment of Jesse White as Federal Co-chair of the Appalachian Regional Commission. To the traditional economic development focus on building infrastructures, Dr. White wants first to build upon the capacities of the region's own people, and then to build vibrant communities and "a strong internally developed entrepreneurial leadership." White is particularly critical of what he terms the "Buffalo Hunt"—the strategy of states and regions that attempt to bring industry in through tax incentives and bounties. White's emphasis on "growing one's own entrepreneurial leadership" seems to fit with the recent initiatives of the University of Kentucky's Appalachian Center and Berea College's Brushy Fork Institute. A most interesting effort has been made by these institutions to identify local leaders and have them explore the needs of their own communities in order to see what projects seem most useful to the local people themselves.

A 1990s concept stemming from the widely read *Our Common Future*—the so-called "Brundstadt Report"—is sustainable development. The concept of sustainable development seems to have sprung in part from the 1992 United Nations Rio Conference on Environment. However, thus far the attempts to define this model are not very precisely drawn. But clearly here is a concept that attempts to "meet the needs of the present without compromising the prosperity of future generations." Thus economic development is tamed by ecological concerns. Many impressed with this approach wish to add community participation and grassroots, democratic decision making as well.

Regional historian Paul Salstrom, in a recent book, *Appalachia's Path to Dependency*, presents a serious search for a region-specific developmental theory, based on a serious reading of certain Third World economists, such as Paul Prebish and W. Arthur Lewis, who together emphasize the need of a strong agricultural base for any area if it is to develop. Salstrom concludes that Appalachia's major alternative to the past's "mistaken developmental strategies and continued dependency," is to foster non-monetized sectors in the regional economy, "so that fewer dollars will suffice to carry on economic exchanges" within the nation and the region. Perhaps, indeed, we need to look to entirely new developmental models that seem to be particularly useful to a region such as Appalachia.

An interesting and apparently successful approach toward integrating community development with community decision making within the Appalachian region had hardly any strictly economic impact at all. The so-called "Ivanhoe Project," which Helen Lewis coordinated, focused on a small southwest Virginia community that had lost nearly all of its industry. During the course of this project, the community discovered its history and found pride in itself. In what amounted to a massive self-study, this community became aware of its uniqueness and produced a large book that won several prizes. Ivanhoe became a much more conscious community in the process, though incomes were not appreciably changed.

Despite the obvious productive successes of modern American corporate capitalism, this system has not worked well for all people and all regions, even within the United States. Our modern corporate system may tolerate too much greed, injustice, and corruption. Therefore, anyone concerned with economic justice rightfully will see a need for significant moderation of this model. It certainly seems appropriate to evaluate seriously the larger, national corporate system when we look at the economic condition of a still poor region within a rich and powerful United States. In fact, the wealth and power of the nation in large measure has been built upon the energy resources of this same poor and relatively powerless region.

Too often the story of corporate actions in Appalachia follow the lines of the Buffalo Creek disaster in West Virginia in February 1972, which produced a major human tragedy with the loss of hundreds of lives because of the careless administration of a gob pile dam, which wiped out a whole valley. More specifically related to ecological disasters were the generations-long operation of the Champion Paper and Fiber Company, which polluted the Pigeon River and fouled the atmosphere west of Asheville, North Carolina. And the Aluminum Company of America all but destroyed Jackson Creek. Even the TVA had its disastrous and expensive foray into nuclear energy, which resulted in a dangerous contamination of large areas in Tennessee.

A particularly telling experience with a major American corporation in the region can summarize the recent Appalachian dilemma concerning greed, modernization, technology, and the lack of corporate concern. The experience involves a corporation born in Appalachia and organized as the Union Carbide Corporation in New York City in 1917.

A Union Carbide subsidiary contracted for the building of the Hawk's Nest Diversion Project for creating electricity on the New–Kanawha River and pushed it through to a rapid completion in December 1931. A three-and-one-half-mile tunnel was driven through Gauley Mountain, and in the process, almost pure silicon sandstone was excavated for most of the distance. The purity of the silicon proved a great economic boon to the Corporation and to West Virginia's rising glass industry. But extracting it caused one of America's major industrial health disasters. Literally hundreds of workers, mostly unknown blacks, were infected with acute silicosis. The total number of persons dying from this disaster of the workplace came to well over one thousand.

More damning than the tragedy itself was Union Carbide's ongoing cover-up of this incident, one of America's principal public health disasters. Union Carbide succeeded in keeping the story out of the press and out of national awareness until Dr. Martin Cherniack told the story in a book published in 1986, over a half-century after the tragedy.

Less than one hundred miles downriver from the Hawk's Nest

lies Institute, West Virginia, the home of West Virginia State University. Here Union Carbide operated a fertilizer plant. The Institute plant was built on the same model as Union Carbide's plant in Bophal, India, where in 1985 the worst accident in the capitalist world occurred and over two thousand people died. At the time of the Bophal tragedy, the Institute plant had a similar malfunction, though no fatalities resulted.

Union Carbide's history of indifference appears to be legend. Is it no accident that its beginnings were in Appalachia? Certainly it is no accident that much of recent Appalachian social science research has developed along radical lines. One cannot study the Appalachian economic story without developing an abiding anger about how events have dealt with the region. It is a region of great and crucial wealth, yet the people of the area have remained, on the whole, poor. The approach of the rich and prosperous America toward a poor Appalachia has, indeed as some have insisted, often resembled that of a colonialist toward a colony, or of a corporate exploiter toward a region that has been kept powerless.

The term "the New Appalachia" has been used by Appalachian Regional Commission staff for some time as they toured about the region on the new developmental highways, stopped at the motels that had developed along this highway network, and shopped at the new regional malls scattered at strategic points along these same highways. To them, this "New Appalachia" seemed little different from the development in the rest of the United States, with its K-Marts, Kroger's, McDonald's and Kentucky Fried Chicken franchises—the last, by the way, a franchise that was begun in Corbin, Kentucky, but remained "isolated" until Louisville developers made the most of its franchising, selling out ultimately to Pepsi-Cola. This "New Appalachia" is indeed becoming essentially like the rest of the nation, except, of course, it is dependent on those it franchises from.

The ARC staff, mostly graduates from America's best eastern colleges, can be forgiven for this self-congratulatory image, since they have been driven by the well-established notion of a New South, which was to be built in the image of the great dominating corporations of the northeast. When the railroads were first driven through these mountains, the institutions of the nation's Victorian market economy then came into the region with the same self-congratulatory messages of hope for our betterment. The region, it seems, has always been renewing itself with outside guidance. Yet the traditions of the area have persisted despite the dynamic of the nation's corporate economy. Even when Wal-Mart comes to an Appalachian hometown, elements of the traditional ways seem to persist.

In the "New Appalachia," too, substantial areas of wilderness remain, substantial enough to attract the filming of Appalachian forests that moviegoers would even see as a pristine eighteenth-century area. Appalachian wilderness areas, however, were not nearly as vast as the West's Rockies or the still largely unspoiled Alaskan wilderness. But the dense undergrowth of Appalachia's forests in areas from northern Pennsylvania to northern Alabama is a convincing wilderness to most. This was especially true of the rugged mountains of western North Carolina.

Since the 1930s, the Appalachian forest has reclaimed many farms begun by numerous yeomen. Their decaying homesteads can still be found throughout the Appalachian forest. But the main encouragement of the Appalachian forest has come from the growth of the national forests. Unlike national forests in the West, the national forests of Appalachia have had to be purchased from private owners. Furthermore, many property owners now have allowed the natural forest growth to return, forgetting any effort to farm the land.

Yet withal, by the 1990s, the Appalachian forest had become a threatened wilderness. Climatic, demographic, and developmental threats have descended even upon its most remote areas. Acid rain and a carbon dioxide-laden atmosphere has killed some forests; and even campers, hikers, birders, kayakers, whitewater rafters, climbers, and fishermen have come to Appalachia's wilderness areas in such numbers that the forests are threatened. The Appalachian wilderness by century's end, in fact, is badly in need of a realistic and sympathetic strategy for a sustainable wilderness.

The Appalachian Mind

TO ATTEMPT TO IDENTIFY any "Appalachian Mind" is disarmingly difficult. Yet as early as the mid-1920s, Baltimore's famous journalist H.L. Mencken, following the lead of "an amiable newspaperwoman of Chattanooga," attempted just that. He was led into an East Tennessee valley, which was, he said, "a place where the old-time religion was genuinely on tap." Mencken found a people who followed their preachers blindly into the world of "the last Day of Judgment." In this place, the reading of books was a source of danger. "Why read a book? If what was in it was true, then everything in it was already in the Bible. If it is false, then reading it would imperil the soul." To Mencken, Appalachia—indeed the whole of the South—was full of boobs and zealots.

Mencken's rhetorical and one-sided evaluation is obviously simplistic and biased. In fact, to attempt any description of the collective "mind" of a complex region is a perilous task. The Appalachian region has such a diversity that any generalizations must be in some ways misleading. What may be said of the thought of a Shenandoah Valley town or Asheville, North Carolina, has little relevance to an eastern Kentucky hollow or to rural Rhea County, Tennessee. Some may suggest that the Appalachian Mind is not even a proper focus for our concern. An Appalachian ideology might prove less elusive. But an Appalachian ideology is not unified either. Some romantically inclined observers, for example, believe that Appalachia has become a kind of embodiment of the best of traditional America and has even become the keeper of the nation's historic individualism, its self-sufficiency, and self-sacrifice. Equally ideological are those concerned for the region's or the nation's future, who see Appalachia as representing everything that is negative about America—the nation's gun-toting violence, its poverty, the exploitation of the environment, its welfare-dependency, its superstition, and its racism.

Several observers, anthropologist Alean Batteau and historian Henry Shapiro principal among them, contend that Appalachia is really but an invention of mainstream American intellectuals who have made of Appalachia an entity that they believe their perceived American society needs. A kind of "Appalachian poetic" has been created, Batteau believes, that takes from the mountain environment those aspects of the notion of "Appalachia" that the "inventor" perceives the nation needs—its dulcimers, log cabins, religious commitment, picturesque speech, even its family feuds and lack of formal education. Thus the region is presented in such a way that outside readers will see the necessity for national reform. Other recent critics of modern America have used Appalachia to present what they perceive to be the worst of America's negative traits. But all, say Batteau and Shapiro, have used the "invented" Appalachia for their own purposes.

Cultural critic David Whisnant claims that the Appalachian values most people have come to accept as authentic have actually been established by certain outside arbiters of taste who have selectively presented Appalachian music, crafts, and culture. As he traces this cultural imperialism, Whisnant believes that an Appalachian aesthetic has been created to fit with certain perceived value that these arbiters of taste desire. Many who have presented Appalachia to the larger world, he claims, have been aesthetically and historically lying for various reasons in order to improve some perceived artistic or political merit.

Surely any attempt to unravel the Appalachian Mind is elusive, and any effort to present this Appalachian Mind probably will be somewhat arbitrary. Clearly the Appalachian people have sung in a richly textured polyphonic chorus. And as we listen, we hear with our own ears. And those who listen have been subject to their own ear training. As a historian born outside the region, I have often had trouble catching the right songs and rhythms. But I have been an interested listener for nearly fifty years.

A recent effort to help us find direction when contemplating the Appalachian Mind is the "collection of first-person writings by Mountaineers," most of whom had responded to the question, "How did you come to discover your Appalachian heritage?" Educator and native Billy Best has compiled fifty such essays, forty of them written specifically for his book, *One Hundred Years of Appalachian Vision,*

1897–1996. In this compilation, the largest number (twelve) believed that the basis for their Appalachian heritage lay in the sense of rurality as they recalled their regional background. English Professor Robert J. Higgs, in a direct reaction to Mencken's deprecating rhetoric, noted that he was clearly a different kind of Southerner and American. As he said, he was "country folk."

The next largest group in Best's compilation (nine) were those who found their mountain heritage in kin. And the third largest group were those shocked and significantly radicalized and committed to the region as they came to realize what had happened to the region and its people.

Another significant group of Best's respondents were led into important writing careers by reacting to teachers and others who made fun of their accents and use of language. A like number of respondents recognized the power of country music and of specific performers in their discovery of Appalachia. Gurney Norman, for example, reported an overwhelming "Damascus Road experience" when he found Roscoe Holcomb's album, "Mountain Music of Kentucky," in a Palo Alto, California, store while he was attending Stanford University.

Some of the most important sounds that reveal the Appalachian Mind must be found in the literature of the region. Until the 1930s, the Appalachian American was usually presented by writers not from the region—mainly the Local Color writers of the late nineteenth and early twentieth centuries, such as Mary Noalles Murfree, John Fox Jr., and Lucy Furman. And the missionaries to the region also told us about the people of the area—William G. Frost, John C. Campbell, James Watt Raine, Willis D. Weatherford, and others. In these years before 1930, "inside voices" were largely lacking except for Emma Bell Miles, a daughter of a local schoolman, who as a young woman had taken art training in St. Louis, but then returned to Walden Ridge, Tennessee, to marry a local man and live a "typical" mountain life. Her *Spirit of the Mountains,* published in 1905, gives a remarkably insightful, but clearly sympathetic, presentation of mountain life. Mrs. Miles saw Appalachians as sensitive, sincere, and without pretension. Though poor, she saw traditional, rural mountain people as survivors in a world increasingly given to materialism and the pursuit of power.

The region did not develop its own clear and strong literary voice until the 1930s, with the appearance of three writers who had graduated from Lincoln Memorial University and gone on for graduate training at Vanderbilt. James Still, Jesse Stuart, and Don West were all sons of the region, yet their voices were very different. Jesse Stuart's muscular, confident, and energetic stories contrasted sharply with Still's sensitive and careful presentation of the clash of the modern life with the traditional yeomanesque culture, with all its foibles and limited exposure to the world. Don West's angry criticism and appeal for radical change dramatically contrasted with the other two.

The clues into the nature of the Appalachian people left by Appalachian regional writers since World War II have been even more varied than the initial voices of Stuart, Still, and West. Wilma Dykeman, for example, gives us strong Appalachian women steadfast in their devotion to the traditional values of family and place, despite the incursion of the modern materialistic world. John Ehle has pursued this same "traditional vs. modern" theme in ways remarkably diverse across a wide spectrum of Appalachian history, from the time of settlement to the early twentieth century.

James Agee and Thomas Wolfe, both sons of Appalachia, but who usually are not considered as Appalachian writers because they made distinguishing literary careers outside the region, have also explored this same tension between traditional rural mountain life and modern forces. Harriette Simpson Arnow has written what is probably the region's epic novel, *The Dollmaker*, which focuses on this same conflict between traditional rural life and modern industrial urbanism. Arnow concludes her epic tragically as modern urban materialism overcomes the yeomanesque and individual creativity of her heroine.

Appalachian literature also reflects a great deal of anger about the pressures that modern corporate capitalism has put upon the Appalachian people. Though writers such as Lee Smith, Mary Lee Settle, and George Ella Lyon, usually show some hopeful way for their characters to work through their stresses, other writers such as Denise Giardina, Breece Pancake, and a host of Appalachian poets— especially the so-called "Soup Bean Poets": Bob Henry Baber, P.J. Laska, Bob Snyder, and others—see Appalachian people tragically overcome by modern pressures and the greed of corporate capitalism.

But these angry sons and daughters of Don West are not the only voices raised by regional poets and short story writers. Jim Wayne Miller, for example, sees himself in continual and creative dialogue with the voices of his tradition, even seeing the help that religion can give to "Briars" as they migrate into the "world beyond the Ohio."

And Gurney Norman, through humor and a "return to the land," sees a way to deal creatively with the stress encountered by those raised in the mountains as they confront modern forces, be they merely behind the "Winchester Curtain" or in faraway California.

Clearly the literary voices of the region are varied, but all have dealt somehow with the conflicts inherent between traditional Appalachian life and modern American culture. The major differences seem to be in the variety of ways that Appalachian writers work out the results of these tensions. Many regional writers can see no way around accommodating to the mainline, corporate culture. Others believe that the resources of family, place, humor, and religious faith provide sufficient resources to allow an Appalachian person to survive and live creatively. Still others believe that radical change in corporate culture is necessary before the Appalachian people should be content. Breece Pancake's suicide was perhaps the most dramatic negative concerning the Appalachian's ability to survive amidst the pressures of modern life.

As we examine regional arts, a key characteristic of the region's artistic mind is that the "lowbrow" folk arts predominate over the "highbrow" fine arts. In urban society the highbrow is clearly given primary status, but in Appalachia the lowbrow is seen as less pretentious and is widely respected. And it appears always to have been thus. In fact, many modern scholarly analysts of folk culture insist that the folk artist when he or she creates has in mind remarkably mature contextual insights, though skeptics sometimes are suspicious of the level of sophistication that folklorists claim to see. But it is certainly true that "democratic" folk arts are remarkably active in the region, and the creations of Appalachian folk artists command a remarkable respect among urban, mainline Americans.

Important "highbrow" artistic groups do exist in Appalachia, such as the Oak Ridge Ballet, the Knoxville Symphony, and the Barter Theater of Virginia. Indeed, Bach's sacred music was sung in Moravian and Lutheran churches in the Shenandoah and North Carolina at least as early at 1800. And many excellent pipe organs now dot the region, some in rural areas. Today you can travel throughout the mountains of West Virginia and not lose the sound of classical music broadcast by West Virginia public radio. But in a region largely "lowbrow," the more typical Appalachian radio voices are country music stations and revivalistic preachers.

As authentic as any of the folk-art voices are those of the chair maker, Chester Cornett; the dulcimer maker, Homer Ledford; and the folk philosopher, Ray Hicks. Of these, Cornett and Ledford are disarmingly shy and self-deprecating, and both are people who use humor to make their most telling points. Cornett, for example, when asked about Appalachia by a visiting journalist, confessed that he had heard of the term but didn't know what it meant. And Homer Ledford is a ham actor of the first order, who regularly entertains in a variety of performing styles, including playing his fiddle behind his head. Yet everyone knows that his real skill is making musical instruments.

Regional philosopher and storyteller Ray Hicks is known to his admirers largely through an Appleshop film "Fixin' to Tell About Jack," where he is at pains to explain the Appalachian people's will to survive. The seed of life itself is the thing that persists, he says. "The galax that I pulled last year is the same galax that's right here in my hand." And Hicks's devotion to the "Jack Tale" emphasizes a mountain hero whose cleverness and matter-of-fact wisdom overcomes all obstacles and enables him to get the better of kings, noblemen, and criminals. The clue to the Appalachian Mind suggested by such folk artists as Cornett, Ledford, and Hicks, is that Appalachian beauty is functional, unpresumptuous, and is related directly to the needs of life. The arts, crafts, philosophy, and humor actually help pull one through life's hard spots.

The oral history tradition represented by North Georgia's *Foxfire* group has given us "Aunt Arie" Carpenter and reveals another corner of the Appalachian Mind. The genuinely humane and unassuming image of Aunt Arie, with her determined opposition to modernity, even made it to Broadway and a movie. Here Jessica Tandy portrayed Annie Nation, the quintessence of a secure mountain personality, who was able to survive the pressures of disappointment, the hard life of the mountains, and the disappointments of family members who succumbed to the temptations of modern life.

Yet any consideration of the Appalachian Mind must also consider that narrow slice of the Appalachian folk mind that seems to be the most remarkable to mainline Americans, and one that even modern photographers such as Shelby Lee Adams feel the need to portray. The folk that Adams's photographs portray are poor materially, are often in bad health, and find solace either in esoteric varieties of the millennial religion or feel compelled to show their rebellion from the dominant culture by purposeful "outrageous behavior." Such folk do exist in Appalachia, and many of the usual stereotypes of hillbillies seem to fit them fairly well. They tend to be anti-intellectual, usually having completed no more schooling than necessary, and their behavior is often characterized by a lack of control. Shelby Lee Adams is quite right to insist that such people do indeed exist. But the danger of such books as Adams's *Appalachian Portraits*, which is a collection of haunting photographs depicting poverty, lack of health, and snake handling, is that those unfamiliar with the region will conclude that this narrow slice of regional life is typical.

Actually the region, as the nation as a whole, has created its share of bizarre and troubled persons. Perhaps the best known such personalities from the region have been Charles Manson and Larry Flynt. Manson's alienation from modern life led him to develop a California cult community that turned vicious, even to the murder of movie star Sharon Tate. Flynt's ambitions led him to founding *Hustler* magazine, and his famous encounter with the Reverend Jerry Falwell. More recently has come the destructive cult of satanic worship in Floyd County, Kentucky, with a teenage leader who believes herself a major anti-Christ sent to lead the youth of America into an Armageddon that will take over the world for evil.

The presentation of Appalachia in the national media reflects a long-standing fascination with the "peculiar people" from the more remote areas of the region. A stereotypically mean and ignorant mountaineer has persisted from the time of William Byrd II in 1728, when he critically described the backwoods people as "Lubbers," to the popularity of the Local Color writers—principally Mary Noalles Murfree and John Fox Jr.—and to the fascination with mountain persons in the comic strips, such as "Lil' Abner" and "Snuffy Smith," or the movies from "Ma and Pa Kettle" (1949–1956 series) to "Deliverance" (1972), and finally even to Robert Schenkkan's Pulitzer Prize-winning *The Kentucky Cycle* (1992).. This stereotypical Appalachian was a person of remarkable laziness, ignorance, and violence. And the national media seems to persist in presenting this clichéd person, which regional scholars have plainly shown to be untypical of most people in the region.

Yet the violent, moonshining, ill-educated, uncouth "bubba" of Appalachian stereotype is not the only stereotypical image that persists. The media is also frequently fascinated by a romantic image of the Appalachian as the keeper of the nation's most precious traditions, as seen in Earl Hamner's television series "The Waltons." Though this romantic theme is also present in some Appalachian "scholarship," this more favorable stereotype is not nearly as frequent in the nation's mass media as the offensive images of Appalachians seen in "Hee Haw" (comic and lazy), "The Dukes of Hazzard" (violence and good-old-boy corruption) and "The Beverly Hillbillies" (innocence in Babylon).

In recent years, the region itself has developed its own media. The first effective regional magazine was the missionary-founded *Mountain Life and Work* begun in 1925. Of course, local weekly newspapers proliferated for a century and more, but most of the region's newspapers have presented a local, middle-class boosterism that attempts to imitate mainstream market developments and to minimize regional differences. Jim Comstock's *West Virginia Hillbilly*, however, had a broader flavor and developed a strong following soon after World War II. Comstock actively celebrated regional uniqueness and wisdom. But the journals and crusading local newspapers that emerged in the 1960s and 1970s—*Appalachian Heritage, Appalachian Journal,* the *Whitesburg Mountain Eagle, The Troublesome Creek Times*—and even the movie-producing Appleshop, have given Appalachia an able media of its own.

The image that appears in this regional media tends to be an angry one (as the Whitesburg *Eagle,* which screams), as it presents a picture of an exploited region. Yet the Appalachian Mind in such regional media is also varied. The anger about how the region has fared is still widely shared in such media, but the method of dealing with Appalachian misfortune varies widely, from seeking rather mild educational and developmental programs, to rather pessimistic projections about what to expect from corporate, exploitive American capitalism.

A major contemporary spokesman for the region, Loyal Jones, has insisted that Appalachian religion "is the key that unlocks mountain culture" and the way that mountain people think. In a region where religion is still taken seriously by the majority of its people, a careful look at Appalachian religion should provide many crucial clues into the way Appalachian people think.

Not surprisingly, the region's churches also reveal a complex picture. There are many mainline, even liberal, churches in the area, with local Presbyterian ministers and Episcopal priests preaching an active Social Gospel to their coal-company parishioners. Strong moral pressure has been brought on those church members who are part of the region's elite, and this moral position is reinforced by cooperative liberal Christian missionary efforts through the Committee on Religion in Appalachia (CORA) and the Appalachian Ministries Educational and Resource Center (AMERC). Yet for the most part, these region-wide ecumenical efforts represent largely modern, mainline-supported mission efforts directed toward an area perceived as exploited.

Most recent scholars of Appalachian religion, however, have focused on the numerous non-mainline churches covering the region. Early scholars of Appalachian religion had been mostly liberal, seminary-trained observers who found most of the churches in the mountains quite unlike the churches they knew. But recent observers, such as Loyal Jones, John Wallhausser, Melanie Sovine, Howard Dorgan, Jeff Titon, and Deborah McCauley, have studied particularly those denominations that are unique to the region.

The recent monumental study *Appalachian Mountain Religion: A History*, by Deborah McCauley, paints a picture of the religious culture of the Appalachian mountain people as quite separate from the mainline religious cultures of Christian America. Along with Jones and Sovine before her, McCauley sees Appalachian religious culture as based upon the "Old Baptist" and camp meeting traditions of the eighteenth and early nineteenth centuries. This is a religious tradition of independent congregations rather than denominational structures, of enthusiastic preaching by informally educated clergy, and a careful but literal reading of the Bible. McCauley sees the missionary efforts of mainline denominations as essentially belittling and destructive of what she deems this admirable mountain religious culture.

One of the Appalachian characteristics agreed upon by most of the early liberal observers of the region was to describe traditional rural Appalachians as "fundamentalist." It is true that in traditional Appalachian religion, the Bible is read literally, thus in this sense "fundamentalist." But as the history of Protestantism shows, the Bible is a complex collection of ancient literature that can be interpreted in a wide variety of ways. This complexity is demonstrated by the more than two hundred different religious denominations in the region.

Like the major nineteenth-century American Protestant churches, most of the Appalachian denominations are products of revivals. Indeed, the revivalism that spawned the Baptist and Methodist growth of the early nineteenth century has continued to produce ever-new manifestations of religious faith in Appalachia, as evidenced by the many varieties of Baptists in the region and the growth and proliferation of Pentecostal churches.

However, Loyal Jones claims that Appalachian people are "closer to Calvinism than any other people." The Calvinistic assertion that human beings are cursed by original sin, he says, enables the Appalachian Calvinist not to be astounded at the human capacity for evil, thus giving him the means to overcome adversity that comes his way. Indeed, the stoic way mountain people take tragedies such as mining accidents and natural disasters led many earlier observers to contend that fatalism was a basic regional characteristic. Several conservative Calvinistic churches do have substantial strength in Appalachia, such as the Old Regular Baptists. Yet the traditional Calvinistic churches are not the churches in the region that have enjoyed the largest growth in recent years. The fastest-growing denominations in Appalachia, as in the nation as a whole, have been the Pentecostal churches.

As a matter of fact, American Pentecostalism is in part rooted in Appalachia. One of the major sources of American Pentecostalism was found in the revivals in the 1890s that resulted in the Church of God of Cleveland, Tennessee. Pentecostalism stems from the very non-Calvinist theology of John Wesley, who believed that Christian perfection was possible for any believer through his/her responses to religious experience. These religious experiences (revivals) could be repeated again and again and could lead the believer toward "sanctification." Sanctification is based on the non-Calvinistic assumption that individual initiative can lead the believer toward salvation and even perfection. This belief has spawned such denominations as Holiness churches, a variety of Churches and Assemblies of God, and other tongue-speaking churches. A certain dramatic but small minority of Pentecostal churches have indeed been led into snake handling and the taking of poison through a literal reading of Mark 16:17–18.

The snake-handling phenomenon within American Pentecostalism originated in Appalachia with a man named George Hensley, of Grasshopper Valley near Chattanooga. Believing that if one were properly prepared, a saved soul could "take up serpents," as Mark 16 notes, the believing snake handler thus takes up serpents to show the strength of his or her belief. There are many Pentecostals, however, who question the propriety of the snake handler's faith. "Thou shalt not tempt the Lord thy God," they say.

The several scholars from outside the rural Appalachian faith tradition who have successfully labored to understand the believers in these "fundamentalist" churches find that only patience and a sincere humility will enable them to enter into and understand the beliefs and practices of these religious people. They accomplish this through a careful listening to their services of worship and their sermons. What Howard Dorgan, Jeff Titon, Deborah McCauley, David Kimbrough, and John Wallhausser seem to show us is that the Appalachian religious mind is quite sophisticated. And their research reveals religious Appalachians with a sincere concern for social justice, despite their reputation of being primarily concerned with individual salvation. Appalachian ministers of such churches have a quite mature recognition of the human dilemma. Whether Calvinist or Wesleyan, the theological beliefs of Appalachia's religious folk are clearly within the bounds of major traditions of Western theological thought. That many moderns choose to denounce Appalachian religion as filled with superstition and infected with "folk belief" is unfortunate.

Champions of reason have pointed out that the Appalachian region has a strong anti-intellectual tradition. There is some legitimacy in this charge, as statistics of regional illiteracy and high truancy rates attest. Yet it is true that the folkish, yeomanesque Appalachian often found little of value in the "book learning" of the school, since what was emphasized at school had relatively little applicability to his real needs. It is also true that a large number of Appalachians still hold to what some refer to as superstitions. Many in the region still "plant by the signs," and a few believe in witches.

Lucy Furman, one of the later Local Color writers, often probed the suspicion of schooling as a part of Appalachian culture as she knew it. She was a teacher at the Hindman Settlement School and had to deal daily with the clash between schoolish and folkish beliefs and about the value of education. Other writers have probed this disagreement as well. The missionary observer John C. Campbell, for example, realized that schooling lifted (or drove) mountaineer students from their culture and ran the risk of making such a student unfit to return to the life he came from.

Nonetheless, the school in Appalachia has been a part of the region's story from the time of first settlement in the mid-eighteenth century. The region's first college, Augusta Academy in Lexington, Virginia—the parent institution of what became Washington and Lee University—was founded in 1749. And as Scotch–Irish settlers moved into East Tennessee, the Presbyterian "log cabin college" system spread with them, with the founding of Greeneville College—later called Tusculum—in 1784, and Blount College in 1794, later to become the University of Tennessee.

Presbyterianism led in the early formation of colleges, but soon the Methodists, Baptists, and the Disciples joined in the formation of institutions of higher learning in the region. By 1850, there were at least twelve denominational colleges in Appalachia. After the Civil War, the national Land Grant College Act located five major state-supported universities within the region—Virginia Polytechnic Institute, Clemson, West Virginia University, West Virginia State, and the University of Tennessee. And the state-supported normal school movement located nineteen other institutions within the region by 1910, institutions that later grew into regional universities. Meanwhile, denominational and private colleges also proliferated throughout the region. Thus there has been a strong college and university presence in the region from a very early date.

On the pre-collegiate level, each state with Appalachian areas developed an increasingly satisfactory system of primary and secondary schools, which by 1900 provided a quite respectable education for students in the towns and the cities of the region. Prior to 1940, some seventeen mostly "outside" Protestant denominations supported about two hundred mission schools located in the predominantly rural places of Appalachia. By World War II, educational opportunities were available to ambitious students in most of Appalachia, and there were then some 100 thousand students going to college within the region. However, the majority of these students studied a curriculum not closely tied to the needs of the area, and most students were not really aware of the region itself. But a few institutions even then saw their mission as particularly related to Appalachia and its problems.

A scholarship focusing on the specific needs, problems, and traditions of Appalachia was slow to develop. The earliest careful scholarship was created predominantly by persons from outside the region who became interested in the area—persons such as William G. Frost, president of Berea College; John C. Campbell, who coordinated the mountain work of the Russell Sage foundation; and the missionary observer, H. Paul Douglass. Elizabeth Hooker's study of the region's religion was funded by northern missionary organizations. The 1935 Department of Agriculture's profile of the region was initiated by a native New Yorker, Professor Helen Dingman of Berea College, and Dean Thomas R. Cooper of the University of Kentucky. But employees of the Department of Agriculture were the ones to actually carry out the studies in this 1935 profile. The "1962 Profile," on the other hand, was initiated by Willis Duke Weatherford of Black Mountain,

North Carolina, with the individual studies prepared predominantly by regional scholars from universities within the region.

Even as the region had found its "inside" literary voice in the 1930s, the area began to find its own scholarly voice soon after World War II. A mature folk-lore, folk-music, and folk-tale scholarship had already arrived much earlier, however, with "inside" and "outside" scholarly collaboration appearing in the early twentieth century in the several folklore journals, as well as widespread collecting.

In the social sciences, James Brown began his pioneering work on the Beech Creek Community in the 1940s. Brown was raised and schooled at Berea, Kentucky, and went to Harvard, where his Ph.D. dissertation began his epic, multigenerational study of several rural families from a single community. Cratis D. Williams of rural Johnson County, Kentucky, was educated at Cumberland College, the University of Kentucky, and New York University. Williams's monumental dissertation, "The Southern Mountaineer in Fact and Fiction," completed in 1961, remains the classical evaluation of the presentation of Appalachia by mostly Local Color writers who had written on the region up to that time. It was Williams's judgment that the "arrival" of Appalachian literature occurred in the 1930s with the appearance of Stuart, Still, and West.

The community studies by anthropologists and sociologists—studies done in the tradition begun by James Brown—reached a widely recognized maturity fairly early. Such studies as Marion Pearsall's *Little Smoky Ridge*, Elmora Matthews's *Neighbor and Kin*, and John Stephenson's *Shiloh*, were insightful evaluations of mountain life and the dynamics of particular mountain communities. Though these community scholars had significant "outside" connections, all became intimately involved with their communities. Better written was John Fetterman's *Stinking Creek*, a study by a Louisville-based journalist.

Then came Harry M. Caudill's *Night Comes to the Cumberlands* in 1963. This was an immensely influential book that probably was more an example of exposé and muckraking than careful scholarship. Surely it was an angry book, a lawyer's brief against the coal industry, which he believed had exploited eastern Kentucky. It was history, too, and history with feeling. Caudill's book was the first of a series of books that narrated various aspects of the history of the region. Caudill himself later pursued further the dynamics of the growth of corporate power in the region, climaxing with his study of the "Moguls of Eastern Kentucky" in a book titled *Theirs Be the Power.*

Caudill's work inspired many from inside and outside the region to look at the dynamics of regional politics and economic growth. Many studies have concentrated on the dynamics of the coal industry such as John Hevener's *Which Side are You On* (1978); David Corbin's *Life, Work and Rebellion in the Coal Fields* (1981); and John Gaventa's *Power and Powerlessness* (1980). More specifically in the tradition pioneered by Caudill was Ron Eller's *Miners, Millhands and Mountaineers* (1982), which did for the region as a whole what Caudill had done for eastern Kentucky, though with more care. More recently has been the very able work of Mary Beth Pudup, Dwight Billings, Kathleen Blee, Wilma Dunaway, and others who have evaluated the society and the economy of the backwoods areas of Appalachia during the nineteenth century. Their important scholarship has given significant new understanding to the dynamics of the spread of the market economy and coming of coal.

Several very significant contributions have come from non-natives of the region to help sort out the dynamics of nineteenth-century Appalachia. Gordon McKinney's Northwestern University dissertation on Mountain Republicans has become the standard account of the region's political story before the New Deal; and Altina Waller's *Feud*, a tour-de-force in the tradition of the "New Social History," presents an exhaustive look at the Hatfield–McCoy wars, which sees the main story related to late nineteenth-century mineral-hunting. Georgia historian John Inscoe's *Mountain Masters* has inaugurated a whole series of careful and scholarly studies on the pre–Civil War and Civil War period in the mountains.

Most of Appalachian scholarship betrays a strong anger against American corporate capitalism. From the early studies of the region by outside, liberal churchmen such as H. Paul Douglass's *Christian Reconstruction of the South* (1904) and the Quaker Malcolm Ross's *The Machine Age in the Hills* (1930), there developed a critical tradition in history that at times has taken on strong socialist overtones. Principal among the recent revolutionary voices, are sociologist Helen Lewis and political scientist Steve Fisher. Fisher's *Fighting Back in Appalachia* (1993) is a collection of studies of and by radical activists who have challenged the basic economic and political arrangements in the region. Lewis's volume, also an edited compilation, *Colonialism in Modern America, the Appalachian Case*, builds a considerable case for Appalachia to be seen simply as a mineral colony of corporate America. And the recent volume by Wilma A. Dunaway, *The First American Frontier: Transition to Capitalism in Southern Appalachia, 1700–*

1860 (1996), is a massive study by a historical sociologist that traces how the area has become a dependent periphery of the World System of corporate capitalism. The sheer ferocity and magnitude of this radical Appalachian scholarship, including also Sam Howie, Allan Banks, Dwight Billings, Herbert Reid, and others, attests to the kind of tragic picture that Appalachian history presents. There is much to be angry about in Appalachia, as the Soup Bean Poets and the various radical organizations active in the region show.

Another angry voice is that of native David Whisnant, whose two books, *Modernizing the Mountaineer* (1980) and *All That is Native and Fine* (1983), attack missionaries, mission schools, and various organizations that have shoved their own values and tastes upon Appalachians and have maneuvered Appalachians into accepting mainstream cultural values. Whisnant treats this cultural politics as a manifestation of basic American imperialism and wonders why dulcimers and recorders have became the proper vehicles for presenting authentic Appalachian music.

Harvard historian Sacvan Bercovitch has recently suggested that the "mind" of any people inevitably involves a struggle for hegemony. Therefore, he sees cultural politics as inherent in any "historically based ideology" or "mind." So any self-conscious group of people, Bercovitch claims, has to recognize where its cultural leadership comes from and needs to work out its relationships with other cultural voices as well.

Following up on the notion that cultural politics brings an inevitable clash, and that cultural taste gives us a clue as to what an Appalachian Mind might be, the work of several recent writers in the region can be most useful. Recognizing that folklore study and collection has provided the region's earliest mature scholarship (as with the able regional articles that appeared in the first years of the twentieth century), it should not be surprising that some of our most useful insights come from this field of scholarship. Loyal Jones, for one, has continued the custom of collecting traditional materials. And along with this collecting he has made studies of key musicians and operators of folk festivals. Jones's biography of Bascom Lamar Lunsford, the leader of the Asheville Folk Festival for years, traces the life and influence of this "arbiter of regional taste." Here, in fact, is a most interesting case of indigenous cultural politics, for clearly some music was "in" for Lunsford, and some was "out." Although there were large aspects of Appalachian life of which he clearly approved, there were also parts of Appalachian life Lunsford did not like. Lunsford gave voice only to those parts of the folk heritage with which he was sympathetic. Any "mind" of a region, Jones reminds us, must be aware of itself and knows what it was and is as well as what it desires to be. Lunsford's suspicions of the faddish and outside influences reveals some of what widely respected native artists valued, while saying something also about the forces that tended to erode traditional values. And what one can say about Lunsford's imposed tastes can also be said of other "inside" leaders of musical taste, such as John Lair of Renfro Valley, Kentucky, and others.

A monumental piece of recent regional scholarship has been the essentially inside voice of Deborah McCauley, as she has traced the development of the religious culture that dominates the more isolated parts of the region. Loyal Jones, in fact, believes that McCauley's study lays bare much of the very soul of Appalachia.

But Appalachians have not always been descendants of Christian European ancestors. Some were Cherokee, as in that remnant in western North Carolina of the 1838 Removal who remained in the mountains within the Qualla Boundary. Traditional Cherokee ways have persisted there in that remarkable cultural island. However, many more Cherokee in Appalachia melded into the dominant culture; thousands of modern Appalachians now proudly claim "Cherokee grandmothers."

Many more non-European Appalachians have African backgrounds. Nearly ten percent of the Appalachian people are African Americans, and many feel as though they are a forgotten minority within the forgotten Appalachian minority. This "Afrilachian" voice has struggled to be heard for more than thirty years, and was probably raised earliest by the John Henry Foundation of West Virginia. Its director and founder, Edward Cabbell, reminds us that John Henry, the steel-driving folk hero who beat the machine, was an African American working on a West Virginia railroad. Appalachian blacks have become scholars, too, as demonstrated by the book Ed Cabbell edited with William Turner, *Blacks in Appalachia*. And a most active group of poets has been the "Affrilachian" group in Kentucky. Though most black-oriented scholarship has followed blacks in coal mining, Turner's scholarship has traced the recent movements and networking of blacks moving from the mountains, yet retaining a connection with the "old homeplace" through the Eastern Kentucky Club. Turner and others are interested in the dynamics and persistence of this network and the role that place, class, and race continue to play in the lives of African Americans who have left the region.

Gurney Norman, an eastern Kentuckian who honed his writing skills in Wallace Stegner's classes at Stanford University in California, speaks frequently of the "Appalachian Conversation." This conversation was started in 1913 when certain missionaries concerned about the region began meeting annually as a "Council of Southern Mountain Workers." Although the conversation was initially conceived rather narrowly, with time it broadened to include educators, business people, and social workers and to become the "Council of the Southern Mountains." The Council began publishing a magazine, *Mountain Life and Work*, in 1925, and its annual meetings brought together everyone interested in the region—educators, students, church people, labor leaders, businessmen, and social workers. During the 1960s, many War on Poverty warriors were brought into the Council's conversation, and in the late 1960s and early 1970s as the War on Poverty was collapsing, these program-oriented reformers actually "captured the Council," hoping to gain financial support. The Council thus became a politically oriented spokesman-agency for this reforming element with its own agenda. With the capture of the region's principal conversational vehicle by a program-oriented minority, the wider Appalachian Conversation was temporarily disrupted.

In the early 1970s, this Appalachian Conversation was renewed first by several new regional journals—*Appalachian Heritage, Appalachian Journal, Appalachian Notes,* and *Mountain Review*—where significant writers, poets, and scholars found outlets for their work. Then in 1976 and 1977, the Appalachian Studies Conference—now the Appalachian Studies Association—took shape, which allowed regional scholars to meet together and provided a forum for action folk who were concerned about regional change. In fact, what some have termed an "Appalachian Studies Industry" has arisen and is focused each year on the meetings of the Appalachian Studies Association. At these meetings, important papers are presented in many academic fields, yet there are also performances of folk musicians, documentaries shown produced by regional movie makers, and teachers and students from regional colleges and high schools share class projects. It is an unusual kind of annual meeting, with the only thing holding the meeting together being an interest in the Appalachian region. The most unusual aspect of this Appalachian Conversation, however, is not that it is diverse or that the voices are so often loud and contentious, but that the persons involved listen to one another. Radicals hear conservatives, and the old listen to the young. And a general good humor pervades the event.

For a few years, part of this Appalachian Conversation revolved around the play by Robert Schenkkan, *The Kentucky Cycle*. Mr. Schenkkan, who never attended an Appalachian Studies Conference, is a Californian who visited eastern Kentucky for two days and apparently confined his regional research to a few of Harry Caudill's books. The Pulitzer Prize for drama for 1992 was awarded to Mr. Schenkkan for this massive, nine-hour play, which purports to cover the Appalachian—even the American—experience from the time of settlement to the War on Poverty. For such a prestigious prize to be awarded to a play that reflects so little of modern scholarship, in fact only the old negative stereotypes about Appalachia—greed, violence, ignorance, selfishness and degradation—has led many in the region to despair of ever selling a more accurate and even mildly sympathetic view of the region to national audiences. Though Schenkkan is at pains to insist that *The Kentucky Cycle* is really a parable about American greed and materialism and that the Appalachian setting is merely a metaphor, even the well-established regional tolerance for hillbilly stereotyping has been severely strained.

Most of the Appalachian voices have rained down on Schenkkan, and Schenkkan has responded with cries of regional conservatism and with attacks on "self-styled experts of the region," whom he has charged with fascism. Gurney Norman and Jim Wayne Miller have been two of many from the region who have written reviews of *The Kentucky Cycle,* and Loyal Jones has not concealed his glee that the play failed on Broadway after only a month's run. Recently Dwight Billings, Gurney Norman, and Katherine Ledford have edited a most insightful book, *Confronting Appalachian Stereotypes: Back Talk from an American Region* (1999), which contains studies by twenty-two regional scholars, many responding in various ways to Schenkkan's play.

Harry Caudill, whom Schenkkan read to reinforce his two-day visit in order to confirm this view of the region, was dead by the time the play appeared. Caudill obviously saw Appalachians as persons with an unfortunate heritage and a tragic present. But *Night Comes to the Cumberlands* ended with the firm hope that a Southern Mountain Authority might lead the region into a better future. Caudill tempered his tragic even "gothic view" of regional history with the hope that tomorrow could be better. In sharp contrast, Schenkkan's play shows no such hope. It is unrelieved gloom.

How would Cratis Williams, for many years our "Dean of Appalachian Studies," have responded? Williams was basically a teacher and a regional advocate. Seldom did he criticize the basic arrangements in the region. Yet he was the first to admit that there was a dark side to the Appalachian character. Appalachians had suffered from much violence in the past, and they had often been greedy and selfish. Williams himself could curse with passion, and he candidly admitted that his family had been involved in feuds. But like Loyal Jones, he presented these darker characteristics of the Appalachian psyche with sensitivity and even humor. Williams was also Calvinist enough to realize that sin was a human condition. Though Cratis Williams was no churchman, he had his suspicions of how far humans could go in improving themselves. Cratis Williams probably would not have said much about Schenkkan's play, but he would have been deeply troubled by the fact that it was awarded a Pulitzer Prize. One cannot control what writers in Los Angeles create, but what were the Pulitzer judges thinking of to award their prize to such an exaggerated collection of negativism? True, similar people and conditions exist in Appalachia. But such total negativism exceeds reality. He probably would have deemed it "naturalism and not realistic," using the literary jargon of his day.

The reaction to any national and derogatory treatment of the region particularly concerns the region's scholars and writers, perhaps overmuch. A CBS documentary on Muddy Gut Creek in eastern Kentucky in 1988 was a major concern of those in the Appalachian Conversation for several months, though this supposedly "in-depth" reporting of the area involved many facets—some of them positive—about life in that hollow. But mostly the image of desperation and poverty prevailed in this documentary. It was not untruthful, but it clearly emphasized the negative side of regional life. But in that same hollow were schools, churches, and families facing life positively and creatively, and these were not mentioned.

Schenkkan's play hit the same nerve. And most of the scholars and writers of the region have responded that all the work they have been doing for years to refute the debilitating stereotypes seems to be for naught. As poet Jim Wayne Miller noted, "Yogi Berra was right. It's deja vu all over again." And the fact that the play received a Pulitzer Prize just added insult to injury.

Loyal Jones's *Appalachian Values*, with photographs by Warren Brunner and published by the Jesse Stuart Foundation in 1994, was in part an answer to Schenkkan's play. Though the sparse text is basically a rewrite of Jones's 1973 *Twigs* essay, there are interesting additions, especially Jones's final evaluation, which admits that some Appalachian values "can be a disadvantage." Appalachian religion, for example, "may cause us to take a 'what will be will be' attitude . . . Our independence often keeps us from getting involved . . . Our attachment to place may keep us from venturing forth."

Anthropologist Allen Batteau has explored the long symbiotic yet ironic relationship between America and Appalachia. The two have been caught in an embrace beginning with the birth of the republic; nonetheless, the twentieth century image of both seems often to be in total contrast. The one is rich, the other is poor; the one is progressive, the other is traditional; the one is a winner, the other a loser and a mineral colony. However, using a more romantic and idealistic dichotomy, the one is materialistic, the other values the spiritual; the one is caught in the rat race of modern life, the other has time for humor and simple pleasures; the one has lost its faith, while the other retains its religious beliefs in spite of life's troubles. Perhaps the trouble comes when the region is painted with those materialistic and cynical colors usually reserved for the nation as a whole. When the poverty and violence of the negative stereotyping is added, the region becomes doubly damned.

But are Americans and Appalachians that different? In truth, both are abstractions, and both often seem to be wrapped in one another. Appalachians are Americans, and Americans are at least partly Appalachians. The racial makeup of the region does not greatly differ from the racial composition of the nation as a whole. In class arrangements, the proportion of poor is perhaps higher in Appalachia. But there are billion-dollar, multinational corporations headquartered in Appalachia as well. And despite the economic growth of the region—its progress—the area does remain remarkably traditional in religion, values, politics, and economic preference. In a way, it is indeed peopled, as William Frost said a hundred years ago, by "Contemporary Ancestors." This explanation is not absolutely true, of course, but it *is* true that the region is more traditional than the nation as a whole—for better or for worse.

14

The Appalachian
Future

IN LOOKING AT THE FUTURE of the people of the Appalachian region, we first need to recognize that there are at least two quite different worlds in the region. Regional scholars have long recognized this Appalachian duality. From the time of John C. Campbell and William G. Frost at the turn of the century, through the radical scholars of the 1960s and 1970s, the two worlds of Appalachia have been noted. Perhaps Harry Caudill said it best when he claimed that there are two kinds of people in Appalachia: the rich and the powerful, who dominate the region's life, and the bulk of the region's people, who are poor and powerless. Scholars of literature have pointed out that most of the disparaging stereotypes of Appalachian people have been foisted onto one particular group or class of "Branchwater Mountaineers," a distinct but colorful minority by the mid-twentieth century.

Following these clues, a recent exploration of the origins of Appalachian stereotypes by historian David C. Hsiung declares that the progressive, commercial elite of East Tennessee towns during the nineteenth century were the earliest to suggest the harshly negative stereotypical judgments about their antiprogressive rural neighbors, which Local Color writers later adopted. Professor Hsiung's useful exploration is essentially on target in suggesting that the animosity between the two worlds of Appalachia was well-established long before the Civil War. This leads me to approach the Appalachian future in two quite different ways: one to emphasize the direction that mainstream, commercial developments will likely go in the region, and the other to contemplate the future of the many people in the region likely to be "left out" as the commercial World System leads us into the New Information Age.

In a remarkably candid and complete assessment of the Appalachian future, historian Gordon McKinney points out that the communication revolution of the New Information Age—the world of computers, cable television, and the World Wide Web—is about to change the way we relate to one another. And this revolution is already impacting the region in major ways. For example, Blacksburg, Virginia, the home of Virginia Tech, has become the most completely connected electronic community in the world. As the people of the region face the global impact of the postindustrial economy, regionally based companies may electronically bill any customer in the world. Clearly, the service-based industries—from the merchandising for Wal-Mart to the world of new services offered on the Internet by regionally based small businesses—will dominate Appalachia's job market in the years to come. As coal and agriculture, the region's dominant industries in the past, move into further decline, the essentially insatiable industries of education, health services, recreation, and tourism will provide the major job opportunities in the future. Since the 1960s, the Community College movement has produced some fifty colleges in the region, with almost two hundred thousand students. And higher education as a whole in the region today serves six hundred thousand students, a figure six times the total of 1940.

Other analyses of the New Information Age emphasize the rising urbanism of the world of the future. Figures for contemporary Appalachia, traditionally a rural region, vary from 40 to 52 percent of the region's population living in Standard Metropolitan Statistical Areas, with many of Appalachia's people living in SMSAs that surround Appalachia, such as Atlanta, Charlotte, and Washington, D.C. This growing urbanization will continue into the future.

Futurologist John Naisbitt's *Megatrends* analysis further suggests impacts on the region from at least four of his ten "megatrends." These are: 1) the move from centralization toward decentralization, which will bring business operations to home and small offices in remote areas; 2) the move away from institutionalized education toward self-help and continuing education in many places; 3) the abandonment of hierarchical bureaucratic arrangements of networking for information and decision making; and 4) a broadening impact of multiple-option solutions and job definitions. In the twenty-first century, all four of these "megatrends" will redefine jobs in ways that can place them in Appalachia.

A *Newsweek* issue in late January 1997 looked at "Beyond 2000: America in the 21st Century." A presidential campaign had just been

fought about the visions for the nation's future. Numerous apoca-
lyptic Christians were debating just what the new millennium would
bring. And an interesting demographic study pointed out that by the
year 2050, the American population might reach more than 500 million, and the percentage of Latino, African American, and Asian
would expand sufficiently to make Euro–Americans a minority within
the United States. Furthermore, the major population growth was
projected to be in the nation's South, rising from the present 91 million to 121 million in the near future. The number of people over the
age of sixty-five by 2050 will have risen from the present 5 percent to
20 percent of the nation's population. Appalachia, however, will probably not show such a dramatic rise in population as the South as a
whole. But a major result will be an immense pressure upon Appalachian lands for recreational and tourist uses, as well as for trash and
garbage disposal, thus presenting immense pressures upon regional
decision making.

Our national parks and forests already betray the marks of abuse
and overuse, with attacks from excess carbon dioxide and acid rain,
extensive clear-cutting, damage by off-road vehicles, trash dump-
ing, and illegal marijuana growing. Without a doubt we will need to
develop more efficient use of the region's natural resources and
beauty as tourism and recreational uses expand. Tourism has become
the world's number one industry, and Appalachia's place in this industry will continue to be an important one. And the services needed
by this industry for guides and instructors in leisure activities will
explode in many directions.

The regional magazine *Now and Then* in 1996 produced its summer issue on the theme "Appalachian Visions: How the Region Sees
Its Future." Though most of the authors saw the region's future in
terms of meeting the challenge of the New Information Age, or of
developing strategies so that the region could move easily into the
better tomorrow, several articles suggested an alternative vision.
Radford University professor Jim Minick, for example, saw the regional future in terms of a place where a person could live with the
"seamless and full cycle" of time's rhythms, and where mountain
culture could be lived and appreciated away from the frantic way of
life of the rest of the nation.

Most regional scholars reflect a view of the region's future that
varies broadly from some optimism to the deep pessimism and fear
of Appalachia's absentee corporate ownership of its principal resources. This wildly diverse view of the Appalachian future reflects

clearly different perception, for if one confines one's vision to the region's commercial and town folk, the future can look quite bright. But the careful regional scholar needs to realize that the region's poorest and least educated will likely be left out of the benefits of the New Information Age.

To deal with this troublesome double vision, we need to consider several theories of regional development and consider what a powerful and humane nation might do for its poorer citizens. Actually, there are important practical reasons to consider the dangers that a divided, "Prince and Pauper" future would pose.

There are those who believe that the United States today has sufficient structures to handle our poverty problem. A free market, some say, distributes goods and services quite justly, for it depends upon individual initiative and hard work. Furthermore, our system of free public schools and public libraries gives ample opportunity for all to acquire the needed information and skills necessary for the world of the future. Indeed, enough of the nation's poor have risen through our present system to give some credence to the view that America is still the land of opportunity.

On the other hand, Social Christians and welfare state apologists remain deeply concerned about the rising income gap and the numbers of people that are mired in deep poverty. Such persons charge that the free market system allows too many people to slip through the cracks of its distributive system and assert that the state should intervene. American theorists from the time of Henry George more than a century ago have sought for ways to enable the poor and the powerless to enjoy their just fruits from the nation's bounty. Only in the 1930s in the United States did we as a nation decide that our national government should make substantial efforts to aid its poor. A climax of these efforts came during the brief years of the War on Poverty in the 1960s.

One of the major battlegrounds during the War on Poverty was in Appalachia, and millions of dollars were expended in this area on programs largely designed in the nation's capital. Two major philosophies for poverty amelioration were followed in these years. The one was the "Culture of Poverty" analysis suggested by sociologist Oscar Lewis, which holds that poverty is largely caused by cultural conditions—large families, poor education, a poor work ethic, and low expectations. So to overcome this cultural trap, programs should be initiated—largely educational—aimed at the poor person's culture. But as many critics have pointed out, this strategy betrays misleading circular thinking that blames the victim and leaves the broader economic structure essentially unexamined.

The other major antipoverty strategy followed during the War on Poverty was the Economic Development Model, a model still followed by most capitalist-oriented economists. The notion here is that for free enterprise, capitalist development to occur, certain preconditions must be present before "take off" occurs. These preconditions—or infrastructures—include ample transportation, health care and educational services, and an adequately prepared work force. This was the strategy followed by the Appalachian Regional Commission and continues to guide that agency's strategy.

The ARC's developments have clearly aided parts of the region, as that agency follows various locally oriented projects generated within the region by the ADDs (Area Development Districts) established within the ARC. Yet most of these projects are tied to various market-oriented strategies promoted by the region's commercial elite. Still, many of the poor within the region remain essentially untouched.

If we are genuinely concerned with the betterment of those in the region left out by existing developmental strategies and likely to be left out in the anticipated developments in the postindustrial, Information Age of the future, some kind of strategy has to be developed to include these folk. In fact, a number of regional and Third World economists have taken it upon themselves to try to devise a strategy that would improve the lot of the poor of the so-called "underdeveloped world." Perhaps a brief survey of some of these ideas might be helpful at this point.

Arturo Escobar, arguing from a Latin American perspective, contends that the "canon of development economics imposed by . . . well-meaning international agencies on underdeveloped economies since the late 1940s," has produced tragic distortions in the Third World. After all, he says, developmental economics is really not a science but rather a strategy imposed by developed economies upon poor areas, which has actually resulted in a "new colonialism" that ignores region-specific conditions.

More specifically related to Appalachia have been regional social scientists who have suggested a number of strategies aimed at ameliorating the region's poverty. One of the well-worked-out systems can be found in Paul Salstrom's *Appalachia's Path to Dependency*. Salstrom holds that thanks to Appalachia's inadequate agricultural development prior to 1880, the industrial development that *did* occur followed an essentially negative path. Beginning with Andre

Gundar Frank's notion that dependency can develop if developmental strategies go awry, Salstrom sees policies followed by the United States government, especially during the Civil War and New Deal periods, as leading the region into dependency rather than economic development.

The broad dissatisfaction with the manner in which economic development theory has operated in poor and underdeveloped regions has been so compelling, that numerous new developmental theories have emerged from many directions. In Catholic countries in Europe, for example, the Christian Democratic Movement, following the ideas of Jacques Maritain, has tried to take the best strategies of socialism but apply them in a Christian way. In Latin America, the Liberation Theology of the Catholic Church sees the Christian Democratic strategy as altogether too tame for the revolutionary change needed in capitalistic countries.

William Greider, after study in Germany, has deep suspicions of how the emerging global economy is likely to operate for most people, even in developed countries. Greider calls for a fundamental reordering of official thought in establishing what he calls a "demand side economics." Such a demand side economics calls for less uncontrolled free trade, more taxing of capital in order to encourage job creation, and forcing the Federal Reserve System to allow higher interest rates and faster economic growth.

A whole new school of world development economics, in fact, has appeared in the 1990s: the so-called "Noetic Science Movement." This movement pushes what it calls a "whole-system perspective," which takes into effect environmental needs as well as a need for democratic decision-making, along with broad guarantees of freedom and equity. Many within more traditional developmental economics have now accepted what has been called "sustainable development," which factors in long-range environmental aspects of development. Specifically related to Appalachia, the ARC Federal Co-chairman, Jesse White, has recently emphasized the need for genuine grassroots participation and the necessity of keeping both wealth and investment under local control.

A host of regional scholars have been so alienated by the negative effects of corporate capitalism upon large segments of the region, that they have been attracted to various programs that focus on the necessity for a pervasive and substantial economic change. The models usually suggested have involved political and community organizing along Populist, and even occasionally Marxian, lines. Taking their clues from the post–War on Poverty victories over the power elite of the region—as in the Homestead Amendment against the broadform deed in Kentucky, various actions against the TVA's policy for moving into wider use of nuclear power, and the defeat of the major dam on the upper New River in North Carolina—these activists are hopeful that even larger victories can be won in the future.

The worldwide difficulties of Communism, as well as the demonstrated devastations brought on the Russian people by their Marxian government, has led many of the region's New Left scholars to abandon strictly Marxian strategies looking toward significant regional change. The leading political activists in the region now usually take what they term a "Neo-Populist" position, which looks toward popular, democratic decision making leading to critical change.

Other New Left scholars of the region are taking what they term a "Post-modernist" position and see a deterioration of the capitalistic World System that has dominated Western civilization since 1500. As these social scientists see it, Post-modernism welcomes the development of a "new sensibility" and recognition that the old ways of thinking and traditional economic structures are unsatisfactory for the new century. It seems that these former New Left scholars are no longer sure about what their science can do to end economic injustice and even question whether any final answers can ever be achieved.

A particularly attractive notion is an idea that seems to promise a quite satisfactory way to accept and even enhance the lives of the "left out" in the several developmental strategies of world capitalism. This is the idea that scholars and governmental agencies alike need to recognize the crucial importance of what sociologist Sally Ward Maggard calls the "Informal Economy." Historian Paul Salstrom, as well, is at pains to describe this kind of system in what he calls rural Appalachia's "Subsistence–Barter and Borrow" system. Both are describing an enhanced self-sufficient economy that would take in those regional folk left out of the postindustrial economy. In Appalachia, because those left out are largely rural, the mere presence of the resource of land and the tradition of yeomanism can provide the essentials of this self-sufficiency.

Some thinking, in fact, has gone into establishing what might be called a "New Free Economy," which recognizes and values the importance of our local, self-sufficient "Informal Economy." If such a notion were accepted, governments at all levels would need to recognize the legitimate role of such a sector within the larger economy and do what they could positively do to preserve the vitality of this Informal Economy. The Swedish sociologist, Gunnar Myrdal, the English economist E.F. Schumacher, the Kentuckian Wendell Berry, and the Third World leader, Mahatma Gandhi, have all contributed substantially toward the building of this alternative model for economic life and development, which would find a significant and continuing role for a healthy, localized barter and self-sufficient economy. Gandhi presents perhaps the most central aspects of this model.

Gandhi's thought begins from the perspective of the poor themselves. Gandhi had a remarkable ability to identify with those in poverty and indeed empowered them successfully against a powerful colonial master. Though India certainly has not solved her poverty problem in the years since independence, from India's perspective her economic problems are not as hopeless as many in the West perceive. In an attempt to systematize Gandhi's economic views, we can draw from his various speeches and articles. His economic ideas do not represent a total system, but they are richly suggestive of a developmental strategy that might prove helpful.

In Gandhi's view, a region suffering from poverty should recognize that it exists in a world of rich and poor, and of the powerful and the powerless, and that differences in both income and political significant will persist into the indefinite future. Gandhi held that economic equality was not possible and indeed probably not even desirable. The only thing that one can really expect from any economic system, he said, is some economic justice for all. To achieve this, he developed several economic principles that need to be accepted. First, the PRINCIPLE OF ECONOMIC PLURALISM; second, the PRINCIPLE OF TRUSTEESHIP; and third, the PRINCIPLE THAT MODERNIZATION MAY NOT BE DESIRABLE.

The PRINCIPLE OF ECONOMIC PLURALISM recognizes that free-enterprise capitalism, though dominant, is not the only economic system that has validity and usefulness. Nor is Marxism the only alternative to capitalism. Marxian planning and state control of the means of production may have valid application in certain situations. Yet a really humane economic system need not be entirely one or the other, but can usefully be a mix—part capitalist and part socialist. A mix of largely free-enterprise operations probably is best, Gandhi thought, but where problems emerge in which state enterprise can work better, as with the TVA or Canadian medicine, we should not be afraid of some governmental ownership or operation.

Yet Gandhi was particularly concerned with another level of economic operation that was neither capitalist nor socialist. This Gandhi termed the "Village Economy." In Appalachia this translates into recognizing the validity of a "Yeoman-oriented Folk Economy" of largely self-sufficient farms, or into Salstrom's "Subsistence–Barter and Borrow" system, or into Maggard's "Informal Economy." Gandhi's suggestion was that it was necessary for the village economy to be integrated and institutionally accepted into the larger national economy, not merely thought of as something an expansive free market economy should replace. We need to develop, Gandhi said, structure and institutions that find a place for this village economy to legitimately exist alongside the capitalist and socialist structures. The folk tradition thus becomes one of the legitimate sectors to build the larger economy upon, not something to cast aside once an advanced capitalist economy develops. If human values are our primary concern, Gandhi said, they can develop as richly in a low income, even a barter-oriented folk economy, as under the affluence of a dynamic market economy.

Gandhi's second principle is the PRINCIPLE OF TRUSTEESHIP. Unlike the Marxians, who contemplated revolution and the confiscation of private property as a way to move toward its kind of "just system" with public ownership of the means of production, Gandhi insisted upon no acts of violence as we move toward a better tomorrow. Instead, Gandhi suggested that we work on the ideas and attitudes, the values and concerns of those persons with the property, wealth, and power. He never let up on the moral responsibilities imposed upon the rich, and he saw there a central role for religion. Nehru, Gandhi's principal lieutenant and a dedicated socialist, thought that this was the most naïve aspect of Gandhi's thought. But this may not be naïve at all. Gandhi's aim was to meet basic needs with fairness, while recognizing that economic equality was probably not possible. But economic justice is eminently attainable.

Gandhi's third principle was that MODERNIZATION AND INDUSTRIALIZATION MAY NOT BE DESIRABLE. In areas of high population concentration and high unemployment, the introduction of modern machinery and computers might not be beneficial. As others have suggested as well, human needs and values should be the major concern of any economic system. Corporations and businesses are only things, as are parties and organizations. Such things have no inherent value in and of themselves, Gandhi reminded us, except as they serve human beings. Technology, thus, is not necessarily positive, nor is it even benign. It may in fact have a profoundly negative impact on people. Therefore, technology should be approached cautiously and even critically if necessary.

The Swedish sociologist Gunnar Myrdal is perhaps the Western theorist who most specifically adopted many of Gandhi's principles. His acceptance of the Principle of Economic Pluralism is perhaps the most thorough. He had little trouble with the mixed economy notion, and it was an easy step to accept the equal validity of the village or folk economy.

Perhaps Wendell Berry is the modern American writer who most effectively presents the unique place that agriculture has in human history and most sensitively presents the place that our relationship to land should play in modern life. Berry is from the Kentucky Bluegrass borderland near Appalachia and celebrates the inherent human endeavor of agricultural cultivation as a way of life. He perhaps best celebrates the small farm and the farmer's mystical relationship to both his land and the process of growing food and fiber on it. Berry also warns us about the profound way in which modern agribusiness has disrupted the nation's proper relationship between the people, the land, and food production. For Berry, farming is essentially a religious act, not a way to pursue profit. Thus as Berry fits Gandhi's thought, he sanctifies the legitimacy of a folk economy based upon the land and its cultivation.

Other less eloquent voices have been raised in America, too, in defense of the small farm, even a yeomanesque return to farm life, or a folk economy in the Gandhian sense. The California farmer/classics professor Victor Davis Hanson raises warnings about the "Latifundiation of American agriculture" and the loss of the free, small farm, and the resulting loss of crucial spiritual and mystical strength. The farmer, Hanson says, "is different, vastly different, from almost every other type of citizen." In the last several years, indeed, a kind of theology of farming has developed among some in the American Church. Among these theologians of farming are Walter Brueggemann, John Carmody, John Hart, Charles Lutts, Bennett D. Poage, and Richard Cartwright Austin. The last two, in fact, are theorists who are specifically concerned with the Appalachian area.

All this suggests that Gandhi's three principles may help to bring a more hopeful future to those likely to be left out of the promise of the upcoming Information Age. There is, and in fact has always been, a place for a viable, yeomanesque-style of life that is attractive to those unwilling or unable to join the mainstream's affluence.

Sources

Introduction

I have mainly depended upon the following for my definition of Appalachia:

Nevil M. Fenneman, *Physiography of Eastern United States*. New York: McGraw–Hill, 1938.

Karl B. Raitz and Richard Ulack, *Appalachia: A Regional Geography; Land, People and Development*. Boulder, Colo.: Westview, 1984.

By far the best discussion of the various definitions of Appalachia is found in Raitz and Ulack, *Appalachia*, p. 9–33.

Much recent literature insists that Appalachia is but an invention of a reforming Northern intelligencia, thus the region should not be considered as an exceptional and distinctive area separate from the rest of the United States. See:

Henry D. Shapiro, *Appalachia on Our Mind: The Southern Mountains and Mountaineers in the American Consciousness, 1870–1920*. Chapel Hill: University of North Carolina Press, 1978; and

Allen W. Batteau, *The Invention of Appalachia*. Tucson: University of Arizona Press, 1990.

Even a recent volume on nineteenth-century Appalachian history holds that the region did not exist until it had been properly conceptualized. See: Mary Beth Pudup, Dwight B. Billings and Altina Waller, editors, *Appalachia in the Making: The Mountain South in the Nineteenth Century*. Chapel Hill: University of North Carolina Press, 1995.

My contention is that Appalachian exceptionalism existed as early as the Backwoods Period, and especially later in what is termed the "Cohee Period." See especially:

Thomas Jefferson Wertenbaker, *The Old South: The Founding of American Civilization*. New York: Scribners, 1942; and

James Kirke Paulding, "Letter X," *Letters from the South* (1817). In Robert Higgs and Ambrose N. Manning, editors, *Voices from the Hills*. New York: Unger, 1975, p. 64–66.

Most recent Appalachian scholarship has been particularly impressed with the colonial economic status of Appalachia. See especially:

Helen M. Lewis, Linda Johnson, and Donald Askins, editors, *Colonialism in Modern America: The Appalachian Case*. Boone, N.C.: Appalachian Consortium Press, 1978; and

Wilma A. Dunaway, *The First American Frontier: Transition to Capitalism in Southern Appalachia, 1700–1860*. Chapel Hill: University of North Carolina Press, 1996. This Dunaway volume fairly convincingly applies the World Systems Theory of Immanual Wallerstein to the Appalachian Experience.Concerning American and regional yeomanry, a massive literature has developed regarding the myth and reality of yeomanry since Jefferson's time. See:

Richard Hofstadter, *The Age of Reform*. New York: Vintage, 1955. Hofstadter holds that yeomanism has always been a misleading myth.

Many of the New Social Historians have studied early American farming in the various sections of the United States, as well as the story of the move from self-sufficient farming to market-oriented agriculture. For our purposes, see especially:

James A. Henretta, "Families and Farms: Mentalite in Pre-Industrial America," *William and Mary Quarterly*, 3rd ser., vol. 35 (1978), p. 3–32; and

Robert D. Mitchell, *Commercialism and Frontier: Perspectives on the Early Shenandoah Valley*. Charlottesville: University Press of Virginia, 1977.

The continuing and changing experience with wilderness is seen in:

Roderick Nash, *Wilderness and the American Mind*. New Haven, Conn.: Yale University Press, 1967; and

Frederick Turner, *Beyond Geography: The Western Spirit Against the Wilderness*. New Brunswick, N.J.: Rutgers University Press, 1994.

Chris Bolgiano, *The Appalachian Forest: A Search for Roots and Renewal*. Mechanicsburg, Pa.: Stackpole, 1998.

The theme of regional misunderstanding, misleading stereotypes and confusing analysis as related to Appalachia is seen in:

Deborah Vansau McCauley, *Appalachian Mountain Religion: A History*. Urbana: University of Illinois Press, 1995; and

Paul Salstrom, *Appalachia's Path to Dependency: Rethinking a Region's Economic History, 1730–1940*. Lexington: University Press of Kentucky, 1994.

Chapter 1: The Indian Era

For this chapter I was dependent primarily upon:

Paul S. Martin, George I. Quigly and Donald Collier, *Indians Before Columbus: Twenty Thousand Years of North American History Revealed by Archaeology*. Chicago: University of Chicago Press, 1947.

Francis Jennings, *The Founders of America from the Earliest Migration to the Present*. New York: Norton, 1993.

Charles Hudson, *The Southeastern Indians*. Knoxville: University of Tennessee Press, 1976.

On Cherokee history, see particularly:

Roy Dickens, *Cherokee Prehistory: The Pisgah Phase in the Appalachian Summit Region*. Knoxville: University of Tennessee Press, 1976.

Bernie C. Keel, *Cherokee Archaeology: A Study of the Appalachian Summit*. Knoxville: University of Tennessee Press, 1976.

Theda Perdue, *Slavery and the Evolution of Cherokee Society*. Knoxville: University of Tennessee Press, 1979.

Theda Perdue, *The Cherokee*. New York: Chelsea House, 1989.

The extent of Iroquois influence is explored by Francis Jennings' trilogy on the Covenant Chain. See especially his *Ambiguous Iroquois Empire: The Covenant Chain Confederation of the Indian Tribes with the English Colonies*. New York: Norton, 1984.

Certain archaeologists have done some very controversial recent research, some of it related to remains found by Michael Johnson at Saltville in southwestern Virginia. The interpretation of these and other remains claim to antedate the ancient Clovis culture of New Mexico and Arizona, and the claim is made that these were not a Mongoloid people. *Newsweek* magazine ran a review of this archaeology on April 26, 1999.

The Indian population estimates are drawn from Russell Thornton, *American Indian Holocaust and Survival: A Population History Since 1492*. Norman: University of Oklahoma Press, 1987. Thornton estimates a population decline in the area of the United States from more than two million in 1492 to less than 150 thousand by 1900.

The quotations in this chapter were drawn from:

Cadwallader Colden, *A History of the Five Nations of Canada which are Dependent upon the Province of New York and are a Barrier between the English and the French in that Part of the World*. New York: Allerton, 1923 reprint; and

Mark Van Doren, editor, *The Travels of William Bartram*. New York: Dover, 1928.

Chapter 2: The Old World Backgrounds

The historical writing about Europe when it began to enter the Modern Period is immense. Particularly useful to me for this chapter were:

Fernand Braudel, *Civilization and Capitalism, 15th to 19th Century*. 3 volumes. New York: Harper and Row, 1982–1984.

Immanual Wallerstein, *The Politics of the World Economy: The States, the Movements and the Civilization: Essays*. Cambridge: Cambridge University Press, 1984.

David Hackett Fischer, *Albion's Seed: Four British Folkways in America*.

New York: Oxford University Press, 1989.

Wallace Notestein, *The English People on the Eve of Colonization, 1603–1630*. New York: Harper, 1962.

Mildred Campbell, *The English Yeoman Under Elizabeth and the Early Stuarts*. New Haven, Conn.: Yale University Press, 1942.

Grady McWhiney, *Cracker Culture: Celtic Ways in the Old South*. University, Ala.: University of Alabama Press, 1988.

Rodger Cunningham, *Apples on the Flood: The Southern Mountain Experience*. Knoxville: University of Tennessee Press, 1987.

Bernard Bailyn, *The Peopling of British North America: An Introduction*. New York: Harper, 1962.

Abbot Emerson Smith, *Colonists in Bondage: White Servitude and Convict Labor in America, 1607–1776*. Chapel Hill: University of North Carolina Press, 1947.

Rudolf Vierhaus, *Germany in the Age of Absolutism*. Translated by Jonathan B. Knudson. New York: Cambridge University Press, 1988.

On religious history, see:

Sidney E. Ahlstrom, *A Religious History of the American People*. 2 volumes. New York: Image, 1975.

A substantial literature is emerging concerning Sub–Saharan Africa from the fifteenth through the eighteenth centuries. I found the following most helpful:

John Hope Franklin, *From Slavery to Freedom*. New York: Knopf, 1956. His early chapters are on Africa.

Roland Oliver, editor, *The Middle Age in Africa*. New York: Oxford University Press, 1970.

Roland Oliver and Anthony Atmore, *The African Middle Age, 1400–1800*. New York: Cambridge University Press, 1981.

Hugh Thomas, *The Slave Trade*. New York: Simon and Schuster, 1997. See especially chapters 12, 17, 18 and 19, particularly the discussions of the states of Benin, Dahomey, Oyo, Congo and Senegambia.

Chapter 3: The Coming of the Europeans

Some of the titles mentioned in the sources for Chapter 2 relate to this chapter as well. Particularly see Bailyn and Fischer.

Other titles that were particularly useful to me were:

Edward Gaylord Bourne, editor, *Narrative on the Career of Hernando De Soto . . . Based on the Diary of Roderigo Ranjel, his Private Secretary*. New York: Allerton, 1904.

John Anthony Caruso, *The Appalachian Frontier: America's First Surge Westward*. Indianapolis: Bobbs–Merrill, 1959.

Verner W. Crane, *The Southern Frontier, 1670–1732*. Ann Arbor: University of Michigan Press, 1956.

Ora Blackmun, *Western North Carolina: Its Mountains and Its People to 1880.* Boone, N.C.: Appalachian Consortium Press, 1980.

John C. Campbell, *Our Southern Highlander and His Homeland.* New York: Russell Sage Foundation, 1921. This is an early classic.

Particularly useful concerning the various peoples who migrated into the Appalachian backwoods are:

James G. Leyburn, *The Scotch–Irish: A Social History.* Chapel Hill: University of North Carolina Press, 1962.

Carl Wittke, *We Who Built America.* Cleveland, Ohio: Western Reserve Press, 1964.

Concerning the emerging backwoods culture and the various conflicts on the Appalachian frontier, see:

Robert D. Mitchell, *Commercialism and Frontier: Perspective on the Early Shenandoah Valley.* Charlottesville: University Press of Virginia, 1977.

Robert D. Mitchell, editor, *Appalachian Frontiers: Settlement, Society, and Development in the Preindustrial Era.* Lexington: University Press of Kentucky, 1991.

Gregory H. Nobles, *American Frontiers: Cultural Encounters and Continental Conquest.* New York: Hill and Wang, 1997.

Michael J. Puglisi, editor, *Diversity and Accommodation: Essays on the Cultural Composition of the Virginia Frontier.* Knoxville: University of Tennessee Press, 1997.

David Colin Crass, Stephen D. Smith, Martha A. Zierden, and Richard D. Brooks, editors, *The Southern Colonial Backcountry: Interdisciplinary Perspectives on Frontier Communities.* Knoxville: University of Tennessee Press, 1998.

For mountain speech, see:

Michael Montgomery, *Exploring the Roots of Appalachian Speech.* Philadelphia: Jon Benjamins, 1989.

Chapter 4: The Wars for Appalachia

Standard treatments of the American frontier and of colonial history deal heavily with the warfare for the American forest, especially the so-called French and Indian Wars (1689–1763). One such treatment of this struggle is Howard H. Peckham, *The Colonial Wars, 1689–1762.* Chicago: University of Chicago Press, 1964. Perhaps the classic of this struggle focuses on the duel between the French and the British in many volumes by Francis Parkman. Most especially see his *History of the Conspiracy of Pontiac.* Boston: Little–Brown, 1855.

See also:

Ray Allen Billington, *Westward Expansion: a History of the American*

Frontier. New York: Macmillan, 1949.

Otis K. Rice, *The Allegheny Frontier: West Virginia Beginnings, 1730–1830*. Lexington: University Press of Kentucky, 1970.

Thomas Perkins Abernethy, *Western Lands and the American Revolution*. New York: Appleton Century, 1937.

John R. Alden, *The American Revolution, 1775–1783*. New York: Harper, 1954.

Ora Blackmun, *Western North Carolina: Its Mountains and its People to 1880*. Boone, N.C.: Appalachian Consortium Press, 1977.

The best treatment of Daniel Boone and his times is John Mack Faragher, *Daniel Boone: The Life and the Legend of an American Pioneer*. New York: Henry Holt, 1992.

For the Indian perspective, see:

Francis Jennings, *The Founders of America from the Earliest Migration to the Present*. New York: Norton, 1993.

Francis Jennings, *The Invasion of America: Indians, Colonialism and the Cant of Conquest*. Chapel Hill: University of North Carolina Press, 1975.

John Sugden, *Tecumseh: A Life*. New York: Henry Holt, 1997. This remarkable biography of Tecumseh deals with the whole of what he terms the Battle for Ohio, 1784–1814, as well as the period following Lord Dunmore's War.

Chapter 5: Backwoods–Cohee Society

The books that helped produce this chapter were:

Robert D. Mitchell, editor, *Appalachian Frontiers: Settlement, Society, and Development in the Preindustrial Era*. Lexington: University Press of Kentucky, 1990.

Wilma A. Dunaway, *The First American Frontier: Transition to Capitalism in Southern Appalachia, 1700–1860*. Chapel Hill: University of North Carolina Press, 1996.

Arthur Tillson, *Gentry and Common Folk: Political Culture on the Virginia Frontier, 1740–1784*. Lexington: University Press of Kentucky, 1991.

Barbara Rasmussen, *Absentee Landowning and Exploitation in West Virginia, 1760–1920*. Lexington: University Press of Kentucky, 1994.

Robert D. Mitchell, *Commercialism and Frontier: Perspectives in the Early Shenandoah Valley*. Charlottesville: University Press of Virginia, 1977.

Stephen Aaron, *How the West Was Lost: The Transformation of Kentucky, Daniel Boone to Henry Clay*. Baltimore: Johns Hopkins University Press, 1996.

Gregory H. Nobles, "Breaking Into the Backcountry: New Approaches to the Early American Frontier, 1750–1800." *William and Mary Quarterly*, 3rd serial, vol. 46 (October 1989), p. 651–70.

Thomas P. Slaughter, *The Whiskey Rebellion: Frontier Epilogue to the American Revolution.* New York: Oxford University Press, 1986.

David Hackett Fischer, *Albion's Seed: Four British Folkways in America.* New York: Oxford University Press, 1989.

Fred A. Shannon, *American Farmer's Movements.* New York: Anvil, 1957.

Durwood Dunn, *Cades Cove: The Life and Death of a Southern Appalachian Community.* Knoxville: University of Tennessee Press, 1988.

John Solomon Otto, "Rediscovering the Southern Hillbilly, Appalachia and the Ozarks." *Appalachian Journal,* vol. 12 (summer 1985), 324–30.

James A. Henretta, "Families and Farms: Mentalite in Preindustrial America." *William and Mary Quarterly,* 3rd ser., vol. 35, no. 1 (1978), p. 3–32.

Allan Kulikoff, *The Agrarian Origins of American Capitalism.* Charlottesville: University Press of Virginia, 1992.

Kenneth E. Koons and Warren Hofstra, *After the Backcountry: Rural Life in the Great Valley of Virginia, 1800–1900.* Knoxville: University of Tennessee Press, 2000.

Theresa Arnott and Julie Mattael, *Race, Gender and Work: A Multicultural Economic History of Women.* Boston: South End Press, 1991.

Ora Blackmun, *Western North Carolina: Its Mountains and Its People to 1800.* Boone, N.C.: Appalachian Consortium Press, 1985.

Otis E. Young, "The Southern Gold Rush, 1828–1836." *Journal of Southern History,* vol. XLVII, no. 3 (August 1982).

Gustavus W. Dyer and John Trotwood Moore, editors, *The Tennessee Civil War Veteran's Questionnaire.* 5 volumes. Easley, S.C.: Southern Historical Press, 1985.

On the Constitutional Convention, see:

Clinton Rossiter, *1787: The Grand Convention.* New York: Macmillan, 1966.

Robert Allen Rutland, *The Struggle of 1787–1788.* Norman: University of Oklahoma Press, 1966.

On the Indian story and Cherokee Removal, see:

Gregory Evans Dowd, *A Spirited Resistance: The North American Indian Struggle for Unity, 1745–1815.* Baltimore: Johns Hopkins University Press, 1992.

John Sugden, *Tecumseh: A Life.* New York: Henry Holt, 1997.

Grant Foreman, *Indian Removal: The Emigration of the Five Civilized Tribes of Indians.* Norman: University of Oklahoma Press, 1976.

Thomas Wilkins, *Cherokee Tragedy: The Ridge Family and the Decimation of a People.* Norman: University of Oklahoma Press, 1986.

Theda Perdue, *The Cherokee.* New York: Chelsea House, 1989.

The quotation is from:

"Birthday Story of Private John B. Burnett, Captain Abraham McClellan's Company, 2nd regiment, 2nd brigade, Mounten Infantry, Cherokee Removal, 1838–1839. Account made on his 80th Birthday, December 11, 1880." Included in Thomas B. Underwood, *Cherokee Legends and the Trail of Tears*. Knoxville: Neuman Printing, 1956.

Andrew Jackson is such a central figure to this period that a careful biography is most useful. I found the following very useful from Remini's multivolume biography of Jackson.

Robert V. Remini, *Andrew Jackson and the Course of American Democracy, 1838–1845*. New York: Harper and Row, 1984.

Chapter 6: The Challenge to Cohee Society, 1820–1860

Thomas Jefferson Wertenbaker's reading of Southern antebellum history is presented in his *The Old South: The Founding of American Civilization*. New York: Scribners, 1942. Other studies with different views about the South and Appalachia's antebellum roles are:

Frank J. Owsley, *Plain People of the Old South*. Baton Rouge: Louisiana State University Press, 1949.

Ralph A. Wooster, *Politicians, Planters and Plain Folk: Courthouse and Statehouse in the Upper South, 1850–1860*. Knoxville: University of Tennessee Press, 1975.

Eugene Genovese, *The World the Slaveholders Made: Two Essays in Interpretation*. 2nd edition. Middletown, Conn.: Wesleyan University Press, 1988.

Allan Kulikoff, *The Agrarian Origins of American Capitalism*. Charlottesville: University Press of Virginia, 1992. Especially see his Chapters 2 and 5.

Concerning Appalachian slavery, the quotations used here come from WPA Narratives, Kentucky, 1938. Microfilm 3119; Ronald Killiam and Charles Waller, *Slavery Times When I was Chillum down on Marsters' Plantation*. Savannah, Ga.: Beehive Press, 1973. The Olmsted quotation is taken from Frederick Law Olmsted, *The Slave States*, edited by Harvey Wish. New York: Capricorn, 1959, p. 226.

More specifically related to Appalachian slavery, see:

Edward W. Phifer, "Slavery in Microcosm: Burke County, North Carolina," *Journal of Southern History*, vol. 28, no. 2 (May 1962), p. 137–65.

John C. Inscoe, *Mountain Masters, Slavery, and the Sectional Crisis in Western North Carolina*. Knoxville: University of Tennessee Press, 1989.

John C. Inscoe, "Race and Racism in Nineteenth Century Appalachia: Myths, Realities and Ambiguities." In Mary Beth Pudup, Dwight B. Billings, and Altina L. Waller, editors, *Appalachian in the Making: The*

Mountain South in the Nineteenth Century. Chapel Hill: University of North Carolina Press, 1995, p. 103–31.

Richard B. Drake, "Slavery and Antislavery in Appalachia." *Appalachian Heritage,* vol. 14 (winter 1986), p. 25–33.

Stephanie McCurry, *Masters of Small Worlds: Yeoman Households, Gender Relations and the Political Culture of the Antebellum South Carolina Low Country.* New York: Oxford University Press, 1995. Despite the emphasis outside Appalachia, and a focus on gender relations, this is a very suggestive study.

There has been a massive literature developed on the nature of slavery and slaveholding in the past few decades. See especially:

Eugene D. Genovese, *Roll Jordan Roll, The World the Slaves Made.* New York: Pantheon, 1976.

Bertram Wyatt–Brown, *Honor and Violence in the Old South.* New York: Oxford University Press, 1986.

Concerning abolitionism in antebellum Appalachia, see especially:

Durwood Dunn, *An Abolitionist in the Appalachian South: Ezekiel Birdseye on Slavery, Capitalism and Separate Statehood in East Tennessee, 1841–1846.* Knoxville: University of Tennessee Press, 1997.

Dwight Lowell Dumond, *Antislavery: The Crusade for Freedom in America.* New York: Norton, 1966.

Lowell H. Harrison, *The Antislavery Movement in Kentucky.* Lexington: University Press of Kentucky, 1978.

Richard D. Sears, *The Day of Small Things: Abolitionism in the Midst of Slavery—Berea, Kentucky, 1854–1864.* New York: University Press of America, 1986.

Chapter 7: The Civil War Era, 1860–1877

The literature on the Civil War is enormous. The particular titles that I depended upon particularly were:

Edward C. Smith, *The Borderland and the Civil War.* Cincinnati: Clarke, 1899.

Kenneth W. Noe and Shannon H. Wilson, editors, *The Civil War in Appalachia: Collected Essays.* Knoxville: University of Tennessee Press, 1997.

James Lee McDonough, *Chattanooga: A Death Grip on the Confederacy.* Knoxville: University of Tennessee Press, 1984.

Charles Faulkner Bryan, "The Civil War in East Tennessee: A Social, Political and Economic Study." Ph.D., dissertation, University of Tennessee, 1978.

Richard E. Beringer, Herman Hattaway, Archer Jones, and William N. Still, Jr. *Why the South Lost the Civil War.* Athens: University of Georgia Press, 1983.

Kenneth W. Noe, *Southwest Virginia's Railway: Modernization and Sectional Crisis*. Urbana: University of Illinois Press, 1994.

Philip Shaw Paludan, *Victims: A True Story of the Civil War*. Knoxville: University of Tennessee Press, 1981.

William Allan, *History of the Campaign of Gen. T.J. (Stonewall) Jackson in the Shenandoah Valley of Virginia*. Reprint. Dayton, Ohio: Morningside Press, 1987.

Richard O'Connor, *Thomas: Rock of Chickamauga*. New York: Prentice Hall, 1948.

James I. Robertson, "The War in Southwestern Virginia." *Now and Then: The Appalachian Magazine* (summer 1993), p. 15–18.

William Davis, "The Massacre at Saltville." *Civil War Times* (April 1972), p. 4–11, 43–48.

Jonathan Sarris, "An Execution in Lumpkin County: Localized Loyalties in North Georgia's Civil War." In Noe and Wilson, editors, *The Civil War in Appalachia*. Knoxville: University of Tennessee Press, 1997.

John G. Barrett, *The Civil War in North Carolina*. Chapel Hill: University of North Carolina Press, 1963.

Gordon McKinney, "Women's Role in Civil War Western North Carolina." *North Carolina Historical Review*, LXIX, no. 1 (January 1992).

John C. Inscoe and Gordon B. McKinney. *The Heart of Confederate Appalachia: Western North Carolina in the Civil War*. Chapel Hill: University of North Carolina Press, 2000.

Ella Lonn, *Desertion During the Civil War*. New York: Century, 1928.

Bessie Martin, *Desertion of Alabama Troops From the Confederate Army*. New York: Columbia, 1932.

Robert T. McKenzie, *One South or Many: Plantation and Upcountry in Civil War Era Tennessee*. New York: Cambridge University Press, 1994.

W. Todd Groce, *Mountain Rebels: East Tennessee Confederates and the Civil War, 1860–1870*. Knoxville: University of Tennessee Press, 1999.

Charles Frazier, *Cold Mountain: A Novel*. New York: Atlantic Monthly Press, 1997. This book won the National Book Award and was on the best-seller list for many weeks. Called by some a "classic," it deals with the return home of a North Carolina soldier who deserted.

On political matters during the Civil War period, see:

Daniel Crofts, *Reluctant Confederates: Upper South Unionists in the Secession Crisis*. Chapel Hill: University of North Carolina Press, 1989.

Richard Nelson Current, *Lincoln's Loyalists: Union Soldiers from the Confederacy*. Boston: Little–Brown, 1992. Current estimates that there were 100,000 Union soldiers from Confederate states, 42,000 of them from Tennessee.

Richard O. Curry, *A House Divided: A Study of Statehood Politics and the Copperhead Movement in West Virginia.* Pittsburgh: University of Pittsburgh Press, 1964.

The Reconstruction writing is much less voluminous than the writing on the Civil War years. The classic presentation of the best modern scholarship is Eric Foner, *Reconstruction: America's Unfinished Revolution, 1863–1877.* New York: Harper and Row, 1988. I have also depended upon the following:

Eric L. McKitrick, *Andrew Johnson and Reconstruction.* New York: Oxford University Press, 1988.

E. Merton Coulter, *William G. Brownlow.* Chapel Hill: University of North Carolina Press, 1937.

Steve Humphrey, *That D . . . d Brownlow.* Boone, N.C.: Appalachian Consortium Press, 1978.

Joseph H. Parks, *Joseph E. Brown of Georgia.* Baton Rouge: Louisiana State University Press, 1977.

Allen W. Trelease, "Who were the Scalawags?" *Journal of Southern History,* XXIX, no. 4 (November 1967), p. 445–68.

Peter Kolchin, "Scalawags, Carpetbaggers and Reconstruction: A Quantitative Look at Southern Congressional Politics, 1868–1872." *Journal of Southern History,* XLV, no. 1 (February 1979), p. 63–76.

Ina W. Van Noppen and John J. Van Noppen, *Western North Carolina Since the Civil War.* Boone, N.C.: Appalachian Consortium Press, 1973.

Horace Mann Bond, *Negro Education in Alabama: A Study in Cotton and Steel.* Washington, D.C.: Associated Publishers, 1939.

Gordon McKinney, *Southern Mountain Republicans, 1865–1900.* Chapel Hill: University of North Carolina Press, 1978.

On the feuds, see:

Altina L. Waller, *Feud: Hatfields, McCoys and Social Change in Appalachia.* Chapel Hill: University of North Carolina Press, 1988.

Otis K. Rice, *The Hatfields and the McCoys.* Lexington: University Press of Kentucky, 1978.

James C. Klotter, "Feuds in Appalachia: an Overview." *Filson Club Quarterly,* vol. 56 (1982), p. 290–317.

Chapter 8: The "Discovery" of Appalachia

A basic analysis that pervades this chapter is that of Cratis D. Williams' great dissertation, "The Southern Mountaineer in Fact and Fiction" (New York University, 1961). This work convincingly evaluates Appalachian literature through the 1950s.

The designation of "Appalachian America" for the region arrived in the late nineteenth century after several decades of description of the area in Local Color fiction and by missionary writers. See especially

William G. Frost, *For the Mountains: an Autobiography*. New York: Revell, 1937. I have also depended quite heavily upon:

Henry D. Shapiro, *Appalachia On Our Mind: The Southern Mountains and Mountaineers in the American Consciousness, 1870–1920*. Chapel Hill: University of North Carolina Press, 1978; and

Allen W. Batteau, *The Invention of Appalachia*. Tucson: University of Arizona Press, 1990.

Major books written in the early, traditional mode of Appalachian scholarship still in print are:

Horace Kephart, *Our Southern Highlanders*. New York: Macmillan, 1913 (1941);

John C. Campbell, *The Southern Highlander and His Homeland*. New York: Russell Sage Foundation, 1921. Reprint. Lexington: University Press of Kentucky, 1969; and

James Watt Raine, *The Land of the Saddle-bags* (1924). Reprint. Lexington: University Press of Kentucky, 1997.

See also, for the "hillbilly" quotes: John Solomon Otto, "Reconsidering the Southern Hillbilly: Appalachia and the Ozarks." *Appalachian Journal*, vol. 12 (September 1985), p. 327.

The definitive work compiling the travel accounts of Appalachia prior to 1865 are three articles by Lawrence S. Thompson that he wrote for *Appalachian Notes*. See:

"From Elvas to Chattanooga: Three Centuries of Travel in Appalachia, 1540–1820." *Appalachian Notes*, vol. 1, no. 2 (1973), p. 1–11.

"Antebellum Appalachia: Three Decades of Travel in Appalachia." *Appalachian Notes*, vol. 2, no. 2 (1974), p. 17–24.

"Appalachia in the Civil War: a Bibliography of Travel Accounts." *Appalachian Notes*, vol. 5, no. 1 (1977), p. 1–8.

David C. Hsiung, *Two Worlds in the Tennessee Mountains: Exploring the Origins of Appalachian Stereotypes*. Lexington: University Press of Kentucky, 1997. This book argues that the origin of Appalachian stereotypes rested with the commercial and town elites inside the region who resented the antiprogressive attitudes of their rural and conservative (yeomanesque) neighbors.

For various topics covered in this chapter, see:

Richard B. Drake, "Documents Relating to the Mission to Appalachia." *Appalachian Notes*, vol. 3, no. 3 (1975), p. 34–38.

William Goodell Frost, "Our Contemporary Ancestors." *Atlantic Monthly*, March 1899, p. 311–19.

James G. Branscome, "Annihilating the Hillbilly: The Appalachian's Struggle with American Institutions." Katallagete: *Journal of the Committee of Southern Churchmen* (winter 1971). This article has been anthologized many times.

David Whisnant, *All That Is Native and Fine: The Politics of Culture in An American Region.* Chapel Hill: University of North Carolina Press, 1983.

Alfred H. Perrin, *Mountain Fiction from Addington to Zugsmith: 924 Works of Fiction by Southern Authors with Southern Appalachian Settings.* Berea, Ky.: Hutchins Library, 1972.

Billy F. Best, "Dogpatch's Capp." *Appalachian Notes,* vol. 7 (1979), p. 21–26.

Thomas R. Ford, "The Passing of Provincialism." In Thomas R. Ford, editor, *The Southern Appalachian Region: a Survey.* Lexington: University of Kentucky Press, 1962, p. 10–25.

Loyal Jones, *Appalachian Values.* Ashland, Ky.: Jesse Stuart Foundation, 1994.

Chapter 9: The Coming of the Machine Age

The title for this chapter comes from a book by a Christian Socialist, the Quaker Malcolm Ross, *Machine Age in the Hills.* New York: Macmillan, 1933. The tradition of seeing the coming of industrialism into Appalachia, especially featuring the development of the coal and timber industries is a long one. This tradition has been continued into the later twentieth century by Harry M. Caudill's influential *Night Comes to the Cumberlands.* Boston: Little–Brown, 1963; and by Ronald D Eller's widely used synthesis, *Miners, Millhands and Mountaineers: Industrialization of the Appalachian South, 1880–1930.* Knoxville: University of Tennessee Press, 1982. I have depended heavily upon Eller's treatment for this chapter.

In recent scholarship, several of Eller's interpretations have been widely challenged, particularly his treatment of preindustrial, yeomanesque agriculture as somewhat idyllic. Some scholars have pointed out that industrialization came to the region much before the New South period. See especially Wilma A. Dunaway, *The First American Frontier: Transition to Capitalism in Southern Appalachia, 1700–1860.* Chapel Hill: University of North Carolina Press, 1966. See also several of the articles in Mary Beth Pudup, Dwight B. Billings, and Altina L. Waller, editors, *Appalachia in the Making: The Mountain South in the Nineteenth Century.* Chapel Hill: University of North Carolina Press, 1995.

The dynamics of the coming of industry into the region have been seen in a number of ways. A frequent pattern used depends heavily upon a Marxian/Populist model to suggest that the region has become a mineral colony of the industrial Northeast. Malcolm Ross early used this model, but more recently it has been summarized in Helen Matthews Lewis, Linda Johnson, and Donald Askins, editors, *Colonialism in Mod-*

ern America: The Appalachian Case. Boone, N.C.: Appalachian Consortium Press, 1978. An important modification of this model is the World Systems Theory developed by Immanual Wallerstein for European economic history. World Systems Theory has been imaginatively applied to the Appalachian case by Wilma Dunaway in her *The First American Frontier.*

The quotations are mostly from Edward King, *The Great South.* Hartford, Conn.: American, 1875.

For other items included in this chapter, see:

Ronald L. Lewis, *Black Coal Miners in America: Race, Class and Community Conflict, 1780–1980.* Lexington: University Press of Kentucky, 1987.

Roy B. Clarkson, *Tumult on the Mountain: Lumbering in West Virginia, 1770–1920.* Parsons, W. Va.: McClain, 1964.

Michael Frome, *Strangers in High Places: The Story of the Smoky Mountains.* New York: Doubleday, 1966.

John Gaventa, *Power and Powerlessness: Quiescence and Rebellion in An Appalachian Valley.* Urbana: University of Illinois Press, 1980.

Crandall Shiflett, *Coal Towns: Life, Work and Culture in Company Towns of Southern Appalachia, 1880–1960.* Knoxville: University of Tennessee Press, 1991.

Harry M. Caudill, *Theirs Be the Power: The Moguls of Eastern Kentucky.* Urbana: University of Illinois Press, 1983.

David Alan Corbin, *Life, Work and Rebellion in the Coal Fields: The Southern West Virginia Miners, 1880–1922.* Urbana: University of Illinois Press, 1981.

Howard B. Lee, *Bloodletting in Appalachia.* Morgantown: University of West Virginia Library, 1969.

David Salstrom, "The Agricultural Origins of Economic Dependency, 1840–1870." In Robert D. Mitchell, editor, *Appalachian Frontiers: Settlement, Society and Development in Preindustrial Appalachia.* Lexington: University Press of Kentucky, 1991.

Mary Beth Pudup, "Social Class and Economic Development in Southeast Kentucky, 1820–1880." In Mitchell, editor, *Appalachian Frontiers.*

Mary Beth Pudup, "Town and Country in the Transformation of Appalachian Kentucky." In Pudup, Billings, and Waller, editors, *Appalachia in the Making.*

Paul F. Cressey, "Social Disorganization in Harlan County." *American Sociological Review,* vol. 14, no. 3 (June 1949), p. 389–92.

The recent book, Ronald L. Lewis, *Transforming the Appalachian Countryside: Railroads, Deforestation, and Social Change in West Virginia, 1880–1920.* Chapel Hill: University of North Carolina Press, 1998; is a masterful analysis of the impact of massive timbering upon West Virginia's "backcounties," and the development of legal and political structures that emerged to protect industry's destructive practices.

Chapter 10: From Plutocracy to Welfare State and Back

The standard treatment of Appalachian politics from the Reconstruction Period to the end of the century is Gordon B. McKinney, *Southern Mountain Republicans, 1865–1900: Politics and the Appalachian Community*. Chapel Hill: University of North Carolina Press, 1978. Various individual state histories are also particularly useful; especially see John Alexander Williams, *West Virginia: A History*. New York: Norton, 1976; Roger L. Hart, *Redeemers, Bourbons and Populists: Tennessee Politics, 1870–1896*. Baton Rouge: Louisiana State University Press, 1975; and James C. Klotter, *William Goebel: The Politics of Wrath*. Lexington: University Press of Kentucky, 1977. See also:

Harry M. Caudill, *Night Comes to the Cumberlands*. Boston: Little–Brown, 1963.

Harry M. Caudill, *Theirs Be the Power: The Moguls of Eastern Kentucky*. Urbana: University of Illinois Press, 1983.

The quotations in this chapter are drawn from:

Norman Pollack, *The Populist Mind*. Indianapolis: Bobbs–Merrill, 1967, p. 230, for the views of Milford Howard.

Theodore H. White, *The Making of the President, 1960*. New York: Atheneum, 1961, p. 106, on Kennedy's response to West Virginia poverty.

Laurel Shackelford and Bill Weinberg, editors, *Our Appalachia: An Oral History*. New York: Hill and Wang, 1977, for various responses to the coming of the Great Depression.

Use has been made in this chapter of several important histories of Southern history and politics. See especially:

C. Vann Woodward, *Origins of the New South, 1877–1913*. Baton Rouge: Louisiana University Press, 1951.

Edward L. Ayers, *The Promise of the New South: Life After Reconstruction*. New York: Oxford University Press, 1992.

George B. Tindall, *The Emergence of the New South 1913–1945*. Baton Rouge: Louisiana University Press, 1967.

Dewey Grantham, *The Democratic South*. New York: Norton, 1967.

Neil R. Peirce, *The Border South: People, Politics and Power in the Five Border States*. New York: Norton, 1975. Peirce calls Appalachia "America's forgotten region."

The Populist Movement is treated by many scholars, but I depended largely upon Lawrence Goodwyn, *The Populist Movement: A Short History of the Agrarian Revolt in America*. New York: Oxford University Press, 1978. See also Stephen Hahn, *The Roots of Southern Populism: The Transformation of the Georgia Upcountry, 1850–1890*. New York: Oxford University Press, 1982; Carl N. Degler, *The Other South*. New York: Harper and Row, 1974; and Robert C. McMath, *Populist Vanguard: A History of the*

Southern Farmers' Alliance. Chapel Hill: University of North Carolina Press, 1975.

The literature on the New Deal is vast. On the aspects of the New Deal that have impacted Appalachia particularly, I have depended especially upon:

David E. Lilienthal, *T.V.A.: Democracy on the March.* New York: Harper, 1944.

Philip Selznick, *T.V.A. and the Grassroots.* New York: Torchbooks, 1966.

George T. Blakey, *Hard Times and the New Deal in Kentucky, 1929–1939.* Lexington: University Press of Kentucky, 1986.

Jerry B. Thomas, *An Appalachian New Deal: West Virginia in the Great Depression, 1929–1941.* Lexington: University Press of Kentucky, 1998.

Milton Derber and Edward Young, *Labor and the New Deal.* Madison: University of Wisconsin Press, 1957.

John W. Hevener, *Which Side Are You On: The Harlan County Coal Miners, 1931–1939.* Urbana: University of Illinois Press, 1978.

Charles W. Johnson and Charles O. Jackson, *City Behind A Fence: Oak Ridge, Tennessee, 1942–1946.* Knoxville: University of Tennessee Press, 1981.

On the War on Poverty, see:

Huey Perry, *They'll Cut Off Your Project: A Mingo County Chronicle.* New York: Praeger, 1972.

David S. Walls and John Stephenson, editors, *Appalachia in the Sixties: Decade of Awakening.* Lexington: University Press of Kentucky, 1972.

Kenneth Clark and Jeannette Hopkins, *A Relevant War Against Poverty: A Study of Community Action Programs and Observable Change.* New York: Harper Torchbacks, 1970.

For Appalachian Regional Commission statistics, see that agency's official magazine, *Appalachia.*

Two evaluations of the effectiveness of the Appalachian Regional Commission are: David Whisnant, *Modernizing the Mountaineer: People, Power and Planning in Appalachia.* New York: Burt Franklin, 1980; and David Bradshaw, *The Appalachian Regional Commission: Twenty-Five Years of Government Policy.* Lexington: University Press of Kentucky, 1992.

Other evaluations of the ARC with vastly different conclusions are:

James Branscome, *The Federal Government in Appalachia.* New York: Field Foundation, 1977.

D. Van Etta, "You Can't Kill a Good Giveaway," *Readers Digest* (August 1993), p. 55–59.

Donald N. Rothblatt, *Regional Planning: The Appalachian Experience.* Lexington, Mass.: Heath Lexington Books, 1971.

Major analyses that see possibilities of a non-conservative future for Appalachia are:

John Gaventa, *Power and Powerlessness: Quiescence and Rebellion in an Appalachian Valley.* Urbana: University of Illinois Press, 1980. This is a most sophisticated analysis of power relationships, which largely equates quiescence with conservatism.

Stephen L. Fisher, editor, *Fighting Back in Appalachia: Tradition, Resistance and Change.* Philadelphia: Temple University Press, 1993.

Richard A. Couto, *Making Democracy Work Better: Mediating Structures, Social Capital, and the Democratic Prospect.* Chapel Hill: University of North Carolina Press, 1999.

For a portrayal of Nixon's Coming-out Party in August 1979, see the Appalshop movie, "The Big Lever."

On the election of 1996, see:

David Sutton, "Politics: Big Dough, Small Change: The Election of 1996." *Appalachian Journal,* vol. 24, no. 3 (spring 1997), p. 296–305.

Chapter 11: Regional Society and Social Change

Cratis Williams' classic dissertation, "The Southern Mountaineer in Fact and Fiction" (Ph.D. dissertation, New York University, 1961), did pioneering work in history and sociology, as well as in Appalachian literature. Yet the study of Appalachian communities was already quite mature by that time, led by James S. Brown's Beech Creek studies begun in the 1940s. Other useful sociological/anthropological community studies have been: Marion Pearsall, *Little Smoky Ridge* (1959), Elmora Matthews, *Neighbor and Kin* (1965), John Stephenson, *Shiloh* (1969), John Fetterman, *Stinking Creek* (1967), and George L. Hicks, *Appalachian Valley* (1976). More recent community studies have been Patricia D. Beaver, *Rural Community in the Appalachian South* (1986), and Shauna L. Scott, "Gender Among Appalachian Kentucky Farm Families," in *The Journal of Appalachian Studies* (spring 1996).

Studies of the region's elite during the nineteenth century are included in three edited volumes—Robert D. Mitchell, editor, Appalachian Frontiers: *Settlement, Society and Development in the Preindustrial Era* (1991); Michael J. Puglisi, editor, Diversity and Accommodation: *Essays on the Cultural Composition of the Virginia Frontier* (1996); and Mary Beth Pudup, Dwight B. Billings, and Altina L. Waller, editors, *Appalachia in the Making: The Mountain South in the Nineteenth Century* (1995).

The discipline of Women's Studies has rather suddenly grown up within Appalachian Studies, and is particularly indebted to Sally Ward Maggard and Barbara Ellen Smith. See especially Smith's "Walk-ons in the Third Act: The Role of Women in Appalachian Historiography," *Journal of Appalachian Studies* (spring 1998).

The field of Black Studies still has a distance to go within Appalachian Studies. Only one major book has been published that surveys the field generally, and this is the edited volume by William H. Turner and Edward J. Cabbell, editors, *Blacks in Appalachia.* Lexington: University Press of Kentucky, 1985.

In fact, the region's story of black-white relations is very complex, for there are many cases of remarkable racial cooperation, yet the region harbors the worst kind of racial violence and intimidation, and such incidents exist in the region from the time of the Ku Klux Klan until the school integration difficulties in Clinton, Tennessee, in 1956. Studies highlighting various aspects of the Appalachian black experience are:

John C. Inscoe, editor. *Appalachians and Race.* Lexington: University Press of Kentucky, 2000.

Robert P. Stuckert, "Racial Violence in Southern Appalachia: 1880–1940." *Appalachian Heritage,* vol. 20 (spring 1992), p. 35–41.

Allen W. Trelease, *White Terror: The Ku Klux Klan and Southern Reconstruction.* Baton Rouge: Louisiana State University Press, 1971.

W. Fitzhugh Brundage, *Lynching in the New South.* Urbana: University of Illinois Press, 1993.

Kenneth T. Jackson, *The Ku Klux Klan in the City, 1915–1930.* New York: Oxford University Press, 1967.

Glenn T. Eskew, "'Bombingham': Black Protest in Birmingham, Alabama." *The Historian,* vol. 59, no. 2 (winter 1997), p. 371–90.

Henry Louis Gates, *Colored People: a Memoir.* New York: Knopf, 1995. This is a particularly useful memoir of an important contemporary black scholar who evaluates his West Virginia childhood and background.

Quite a literature has developed over just how pleasant life was for the black coal miners in West Virginia and their families. A general review of this issue is in Ronald L. Lewis, *Black Coal Miners in America: Race, Class and Community Conflict, 1780–1980.* Lexington: University Press of Kentucky, 1987. Particularly see his pages 143–56. David Alan Corbin in *Life, Work and Rebellion in the Coal Fields: The Southern West Virginia Miners, 1880–1922.* Urbana: University of Illinois Press, 1981, is particularly optimistic about the solidarity that developed between black and white coal miners, and the essential equality enjoyed by blacks in the West Virginia mine fields during the Jim Crow era.

Studies relating to other Appalachian minorities are:

N. Brent Kennedy, *The Melungeons: The Resurrection of a Proud People: An Untold Story of Ethnic Cleansing in America.* Macon, Ga.: Mercer University Press, 1994.

Theda Perdue, *The Cherokee.* New York: Chelsea House, 1989. Her chapter 6 deals with the Eastern Band.

Studies of the region's urbanization represent a relatively untried field thus far within Appalachian Studies scholarship, but it is a familiar theme within Appalachian literature. Traditional folk society's relationship to regional urban culture is probed by James Agee, Thomas Wolfe, Wilma Dykeman, Lee Smith, and numerous other writers. Furthermore, very fine data is easily available in the region's major modern geographic study, Karl B. Raitz and Richard Ulack, *Appalachia: a Regional Geography—Land, People and Development* (1984).

The social impact that the coal town brought to regional culture is followed in regional fiction, especially in James Still's *River of Earth*. But historians have also probed those changes brought to traditional life. Especially see Crandall A. Shifflett, *Coal Towns: Life, Work and Culture in Company Towns of Southern Appalachia, 1880–1960* (1991); and David A. Corbin, *Life, Work and Rebellion in the Coal Fields: Southern West Virginia Miners, 1880–1922* (1981).

Regional health care is a field essentially untapped by serious scholarship thus far. But see especially the following:

The various studies of the Frontier Nursing Service, so far largely promotional in nature.

"Health in Appalachia: Proceedings from the 1988 Conference on Appalachia." Lexington: University of Kentucky Appalachian Center, 1989.

Sandra Lee Barney, *Authorized to Heal: Gender, Class, and the Transformation of Medicine in Appalachia, 1880–1930*. Chapel Hill: University of North Carolina Press, 2000.

Chapter 12: "The New Appalachia," 1930–2000

The difficulties of the region and the miscarriage of developmental strategies is best shown in Paul Salstrom, *Appalachia's Path to Dependency: Rethinking a Region's Economic History, 1730–1940*. Lexington: University Press of Kentucky, 1994. See also Dwight B. Billings and Kathleen Blee, *The Road to Poverty: The Making of Wealth and Hardship in Appalachia*. New York: Cambridge, 2000.

The quotation reinforcing the persistence of agricultural self-sufficiency in the 1930s is from Ronald L. Heinemann, *Depression and New Deal in Virginia: The Enduring Dominion*. Charlottesville: University Press of Virginia, 1983, p. 173.

More specific aspects of the problems of the region are traced in:

Frances Kane, *Textiles in Transition: Technology, Wages and Industry Relations in the U.S. Textile Industry, 1880–1930*. New York: Greenwood, 1988.

Donald E. Lundberg, M. Krishnamoorthy and Mink W. Stavenga, *Tourism Economics*. New York: Wiley, 1995.

There are many evaluations of the New Deal's policies. See especially David Eugene Conrad, *The Forgotten Farmers: The Story of Share-croppers in the New Deal.* Urbana: University of Illinois Press, 1965. See also Salstrom's *Appalachia's Path to Dependency;* his sixth chapter, "The New Deal and Appalachian Agriculture" (p. 94–110) is a very critical evaluation. Less critical are Harold B. Row, *Tobacco Under the A.A.A.* Washington, D.C.: Brookings Institution, 1935; and George T. Blakey, *Hard Times and New Deal in Kentucky, 1929–1939.* Lexington: University Press of Kentucky, 1986. I have found Arthur M. Schlesinger Jr.'s *The Coming of the New Deal,* volume 2, of his *Age of Roosevelt,* New York: Houghton Mifflin, 1958, pages 27–84, to be most helpful.

On the Appalachian Great Migration, see James S. Brown and George H. Hillery Jr., "The Great Migration, 1940–1960," in Thomas R. Ford, editor, *The Southern Appalachian Region: A Survey.* Lexington: University of Kentucky Press, 1962.

On Economic Development theory, see Walt W. Rostow, *The Stages of Economic Growth.* New York: Cambridge University Press, 1971; and Niles M. Hansen, *Rural Poverty and the Urban Crisis: A Strategy for Regional Development.* Bloomington: University of Indiana Press, 1970.

The widely available journal, *Appalachia: A Journal of the Appalachian Regional Commission,* gives a running account of ARC strategies and its progress toward the "New Appalachia." The difficulties of the ARC strategies are pointed out by David Whisnant, *Modernizing the Mountaineer: People, Power and Planning in Appalachia.* New York: Burt Franklin, 1980; Paul Salstrom in *Appalachia's Path to Dependency* (1994), and others. Sympathetic evaluations are also available, as Donald N. Rothblatt, *Regional Planning: The Appalachian Experience.* Lexington, Mass.: Heath, 1971; and Michael Bradshaw, *The Appalachian Regional Commission: Twenty-five Years of Government Policy.* Lexington: University Press of Kentucky, 1992.

See also:

Charles W. Johnson and Charles O. Jackson, *City Behind a Fence: Oak Ridge, Tennessee, 1942–1946.* Knoxville: University of Tennessee Press, 1981.

A discussion of the war veterans of Appalachia and the regional soldier's heroic record is in *Now and Then: The Appalachian Magazine,* vol. 4, no. 2 (fall 1987), edited by Bertram Allen.

Durwood Dunn, *Cades Cove: The Life and Death of a Southern Appalachian Community, 1818–1937.* Knoxville: University of Tennessee Press, 1988. His final chapter is entitled "Death by Eminent Domain."

T.N. Bethhell, "Conspiracy in Coal," Washington Monthly, 1969. In David S. Walls and John B. Stephenson, editors, *Appalachia in the Sixties.* Lexington: University Press of Kentucky, 1972, p. 80–86.

Joseph E. Finley, *The Corrupt Kingdom: The Rise and Fall of the United Mine Workers.* New York: Simon and Schuster, 1972.

Linda Ann Ewen, *Which Side Are You On? The Brookside Mine Strike in Harlan County, Kentucky, 1973–1974.* Chicago: Vanguard, 1979.

Richard B. Drake, "Documents Relating to the Broadform Deed." *Appalachian Notes,* vol. 2, no. 1 (First Quarter 1974), p. 1–7.

Stephen L. Fisher, editor, *Fighting Back in Appalachia: Traditions of Resistance and Change.* Philadelphia: Temple University Press, 1993.

Dwight Billings, "Culture of Poverty in Appalachia." *Social Forces,* December 1974, p. 315–23.

Stephen L. Fisher, "Victim-Blaming in Appalachia: Cultural Theories and the Southern Mountaineer." In Bruce Ergood and Bruce E. Kuhre, editors. *Appalachia: Social Context Past and Present.* Dubuque, Iowa: Kendall/Hunt, 1976, p. 139–48.

Treatments of the alternative to the Appalachian Regional Commission, the Congress for Appalachian Development (CAD), which was rejected, are:

Harry M. Caudill, *Night Comes to the Cumberlands: A Biography of a Depressed Area.* Boston: Little–Brown, 1963. His chapter 22 is entitled: "The Case for a Southern Mountain Authority."

David Whisnant treats Caudill's and Gordon Ebersole's efforts for CAD in *Modernizing the Mountaineer* (1980), p. 220–37.

The Jesse White interview was with Jean Haskell Speer, and reported in her article, "On Continuing the Highway and Exploring Some Less Travelled," in *Now and Then: The Appalachian Magazine,* vol. 11, no. 11 (spring 1994), p. 5, 35–36.

See also:

Agenda 21: Program of Action for Sustainable Development. New York: United Nations Publications, 1993.

Ivanhoe, Virginia, Civic League, *Telling Our Stories, Sharing Our Lives.* Ivanhoe, Virginia, Civic League, 1991.

Kai T. Erickson, *Everything In Its Path: Destruction of Community in the Buffalo Creek Flood.* New York: Simon Schuster, 1976.

Martin Cherniack, *The Hawk's Nest Incident: America's Worst Industrial Disaster.* New Haven, Conn.: Yale University Press, 1986.

On the matter of a sustainable wilderness in Appalachia, note the following:

G. Forest, *Great Adventures in the Southern Appalachians.* Winston-Salem: John F. Blair, 1994. This book is one of many, generally providing a guide for the many recreational uses of the Southern Appalachians. Every particular type of recreation—fishing, canoeing, birding, etc.—has published guides telling of proper equipment, places to go, and special skills and training needed in order to get the most from one's visit to Appalachia.

Chapter 13: The Appalachian Mind

The Mencken quotations are from H.L. Mencken, "Among the Believers," July 14, 1925, Dayton, Tennessee. In David Colbert, editor, *Eyewitness to America: 500 Years of America in the Words of those Who Saw It Happen.* New York: Pantheon, 1997, p. 348–49.

For the presentation of the thesis of the "invention of Appalachia," see Allen W. Batteau, *The Invention of Appalachia.* Tucson: University of Arizona Press, 1990; and Henry D. Shapiro, *Appalachia on Our Mind: The Southern Mountains and Mountaineers in American Consciousness, 1870–1920.* Chapel Hill: University of North Carolina Press, 1978.

David Whisnant, *All That Is Native and Fine.* Chapel Hill: University of North Carolina Press, 1983, is a fascinating study of cultural politics in the defining of things Appalachian.

There are several important recent compilations of Appalachian literature, and efforts to get at the thinking of those who write about the region to understand the influence of the region upon them. See especially:

Cratis D. Williams, "The Southern Mountaineer in Fact and Fiction." Three volumes. Ph.D. dissertation, New York University, 1961.

Robert J. Higgs and Ambrose Manning, editors. *Voices from the Hills.* New York: Ungar, 1975.

Robert J. Higgs, Ambrose Manning, and Jim Wayne Miller, editors. *Appalachia Inside Out: A Sequel to Voices from the Hills.* Knoxville: University of Tennessee Press, 1995. Two volumes.

Bill Best, compiler. *One Hundred Years of Appalachian Visions, 1897–1996.* Berea, Ky.: Appalachian Imprints, 1997.

Joyce Dyer, editor, *Bloodroot: Reflections on Place by Appalachian Women Writers.* Lexington: University Press of Kentucky, 1998.

On individual writers, see:

Grace Toney Edwards, "Emma Bell Miles: Appalachian Author, Artist, and Interpreter of Folk Culture." Ph. D. dissertation, University of Virginia, 1981.

Wilma Dykeman, *The Tall Woman* (1962); *The Far Family* (1965), *Return the Innocent Earth* (1973).

John Ehle, *The Land Breakers* (1964); *The Journey of August King* (1971); *The Road* (1967); and *The Winter People* (1981).

James Agee, *A Death in the Family* (1957).

Thomas Wolfe, *Look Homeward Angel: A Story of a Buried Life* (1929); *Of Time and the River* (1935); *The Web and the Rock* (1939); *You Can't Go Home Again* (1940); and *The Hills Beyond* (1941).

Harriette Simpson Arnow, *The Mountain Path*; and *The Dollmaker* (1954).

Lee Smith, *Oral History* (1983); *Fair and Tender Ladies* (1988); *Black Mountain Breakdown* (1980); and *Saving Grace* (1995).

Mary Lee Settle, the "Beulah Quintet": *Prisons* (1973); *O Beulah Land* (1956); *Know Nothing* (1960); *Scapegoat* (1980); and *The Killing Ground* (1982).Denise Giardina, *Storming Heaven: a Novel* (1987); and *The Unquiet Earth: a Novel* (1992).

The Stories of Breece D'J Pancake. Boston: Little–Brown, 1983.

Soupbean: An Anthology of Contemporary Appalachian Literature. Beckley, W.V.: Mountain Union Books, 1977.

Jim Wayne Miller, *Dialogue With a Dead Man* (1978); *The More Things Change the More They Stay the Same* (1971); and *The Brier, His Book: Poems* (1988).

Gurney Norman, *Divine Rights Trip: A Folk Tale* (1973); *Kinfolk: The Wilgus Stories* (1986).

Concerning the insights of folk creators, see:

Richard Blaustein, Review of Batteau's *The Invention of Appalachia* in *Now and Then: The Appalachian Magazine*, vol. 8, no. 3 (fall 1991), p. 36–38.

Lawrence W. Levine, *Highbrow/Lowbrow: The Emergence of Cultural Hierarchy in America*. Cambridge, Mass.: Harvard University Press, 1988.

Gerald Alvey, *Dulcimer Maker: The Craft of Homer Ledford*. Lexington: University Press of Kentucky, 1984.

Linda Garland Page and Eliot Wigginton, editors. *Aunt Arie: A Foxfire Portrait*. New York: E.P. Dutton, 1983.

Contemporary presentations of some of the negative stereotypes of Appalachia are:

Shelby Lee Adams, narrative by Lee Smith, *Appalachian Portraits*. Jackson: University of Mississippi Press, 1993.

Robert Schenkkan, *The Kentucky Cycle* (1992).

For Loyal Jones' dealing with Appalachian values and strategies, see (with Billy Edd Wheeler) *Curing the Crosseyed Mule: Appalachia* (1989); *Laughter in Appalachia* (1987); and *The Preacher Jokebook* (1989). Books under his authorship are *Minstrel of the Appalachians: The Story of Bascom Lamar Lunsford*. Boone, N.C.: Appalachian Consortium Press, 1984; and *Appalachian Values*. Ashland, Ky.: Jesse Stuart Foundation, 1994.

On religion in Appalachia, recent books are:

Howard Dorgan, *Giving God the Glory in Appalachia: Worship Practices of Six Baptist Subdenominations*. Knoxville: University of Tennessee Press, 1987.

Howard Dorgan, *The Old Regular Baptists of Central Appalachia: Brothers and Sisters in Hope*. Knoxville: University of Tennessee Press, 1989.

Jeff Todd Titon, *Powerhouse for God: Sacred Speech, Chant and Song in an Appalachian Baptist Church*. Chapel Hill: University of North Carolina Press, 1982.

Loyal Jones, "Appalachian Religion." In Samuel S. Hill, editor, *Encyclopedia of Religion in the South*. Macon, Ga.: Mercer University Press, 1984.

Loyal Jones, *Faith and Meaning in the Southern Uplands*. Urbana: University of Illinois Press, 1999.

John Wallhausser, "I Can Almost See Heaven from Here." *Katallagete*, vol. 8, no. 2, p. 2–10.

Deborah Vansau McCauley, *Appalachian Mountain Religion: A History*. Urbana: University of Illinois Press, 1995.

On snake handling, the literature is quite sensational. The most dependable study is David Kimbrough, *Taking Up Serpents: Snake Handlers of Eastern Kentucky*. Chapel Hill: University of North Carolina Press, 1995.

The two profiles made of the region thus far are:

1) U.S. Department of Agriculture, *Economic and Social Problems and Conditions in the Southern Appalachians*. Washington, D.C.: U.S. Government Printing Office, 1935. Miscellaneous publication 205.

2) Thomas R. Ford, editor, *The Southern Appalachian Region: A Survey*. Lexington: University of Kentucky Press, 1962.

For the various studies made of Appalachian communities, see:

James Brown, "Social Organizations in an Isolated Mountain Neighborhood." Ph.D. dissertation, Harvard University, 1950.

Marion Pearsall, *Little Smoky Ridge: The Natural History of a Southern Appalachian Neighborhood*. University: University of Alabama Press, 1959.

Elmora Messer Matthews, *Neighbor and Kin: Life in a Tennessee Ridge Community*. Nashville: Vanderbilt University Press, 1965.

John B. Stephenson, *Shiloh: A Mountain Community*. Lexington: University of Kentucky Press, 1968.

John Fetterman, *Stinking Creek*, New York: Dutton, 1967.

The publication of the continuing Beech Creek study begun by Brown is Dwight B. Billings and Kathleen M. Blee, *The Road to Poverty: The Making of Wealth and Hardship in Appalachia*. New York: Cambridge University Press, 2000.

The principal studies that have developed the colonial model as a way of seeing how the Appalachian Experience should be interpreted are:

Helen M. Lewis, Linda Johnson, and Donald Askins, editors. *Colonialism in Modern America: The Appalachian Case*. Boone, N.C.: Appalachian Consortium Press, 1978.

John Gaventa, *Power and Powerlessness: Quiescence and Rebellion in an Appalachian Valley*. Urbana: University of Illinois Press, 1980.

Wilma A. Dunaway, *The First American Frontier: Transition to Capitalism in Southern Appalachia, 1700–1860*. Chapel Hill: University of North Carolina Press, 1996.

The story of the black minority in Appalachia is best approached through:

William H. Turner and Edward J. Cabbell, editors, *Blacks in Appalachia*. Lexington: University Press of Kentucky, 1985. The term "Afrilachian" is a term invented by black poets at the University of Kentucky in the mid-1990s.

A fair literature has developed in various regional books and journals around awarding Robert Schenkkan's *The Kentucky Cycle* the Pulitzer Prize. See:

Jim Wayne Miller, The Kentucky (Re)Cycle," *Appalachian Heritage*, vol. 21, no. 2 (spring 1993), p. 59–66.

Several reviews have come from various mountain reviewers—Wilma Dykeman, Gurney Norman, Herbert Reid, John Alexander Williams and others—that have appeared in such disparate places as the *Knoxville News-Sentinel*, the *New York Review of Books*, and *Appalachian Journal*. A heated discussion of the Schenkkan play occurred at the Appalachian Studies Association meeting in Blacksburg, Virginia, on March 11, 1994. Schenkkan was not present.

Dwight B. Billings, Gurney Norman, and Katherine Ledford, editors, *Confronting Appalachian Stereotypes: Back Talk from an American Region*. Lexington: University Press of Kentucky, 1999. This will probably become the region's official response.

See also J.W. Williamson, *Hillbillyland: What the Movies Did to the Mountains and What the Mountains Did to the Movies.* Chapel Hill: University of North Carolina Press, 1995.

Chapter 14: The Appalachian Future

The contrasting futures of those in the southern mountain area seems so compelling, that I have begun this chapter with the image of Appalachia's two worlds. See:

Harry M. Caudill, *Theirs Be the Power: The Moguls of Eastern Kentucky.* Urbana: University of Illinois Press, 1983; and

David C. Hsiung, *Two Worlds In the Tennessee Mountains.* Lexington: University Press of Kentucky, 1997.

For visions of the Appalachian future, see:

Gordon McKinney, "No Longer the Land Where Time Stands Still," *Berea Alumnus* (winter 1996), p. 508.

Now and Then: The Appalachian Magazine. Special issue, "Appalachian Visions: How the Region Sees Its Future." Summer 1996, vol. 13, no. 3.

The Appalachian Reader: The Independent Journal of Citizens Organizing in the Mountains, "Special Report: Who's Making Policy." (April–May 1998.)

Stephen Fisher, editor, *Fighting Back in Appalachia: Traditions and Resistance and Change.* Philadelphia: Temple University Press, 1993.

Wilma A. Dunaway, "Interview: Crisis, Transition and Resistance Movements: A Conversation with Immanual Wallerstein," *Appalachian Journal,* vol. 26, no. 3 (spring 1999), p. 284–305.

Paul Salstrom, *Appalachia's Path to Dependency: Rethinking a Region's Economic History, 1730–1940.* Lexington: University Press of Kentucky, 1994.

On the economic theories of development, see:

Oscar Aries Sanchez (former president of Costa Rica) in Prague Forum of 1997 in *Civilization: The Magazine of the Library of Congress.* (April–May 1997), p. 60–61.

Arturo Escobar, *Encountering Development: The Making and the Unmaking of the Third World.* Princeton, N.J.: Princeton University Press, 1995.

Walter W. Rostow, *The Stages of Economic Growth: A Non-Communist Manifesto.* Cambridge: Cambridge University Press, 1961.

Various analyses of the future are:

John Naisbitt, *Megatrends: Ten New Directions Transforming Our Times.* New York: Warner, 1984.

Lester Thurow, *The Future of Capitalism: How Today's Economic Focus Shapes Tomorrow's World.* New York: William Morrow, 1996.

Alvin Toffler and Heidi Toffler, *War and Anti-War: Survival at the Dawn of the 21st Century.* Boston: Little–Brown, 1993.

Jennifer L. Hochschild, *Facing Up to the American Dream: Race, Class and the Soul of the Nation.* Princeton, N.J.: Princeton University Press, 1995.

Robert Wuthnow, *Poor Richard's Principle: Recovering the American Dream and Moral Dimensions of Work, Business and Money.* Princeton, N.J.: Princeton University Press, 1996.

George Soras, "The Danger of Ideological Laissez-Faire." *Atlantic* (January 1998), p. 23–25.

Lester T. Brown, *Saving the Planet: How to Shape an Environmentally Sustainable Global Economy.* New York: Norton, 1991.

On Gandhi's economic philosophy, see *Amrita Bazar Patrike* (June 30, 1994), *Harijan* (November 15, 1934 and August 25, 1940), and *Young India* (March 17, 1927). Perhaps the major economists who follow up on Gandhi's ideas are:

Gunnar Myrdal, *Asian Drama: An Inquiry Into the Poverty of Nations.* Three volumes. New York: Pantheon, 1968.

E.F. Schumacher, *Small Is Beautiful: Economics as if People Mattered.* New York: Harper Colophon, 1975.

More specifically as related to Appalachia, see:

Paul Salstrom, *Appalachia's Path to Dependency* (1994). Various warnings are discussed in this book.

Rhoda Halperin, *The Livelihood of Kin: Making Ends Meet "The Kentucky Way."* Austin: University of Texas Press, 1990.

Sally Ward Maggard, "The Informal Economy and the Formal Economy." Appalachian Studies Association Paper, March 1996.

Steve Fisher and Jim Foster, "Models for Furthering Revolutionary Praxis in Appalachia." *Appalachian Journal*, vol. 6 (1979), p. 170–94.

Si Khan, "New Strategies for Appalachia." *New South*, vol. 25 (summer 1970), p. 57–64.

Helen M. Lewis and John Gaventa, *The Jellico Handbook: A Teachers's Guide to Community-Based Economics.* New Market, Tenn.: Highlander Center, 1988.

On the emerging philosophies of agriculture, see:

Wendell Berry, *The Unsettling of America: Culture and Agriculture.* New York: Avon, 1977.

Walter Brueggemann, *The Land.* Philadelphia: Fortress Press, 1977.

Charles P. Lutts, editor, *Farming the Lord's Land: Christian Perspectives of Agriculture.* Minneapolis: Augsburg, 1980.

Richard Cartwright Austin, *Reclaiming America: Restoring Nature to Culture.* Abingdon, Va.: Creekside Press, 1990.

Index

Italicized page numbers refer to maps.